JOURNAL OF THE PLAGUE YEAR

JOURNAL OF THE PLAGUE YEAR

An Insider's Chronicle of
Eliot Spitzer's Short and Tragic Reign

by

Lloyd Constantine

KAPLAN PUBLISHING

New York

© 2010 by Lloyd Constantine

Published by Kaplan Publishing, a division of Kaplan, Inc.
1 Liberty Plaza, 24th Floor
New York, NY 10006

Library of Congress Cataloging-in-Publication Data has been applied for.

Printed in the United States of America

10 9 8 7 6 5 4 3 2 1

ISBN: 978-1-60714-615-5

Kaplan Publishing books are available at special quantity discounts to use for sales promotions, employee premiums, or educational purposes. For more information or to purchase books, please call the Simon & Schuster special sales department at 866-506-1949.

.....

DEDICATION

THIS BOOK IS DEDICATED to the hundreds of men and women
who followed Eliot Spitzer to Albany in 2007 in an effort to
improve New York State; and also to the staff of the Second
Floor, who schooled us when we arrived and continued their fine
work after we departed.

....

TABLE OF CONTENTS

"A dreadful plague in London was
   In the year sixty-five,
Which swept an hundred thousand souls
   Away; yet I alive!"
                              —Daniel Defoe

.....

PROLOGUE

On sunday morning, March 9, 2008, I awoke in my massive bed in Chatham, New York, in the arms of Jan, my wife. I had slept the recently rare deep, uninterrupted and comforting sleep of an untroubled and prosperous man, in spitting distance of his 61st birthday.

The weekend had been very sweet. We had ritualistically made successful contact with each of our three children, living in San Francisco, Thailand and Wisconsin. Each seemed to be in a good place. One major reason I continued to work, after the economic imperative for my gainful employment ended, was to avoid worrying about my kids full-time and obsessively, and annoying them even more than I already did with my frequent advice.

The rare trifecta, all my kids happy at one moment, had been an important, but not the only, soporific. The previous day's company — including two wonderful young protégés, who were friends of the entire Constantine family and of each other, augmented that comforting circumstance. We had spent the day at our weekend home in the Berkshires discussing their extensive humanitarian work, including the girl's early departure from Boston the next morning to New Orleans for a Katrina-related mission. As she was preparing to depart in a heavy rain to face the Massachusetts Turnpike alone, I had merely to glance at the other guest, a 32-year-old boy and veteran of the Peace Corps, who was an associate in my former law firm, Constantine Cannon, seemingly still bearing my name.

I knew that he would decipher my subtle glance, sacrifice the skiing we had planned for Sunday and immediately insist that he drive with the girl to Boston, then take the cheap and infamous "Chinatown bus" for the six-hour ride back to Manhattan.

That everyone was behaving admirably that Saturday, my kids by being happy or feigning happiness, our guests by being such sensitive and humane people and Jan and me by appreciating all this, rounded out what had been a very rare, very good week, in my job as senior advisor to New York Governor Eliot Spitzer—my closest male friend, protégé and former law partner. The 17 months preceding that very good week in early March 2008 had been very, very bad for Eliot, his administration and our friendship. Consistently feeling that my senior advice was unheeded or undermined by others in Eliot's inner circle, I had steadily assaulted him with strident and sarcastic critiques of the administration's transition to office and its performance after taking charge. These critiques had been delivered in person, on the phone, by email and, when they were particularly harsh, by handwritten memo.

At various times during this period, I thought of beginning a diary with the code name *A Journal of the Plague Year* borrowed from the 18th-century novel about the Black Plague written by Daniel Defoe. But each time I got that urge, I had suppressed it as being puerile and premature—since there was still loads of time in the presumptive eight or 12 years of the Spitzer governorship to get things on track, begin to fulfill the promises Eliot had made to the people of New York and then take our successes on the road to the White House. I told Jan that the very good week was possibly the beginning of the extravagant success that had been expected by the unprecedented majority that had elected Eliot and by the hundreds of talented people who had left big jobs, often abandoning lucrative compensation (as I had) to work for Eliot. Many of these people had moved less-than-enthusiastic families to Albany or, failing to do so, were shuttling between New York City and its suburbs to the state capital, where they inhabited Spartan quarters.

The very good week at the governor's office had included major progress toward the passage of an austere, but on-time, budget, due April 1. In this budget, Eliot would close a $5 billion budget deficit by making tough, skillful and intelligent choices. He would wisely administer pain on many agencies and constituencies while maintaining progress in certain programs vital for the social and economic progress of New York, such as higher education. This was one of the areas I directed for the Spitzer Administration and the portfolio I enjoyed and cared about most.

My portion of the very good week had been filled with higher ed. budget negotiations, speeches and meetings with college officials, faculty, students and representatives of the

Bill and Melinda Gates Foundation. Albany's *Times Union*, the capital's powerful and only daily, had spent much of the past year chronicling the Spitzer Administration's problems and had even become an unhappy participant in our most prominent fiasco, known as Troopergate. But during this rare very good week, the *TU* was reporting our newfound toughness and skill, and three days before had profiled me and spotlighted Eliot's higher education program, front page, front and center and above the fold.

So Sunday, March 9, 2007, preceded by the deep and restful sleep, the wonderful Saturday, and the very good week at the office, was gentle, fun and uneventful until 7:35 P.M., when I received the first of several email... from Eliot. The first was innocuous and routine, asking where he could call me on a landline, since he virtually always had access to me on my cell phone. But Eliot, generally courteous and respectful of me, even in the worst moments of the preceding year, and even when I was not of him, rarely just called. Instead, Eliot would send a less obtrusive email asking when and at what number he could reach me. I thought nothing of this opening volley that Sunday evening, since I received an email like this on most days when we did not actually see each other. Since both of our BlackBerrys were appendages, I would quickly respond to his inquiry (as I did this time with my 518 Chatham number), and he would call me within minutes. But not this time. Instead, Eliot sent several more email... as the evening progressed, repeating the question of whether I was available for a call. I responded affirmatively each time, but he didn't call. At 10:37 P.M. Eliot emailed, once again, but this time asked me to be at his Fifth Avenue apartment in Manhattan at 7:00 A.M. the next morning. At that moment, I assumed that something bad was happening. Eliot knew I was in the Berkshires with Jan and that we would have to leave at 4:00 A.M. to guarantee arrival by 7. Being a gentleman and respectful of Jan, Eliot would normally travel in the middle of the night himself rather than ask us to do it. That is, unless something was wrong. So I called Eliot straightaway and asked what was happening.

Eliot was crying and said two jangling if not necessarily inconsistent things. He said, "You can throw me over if you want to, and I won't blame you if you do," and then said, "As of now, you are my counsel."

Eliot's counsel — the governor's counsel — was a colleague named David Nocenti. So for an instant I interpreted Eliot's crying as indicating that David had been hurt or killed. But then the part about *"throw[ing]"* Eliot *"over"* (which then and now seemed oddly phrased and almost Victorian) didn't make sense. Unless Eliot had killed David, literally or figuratively, by throwing him under the bus for something Eliot had done, perhaps connected to Troopergate, a scandal from 2007 that continued to burden all our efforts. Each of these bizarre possibilities crossed my mind in the less than two seconds of silence, and then Eliot continued, *"I have to resign — as early as tomorrow, the Times will report that I have been involved with prostitutes — I can't continue as governor and must resign."* I first ascertained that Silda (Eliot's wife) and his three teenage daughters knew what he had just told me, and then said, *"I won't abandon you — you don't have to resign — it's late, try to get some sleep — I will be at your place by seven."*

My sleepless hours between that conversation at 10:37 P.M. and our departure at 4:00 A.M. were spent sifting through the little bit of information I had and conjuring lurid details and dire consequences. However, none of the imagined encounters or imminent consequences approached the terrible reality that unfolded in the days and weeks that followed.

But the horrors inadequately imagined that night were simultaneously balanced by an opposing and oddly comforting stream of thoughts that began to dissipate the disappointment and disillusionment with Eliot, which had been building in me over the preceding year and a half. Finally, I had a reasonable working hypothesis to help explain the emergence of the "Impostor" who had been masquerading as my cherished friend. Eliot had never been out of control, erratic, vacillating, equivocating, or, worst of all, confused about who he was or ambivalent about his desire to be New York's Governor, and yet these traits were frequently exhibited by the Impostor. At lunch a year before, Silda had asked me, "Who is this guy?" I had tried to comfort her, and myself, with some hopeful platitude about "the intoxication of the moment."

Now, if not an explanation, at least I had this plausible hypothesis. The secret things Eliot had been doing and my assumption — no, certainty — that Eliot understood that they inevitably would come to light and bring him down, and all of us with him, had been steadily dripping venom into his mind. This poisonous intravenous drip had produced the Impostor of the brilliant, dedicated and decisive man I had known and loved for more than a quarter century.

This book is about the 17 months that preceded the phone call with Eliot at 10:37 P.M., March 9, 2008, encompassing the Spitzer gubernatorial transition, which I co-chaired, and the short, unhappy Spitzer Administration. It is also about the 61 hours between the call and Eliot's resignation on March 12, 2008, and the month that followed his and my resignations. To say that I had no choice but to write this book would be an overstatement. An honest and well-informed book about the Spitzer Administration would serve an important purpose, as Eliot's administration was widely and realistically viewed as a future national government in formation. This purpose coincided with my personal need to attempt to solve the puzzle of why an endeavor invested with so much hope and potential went quickly and tragically off course. The book is an honest account providing information and insight otherwise unavailable. However, this candor and information comes from only one source. Facts were checked, but no opinion other than the author's is reflected. I crossed some lines that may make certain people very dear to me unhappy. I refused to cross others, which may frustrate or anger other people. The most important reason for writing this or any book worth its salt is to learn something about the subject matter. I achieved that goal, and others will decide whether the effort has also illuminated the subject for them.

■ ■ ■

····

How I Came
to Be the Old Guy

BEFORE I RECITE the essential dated history of the Spitzer/ Constantine relationship, I would like to answer the one question most often asked of me since that terrible day in March 2008: *"Did you know Eliot was doing this?"* I did not know nor did I suspect it. And with only two exceptions, I did not and do not resent the question; it didn't cause me pain to hear it or to answer it. For months afterward, it was almost the first question asked in most of my conversations with friends and associates. It was an obvious and natural question. For most of that first month, I wasn't feeling much of anything, let alone resentment or hurt feelings; I was just reacting to the demands of the moment.

My specialty as a lawyer is litigation, and I am good at it, but the role Eliot suddenly asked me to assume when he said, "As of now, you are my counsel" was a new one for me. It was the role of sage old guy—"the person you call when your son has been arrested for *fill in the blank*" is the way this role is usually described. It is one of the last remaining exclusive men's clubs.

Men like Vernon Jordan, George Mitchell and Bob Bennett come to mind.

When I would read profiles and puff pieces about reputedly great lawyers, the stock in trade of legal profession periodicals, I never felt jealous, except when I read the profiles of the sage old guys. Now suddenly I was being drafted into that role by Eliot, and designated for a mess exponentially greater than some teenage DWI, and something reported with more intense media scrutiny than any scandal before. I immediately discovered that the job requires you to detach from your "client," which in this case was an entire family of people I love. The old man also must defer consideration of the effect the scandal is having on him and his family, a posture quickly noticed and gently, but firmly, resisted by Jan. The required numbness screened out most of the pain I might otherwise have felt every time I was asked whether I knew about what Eliot had been doing. It also muted any anger that I otherwise might have felt when my friends and kids told me that "the blogs" were speculating that I was also a client of the prostitutes patronized by Eliot.

But there were moments when the full suite of human emotions flooded through. In particular, when Jan and Silda each asked me whether I knew about or suspected Eliot's behavior. To say that being asked that question by them were daggers to the heart is an understatement, but the one thrust by Silda felt worse. Jan was merely confirming the widely held and well-founded belief among women that men protect other men's secrets, while indulging the misinformed assumption that men, like women, share their intimate secrets with others of their gender. But it still hurt that my wife of almost 33 years would suspect that I would let a friend as loved, and as important to our lives, as Eliot ruin his, and screw up ours, without at least a valiant attempt at stopping him. With Silda, there was all that, but additionally our friendship—and my responsibility to her children—three great teenage girls whom Jan and I called the "Flying Squirrels." My concern for all those relationships and responsibilities was called into question by Silda's inquiry.

This is how those relationships came to be: In 1996, two years after I and a small group of friends, including Eliot, broke away from very large law firms to form an antitrust boutique called Constantine & Partners, the firm had been profiled in *Crain's New York* business magazine, replete with a large color picture posed in front of the firm's signature decoration—a triptych with three versions of an American flag rendered Impressionistically. The three lawyers posed in front of the flag were Eliot, Bob Beglciter (another prominent partner) and me.

The article was written 14 years after Eliot first came to work in the Office of the Attorney General as my intern and two years after his unsuccessful first attempt to become AG. Still, at that relatively late date, the coverage had annoyingly focused almost exclusively on me, my background and my aspirations for the new law firm. In two years, Eliot would run again for that office and win. He would build the most powerful and effective Office of state attorney general in the history of the United States—encompassing some 1,550 distinct state AG administrations since 1789.

As Eliot's hard-earned and well-deserved success as attorney general mounted, I, in many people's minds, began to lose my distinct professional identity. Every time I was mentioned in the press and praised or blamed for something I had done (something that had nothing to do with Eliot), the Spitzer name and connection were nevertheless invoked. All but my immediate family and closest friends would mention or inquire about Eliot at the top of almost every communication. This intensified after Eliot was elected governor. Then I abandoned my law firm and high-powered career to become just one of the governor's men and totally lost the last vestige of my separate professional identity. This made and makes my efforts to move on much more difficult. I do so as *former senior advisor to disgraced former Governor Eliot Spitzer.*

I met Eliot in late spring 1982 when he became my student-intern in the New York attorney general's office. I was then head of the AG's Antitrust Bureau, and Eliot had just completed his first year at Harvard Law, with election to the prestigious Law Review. An intern with Eliot's pedigree, Princeton and Harvard Law, almost always gets the assignment he wants. Among the substantive areas of law Eliot might have selected, he chose antitrust and was assigned to me. Given a choice, I probably would have resisted the pairing, because of my bad experience the previous summer with an intern whose pedigree was very similar to Eliot's. Just replace Harvard with Yale. Like Eliot, Mr. 1981 was a rich kid with famous parents. Guys with résumés like that could work at just about any law firm and earn ten-fold the paltry stipend paid by the New York AG. When they decide to work in government, they tend to expect some psychic compensation to make up for the low wages. The Yalie had expected a "fun summer." On paper, at least, Eliot looked like he might present a similar problem.

When Eliot strode into my corner office on the 45th floor of the South Tower of the World Trade Center, he needed only five minutes to dispel my prejudices. We quickly exchanged names, schools and favored sports, and played a quick game of "Jewish Geography." I understood the subtext of Eliot's words as "Hey, old man [I was 35, and he was just 23], I can beat you at your chosen games of tennis, squash or just about any other you might be so foolish as to play with me." As for me, it was "Good luck—give it your best shot." Almost three decades later, and after several thousand rounds, the contest is unresolved.

I sensed that Eliot and I were kindred spirits, despite the age difference. We soon discovered similar motivations beyond the athletic field and especially in our view of the law as an instrument of social change. But I could see from the outset that Eliot had attributes, beyond his youth, that I lacked. He had been president of the Princeton student government—a sign that he aspired to public office. Eliot had money, but clearly no desire to accumulate more wealth for its own sake. He also loved constitutional law, as I did. Legal discussion and debate became one of our games. However, Eliot, more than I, believed in the power of government to help people. In 1982, I was still a skeptical outsider, relatively new in my government job and still clinging to my technical status as on "leave of absence" from South Brooklyn Legal Services, where I had spent my early career battling the government on behalf of impoverished clients.

Eliot and I instinctively understood our differences and our more predominant similarities—most importantly similar worldviews and the mutual realization that we had each found an ultra-competitive other. After spending the summer of 1982 working mostly on a criminal antitrust prosecution of ambulance companies that had divided the Syracuse, New York, region into little fiefdoms where they would not compete, Eliot returned to Harvard. We stayed in touch, not frequently but regularly. I had been impressed by Eliot and knew he would rise quickly in the profession.

After graduation, Eliot clerked for United States District Judge Bob Sweet in the Southern District courthouse, within walking distance of my office in the Trade Center. As he was leaving that post and pondering his virtually unlimited options (my office not among them, as Attorney General Bob Abrams had a strict rule requiring two years at the bar before joining his AG's staff), I strongly advised Eliot to take the best job in government that he could find, preferably in a prosecutorial role. It took no exceptional analytical skill to see that Eliot would be a great prosecutor. I didn't think Eliot would enjoy the menial tasks that make up the bulk of the work assigned to junior associates at large law firms, and told him that if he took that path, he would become bored very quickly. Brushing aside this advice, Eliot went to Paul Weiss, then perhaps the most cerebral of New York law firms. He left the law firm in less than a year to join Bob Morgenthau's staff in the office of the New York County (Manhattan) District Attorney.

Eliot quickly rose to head Morgenthau's labor racketeering bureau, and in that role I deputized him to act as a "Special assistant attorney general" so that he could utilize New York's antitrust law in his prosecution of the Gambino crime family and their control of the garment-center trucking business. The AG jealously guarded this prosecutorial tool. Attorney General Abrams and I had denied requests by other district attorneys for permission to prosecute other traditional crimes, such as arson and bribery, as antitrust offenses. However, when Eliot approached us, Bob and I resisted the urge to protect our jurisdictional turf. We considered Eliot as one of our own.

In the early 1990s, Eliot left the DA, and I left the AG, both to join big law firms. He went to Skadden Arps, and I became a partner in the New York City branch of Chicago-based McDermott Will & Emery. Within a short time we both became dissatisfied, through no fault of those fine firms. I had been constantly conflicted out of representing the big companies who sought my skills in antitrust cases, generally though not always as plaintiffs' counsel. The prospective clients I reluctantly turned down had included American Express, General Electric, Dean Witter and Visa. Eliot, for his part, had been a fish out of water, primarily defending "white collar" criminal defendants. He was a little fish at that, toiling as a Skadden "associate" despite his already bejeweled curriculum vitae, which included litigation experience superior to many partners at his firm. Beyond the status issue and the mismatch of assignment and temperament, as Eliot was a natural prosecutor/plaintiff rather than a defender, Eliot was merely treading water until running for elective office.

In early 1994, Eliot and I had a before-sunrise squash game. Later, over breakfast at the Princeton Club on East 43rd Street, we commiserated and discussed a plan. I wanted to leave my big law firm and form an antitrust law boutique. A wealthy prospective client, whom I could not represent while at McDermott, awaited me with a big juicy plaintiff's antitrust case against cable television monopolist Time Warner. Eliot was pondering an exit from Skadden to enter the Democratic primary for attorney general. Bob Abrams had resigned a few months earlier, leaving a caretaker AG, former Assemblyman Oliver Koppel, who had been "elected" by his legislative colleagues to serve out Bob's unexpired term. It was no surprise to me that Eliot thought he could win the primary and general election; I would have been disappointed had he thought otherwise, although I did not think he would win in his first run. I told him that when he lost the primary he should become one of the founding partners in the new law firm I was forming. His response was polite, but appropriately dismissive, to an offer that he could not seriously contemplate as he launched body and soul into his first political campaign.

Eliot's goal, at least as I saw it, should have been to establish his visibility and lay the groundwork for his second run for statewide office, four years later. I told Eliot that our new firm would give him all the room, time and flexibility he needed to make what I expected would be his second and successful run for elective office.

The plan worked perfectly for everybody. Eliot did much better than expected in the 1994 Democratic primary. Although he did not win, he got over 20 percent of the votes in a four-way race and earned the endorsement of both the *New York Daily News* and the *New York Post*. Eliot joined us as one of the founding and, we joked, name partners of Constantine & Partners

(C&P) during the first few months of its existence. For the next three and one-quarter years, Eliot billed about two thousand hours annually, good years for most lawyers, but about half the time Eliot actually worked during that period. The balance of his time was spent constantly crisscrossing New York State, laying the foundation for his next and successful run to become New York's attorney general.

At C&P, Eliot took a major role in representing Liberty Cable in its battles with Time Warner, did antitrust work for Rupert Murdoch's News Corporation, and most enjoyably represented William "Kid Chocolate" Guthrie, a "contenda" for the World Light Heavyweight Boxing Championship. Guthrie had been deprived of a shot at the title because of alleged restraints of trade involving boxing promoter Don King. When C&P won Guthrie's antitrust case, the kid got his shot, knocked out the champ and thanked Eliot and the firm from the ring on national TV.

During the formative years of our law firm, the personal relationships between Eliot and me and among Jan, Silda and the kids in our families deepened. We came to count on each other without reservation or question. Jan and I and our daughter, Elizabeth, sat on the board of Silda's charity, Children for Children Foundation. We were fixtures at Eliot's events and members of his various committees. My son, Isaac, drove for Eliot during his second AG campaign, during a year off from Williams College, where he and our older daughter, Sarah, got their B.A.s. The Spitzer and Constantine families became the constant source of meals, advice and other forms of sustenance for each other.

Eliot's 1998 AG campaign, with all its twists, turns, valleys and ultimate triumph, was felt more personally and acutely in the Constantines' home than in any other except the Spitzers'. Eliot was more than just our guy, he was the one who shared our beliefs and values and vision of greatness for the city, state and nation. He was the one who we all felt would eventually go all the way.

The first seven triumphant years of Eliot's eight as New York's attorney general (1999 through 2005) deepened the already intimate connections and served to confirm our belief that Eliot's political future was boundless, that it would include terms as governor and president, and that these would be as full of achievement as his AG years had been.

By the fourth year of Eliot's first term as AG, I was telling anyone who would listen that the American presidency was Eliot's manifest destiny. At a fundraiser at our home during the spring of 2002, I told the attendees at our Upper West Side Manhattan apartment that if they wondered why Eliot needed their money for his AG campaign, against an as-yet-unnamed sacrificial lamb, that they weren't thinking straight. In truth, they were investing in the "long run," and if any among them doubted that or needed that term defined, I was glad to both refund their money and validate their parking receipts. Eliot did not look even a bit uncomfortable as I made these comments.

In November 2004, I sat down with my law partners for a heart-to-heart in our offices at Madison Avenue and 51st Street. I told them that it was a foregone conclusion that Eliot would be elected governor two years hence. I also told them that, unlike

1998, when after chairing Eliot's transition to attorney general I had declined his offer of a position in the administration, in November 2006 I might well accept. Things needed to be done at a firm then called Constantine & Partners not merely to survive but thrive when the old man left. Beginning that night, we planned those things and began doing them.

The eighth year of Eliot's term as AG, 2006, was election year for New York's statewide offices. For Eliot, who had amassed a huge war chest and a dazzling national and international reputation as "the Sheriff of Wall Street," the primary and general elections seemed to have been mere formalities in a governor's race that was really over before it had begun. The year also marked a distinct deterioration in my relationship with Eliot. At first, I hadn't understood why that had occurred. As 2006 progressed, I convinced myself that detractors from Eliot's AG staff had been the cause. That was a partial explanation, but I now also believe it was Eliot's secret life and his awareness of the consequences, which at first changed him in subtle, and later, not-so-subtle ways.

■ ■ ■

....

Damaged on Arrival:
The Spitzer Transition

L ATER, I SAY that words spoken by Eliot in his inaugural
address, barely a minute after taking the oath of office as
New York's governor on January 1, 2007, sowed the seeds of
his administration's failure. In truth, the bitter harvest was
being planted even earlier in the badly conceived and badly
executed gubernatorial transition, which I co-chaired. Transitions to American political office are important. This was
recently demonstrated by Team Obama as they began to run a
distressed country during the 2008–09 transition, despite the
president-elect's protestations, the day after being elected, that
"there can only be one president at a time." This crucial transition was facilitated by the grace and professionalism exhibited
by President Bush's departing team, one of their finest, among
few, fine moments. That class was in stark contrast to the petty
and childish games played by the Clinton Administration as
they left office in January 2001, in a sad departure from a great
tradition.

"The American tradition of orderly, peaceful and non-partisan transition is one of the many things that make us the greatest nation in the world and still its best hope." When I wrote that sentence in my letter of resignation to David Paterson, and transmitted it five minutes after Eliot had publicly stated his intention to resign, I had the sweet and bitter memories of three previous transitions dancing in a head convulsing from the revelations, events and debates of the preceding 61 hours. My role in the first of these, the 1994 transition from Oliver Koppel to Dennis Vacco as New York's attorney general, had been brief and comic. By virtue of my old friendship with James Ortenzio, Vacco's chief fundraiser and political advisor, ironically I had conducted a series of master classes for Attorney General–Elect Vacco soon after the November 1994 election. The irony stemmed from the fact that he and I were polar opposites, both ideologically and politically. However, after these tutorials, Vacco had asked me to be his first assistant and, after I declined, had convinced me to serve on his transition committee. When Dennis finally figured out who I actually was and that my closest friend and newest law partner was Eliot Spitzer, a recent and future candidate for his new job, I was removed from the Vacco transition committee, with no hard feelings on either side. My second transition occurred in 1998, after Eliot narrowly defeated Vacco in his bid for reelection. Vacco, claiming election fraud, refused to concede for six weeks, until December 15, 1998. That was just 16 days before Eliot's inauguration. I, as head of Eliot's transition, had done the best that I could before Vacco's tardy concession, to assess Vacco's staff and the cases pending in the attorney general's office and convince people to accept positions in Eliot's new administration. All the while Vacco, backed by Governor George Pataki and New York City Mayor Rudy Giuliani, had vowed that Eliot would not actually have any jobs to offer, as his electoral victory would not hold up. After the Vacco concession, the many enormous transition tasks were all accomplished in those 16 days. We—Eliot, I, and the transition team—did them so well that a staff of unparalleled quality was recruited and seated in January 1999. That staff, under Eliot's leadership, became the most powerful and effective state attorney general's office in the history of the United States.

Eliot's AG's office supplanted numerous regulatory bodies in Washington, D.C., as the place the business community respected, feared and/or loathed but knew had to be reckoned with. That unparalleled performance was the reason Eliot Spitzer was elected New York's governor by the greatest plurality in the history of the state, far outdistancing even Teddy and Franklin Roosevelt. It also explains why, in the period before Eliot took office, many political junkies predicted that, like the Roosevelts, he would eventually run for and be elected president. Indeed, the most frequently mentioned post-2008 Democratic presidential contenders during the fall of 2006 were Eliot and Barack Obama. It was assumed that Hillary Clinton would be the Democratic Party's nominee in 2008. Of the two future kings, most political types expected that Eliot's reign would come first.

That Eliot would someday be president was the general opinion the day before he took the oath of office as News York's 54th governor. But by that date I, who had begun publicly describing Eliot as a future president in the spring of 2002, no longer thought his future prospects were quite as bright as I once had. My third transition, Pataki to Spitzer as New York's governor, was coming to a close with poor results, which unfortunately laid the foundation for a rocky start.

On December 29, 2006, at the very end of the transition that I co-chaired, I had handwritten a letter to Eliot detailing many of the flaws in the process and informing him that I would not take the "senior advisor" position in the administration, which we had agreed on earlier in the fall. I decided not to send the letter or personally discuss my decision with him until after the inauguration and the January 3 State of the State message. The announcement of my appointment had been postponed three times and was scheduled for January 5, 2007. On January 4, I called my law firm colleagues together for a meeting and informed them that, contrary to what I had told them two weeks before, at a solemn special partners meeting, I would not be leaving the firm to join Eliot, their friend and former partner.

They were shocked, some happily and others less so, especially those who had been designated to replace me as the firm's chair, as the managing partner of our New York City office, and those who would inherit my lucrative relationships with major clients. But in any event, they all feigned happiness, and I did not go into great detail about my reasons for abandoning the position they all knew I had been working to create for at least a dozen years. I left the meeting, called Eliot's office, and scheduled an 11:00 P.M. phone call to tell him of my decision. I then reread the letter to see whether anything needed to be added or deleted. As I began to do this, a Google Alert flashed across my computer screen announcing my appointment as Eliot's senior advisor. This shocked me, since the announcement had been scheduled for the next day, January 5, after having been delayed three times by the administration's communications director, Darren Dopp. One of the reasons for the 11:00 P.M. call with Eliot had been to pull the plug on the press release and spare Eliot and me the embarrassment of explaining to the press what actually had happened, or far more likely, dissembling about it.

However, because of the "mistaken" announcement (as was explained to me by Christine Anderson, the press secretary who reported to Darren Dopp), I was confronted with that precise unpleasant scenario. I abandoned my decision to withdraw and did so, stupidly, because it was the easiest thing to do at that moment. Nothing about this comedy of errors or pranks changed the reasoning and feelings spit out in my letter. Here are a few excerpts, written in a rage, but which evoke even stronger emotions now, given all that subsequently happened:

> **Dear Eliot,**
>
> **With this letter I withdraw my job application and do so at a time and with the hope that our friendship can be salvaged. You have handled this badly [the Transition]...**
>
> **It hurts and saddens me to now recognize how correct Silda was in her observation/prediction of your inability to handle this [being my boss]. It should make you happy to contemplate how well this marvelous woman understands you and embraces such failings—because they are yours....**

I am not going to spend any more time thinking about what this problem of yours may or may not be. I realize now that I have been overly concerned with your success and welfare. That degree of concern only makes sense if it is mutual. Perhaps in the future we can return to that happy symbiosis.

This withdrawal of my job application gives me the freedom to once again candidly advise you as I formerly did. My first advice is that this big Transition has been badly conceived and badly executed. I will not compare it to the small Transition in 98-99, which you and I did very well, under extraordinarily difficult conditions and which produced now world famous results. On its own merits this big Transition has been bad. No single person has the whole picture in his head. The incredible lead you had and sustained gave you tremendous advantages in designing a Transition. These advantages were squandered and the time used to construct a complicated structure mostly devoid of substance and which is incubating resentment and enemies which will become manifest in years to come.

...[Y]ou have stocked the PACs [policy advisory committees] with world class experts. These really smart people are getting the distinct impression that they are expending a lot of effort and energy in a process basically for show.

...All the people (at least the outsiders) are big people with big careers and egos. They are smart. They figure out that there [sic] time has been wasted when for example they spend a week checking references for candidates for a position promised and awarded to someone else before they began. I have quietly but firmly tried to correct as many of these situations as I could and while I think I have headed off some train wrecks, like the unnecessary mass resignation demand, in most cases my advice has been impolitely ignored or treated like a vile of anthrax. For example, that's exactly how my persistent advice on the retention of outside ethics counsel was treated and this was explained as not wanting to replicate the shackles that you had to operate under at the OAG *[Office of Attorney General]* after we (you and I) agreed to certain restrictions after the '98 Transition. These types of shackles keep you safe and represent one prong of the ethical paradigm shift you will attempt in Albany. You know it, I know it — and others who work for you have to figure that out or you will fail.

...

As my mother said to me a few times I love you but I don't like you very much. That's the truth right now.

...

And I am still proud of you.

Lloyd

My letter had been preceded by several uncomfortable months in a long relationship otherwise characterized by straight talk and gentle camaraderie. In the run-up to the 2006 Democratic primary and general election, Eliot suspended a regular tennis game he and I had maintained for almost two decades.

His reason was valid; his right hamstring was tender, and he didn't want to hobble around on the campaign trail. But this suspension had a bad effect on our relationship and on Eliot.

Competitive sports is a great status leveler, especially for alpha males. It had worked that way for us on the squash and tennis courts during the years when Eliot was my subordinate. It continued to level things as the power shifted from the older to the younger man. Without our weekly tennis game, I had to schedule time with the great man, even to have the simplest conversation or render unsolicited advice, which I always had done right after tennis, and most emphatically after I won. I had employed this technique for years, saving important advice for the 15 minutes or the occasional breakfast we shared right after the 6:00 A.M. tennis match had concluded. When I thought that the advice was particularly important, I tried even harder to win on the court. He seemed more receptive to my opinions when this worked.

After years of employing this strategy, Eliot said something that validated my method. He asked about a mutual acquaintance who was much closer to me than to him. Like Eliot, the guy was my partner in a decades-long athletic contest, only on the squash court, not tennis. Eliot knew that in the first decade or so of our matches my friend had almost always won, but that in recent years the tide had turned. "Who's winning these days?" Eliot asked.

"Why does it matter?" I replied, to which Eliot said, "That's all that matters." Of course, I agreed with him and had merely feigned the attitude of an adult. The conversation confirmed for me who this guy was and how best to deal with him as his triumphs and ego soared to the heavens.

In 2006, the lack of tennis with me, or anyone else, had also deprived Eliot of an important physical release, leaving just his daily run in the park. Running provided him less of an outlet for physical aggression and achievement. Although we found some time to talk at scheduled, cancelled, rescheduled and always hurried breakfasts and coffees, the relationship became strained as the year went on. I thought that I knew the source of the problem. Staff at the AG's office who would move with Eliot to the "Second Floor" (as the governor's office in the Capitol is called) were worried about me. By and large, they were people whose entire professional lives were defined by and depended on Eliot and their relationship to him. I had recruited some of these people back in the '98 transition and liked most of them. With some, the affection was reciprocated, but being an "outsider," a particularly rambunctious one who was very close to Eliot, I still worried them.

I did not work for Attorney General Spitzer. After the '98 transition, I went back to my law firm and continued my career, which had gotten bigger and more lucrative as time passed. After Eliot's departure, C&P had litigated a series of high-profile antitrust cases against Time Warner, AOL and the bank cartel jointly run by Visa and MasterCard, which resulted in a historic multi-billion-dollar settlement and a nine-figure attorney's fee for our law firm, the behest of Rupert Murdoch, had orchestrated a multiple-pronged attack on the merger of DirecTV and Dish Network, resulting in its collapse.

At times, I took public positions that to Eliot's staff (but not to Eliot) seemed strange. I devised and helped execute the legal strategy which saved the liberal-reviled Fox News from the early death planned for it by Ted Turner. I had testified in the Senate in opposition to Stephen Breyer's Supreme Court nomination, had attacked the Clinton antitrust agencies for their docile response to telecommunications mergers, and had conducted a very public and zealous defense of Aon, one of Eliot's targets in the insurance industry. The *New York Post* reported that this representation had resulted in his administering a mere "slap on the wrist"—to Aon—a ludicrous charge given the $190 million "fine" they had paid.

Eliot's staff saw my name and face in the papers all the time, often linked to these controversial cases and public debates. That I was a source of their worries was understandable for what were silly, petty, selfish and selfless reasons. I suspect their biggest worry was that I might supplant, or at least diminish, their own importance to the next governor. As 2006 passed and the Spitzer avalanche began to roll down the mountain, staff concerns about me, communicated to Eliot in myriad ways, were given energy by some stupid things that I did. I was always called for a quote in articles about Eliot. These quotes were generally good, positive and appreciated, at least by Eliot. But, in one article in the *New York Observer*, a left-leaning political weekly, I told the reporter an anecdote that I thought illustrated good things about both Eliot and me. It was a mistake.

I and my law firm had been offered $1 million to attend one meeting between Eliot and a target of one of his highly publicized corporate probes. This showdown meeting was coming toward the conclusion of a long process of investigation and the negotiation of a potential settlement in lieu of Eliot suing the company. I had told the guy who contacted me that if I showed up for the very first time at a meeting so late in the process, Eliot and his staff would become enraged. I said, "I don't know what the bid and ask for a settlement is, but if he's been asking for a half-billion, when he sees me it will go up by 50 to 100 million. My cameo will cost you that plus the million you pay me."

I refused the assignment, as I always did for any proposed meeting with any government official, unless I and my firm performed the substantive legal work leading up to the meeting. We refused to be influence peddlers. However, I should have realized that telling this story to the reporter was a mistake. I should have had enough self-awareness to understand that my comments were more about my ego than about confirming Eliot's integrity. I had been implicitly flaunting my new status as a rich guy who didn't need the extra million. The *Observer* article worried Eliot's staff because it suggested that there was a market for the purchase and sale of influence with the AG. The press and Eliot's many enemies were desperate to find something to stop, or at least slow the pace of, the Spitzer juggernaut.

My other press gaffe was worse. It involved the race to succeed Eliot as attorney general. Eliot's unprecedented success and worldwide visibility made the position of New York attorney general a much more desirable office and stepping-stone than it had ever been. In two successive years prior to the 2006 election, Eliot had been runner-up as *Time* magazine's "Person of the Year." During the Democratic primary campaign, I had been approached by most of the major candidates for my support. Like all candidates, they wanted money, but my support was primarily sought as a path to Eliot, who had stated that he would not take sides in the primary.

When these candidates, including Assemblymen Mike Gianaris and Richard Brodsky, former U.S. Attorney Denise O'Donnell and perpetual candidate for everything Mark Green, called or met with me, each stated in the first breath that they knew Eliot would remain neutral. The fact they were saying it to me meant that they hoped that my support might change that neutrality. More realistically, they would attempt to spin the support of Eliot's mentor, a person so closely identified with him, as connoting Eliot's tacit support for their candidacy.

I had witnessed such an attempt by Mark Green at a fundraiser hosted by David Boies, the famous litigator who had vanquished Microsoft in the Justice Department's antitrust case and unsuccessfully, but valiantly, represented Al Gore in the *Bush v. Gore* litigation over the outcome of the 2000 presidential election. When I showed up unannounced at Boies' event, Green stopped lauding his host in mid-sentence and started repeating my name in conjunction with Eliot's at an astonishing rate of about 50 mentions per minute. Green said, "And here's Lloyd Constantine, who's a close advisor to Attorney General *Spitzer*. Lloyd knows more about the AG's office than just about anyone, except maybe *Eliot*. Lloyd was *Eliot's* boss in the Attorney General's office back in the eighties," and so on. The Eliot/Lloyd relationship was well established and could be spun and misrepresented.

For instance, in 2008, while Eliot's senior advisor, I worked hard to convince *New York Times* reporter Danny Hakim not to write that my early support of Barack Obama was an indication that Eliot's endorsement of Hillary Clinton was lukewarm, and showed a lack of discipline in Eliot's ranks. Christine Anderson, our communications director, had tipped me off that Hakim was writing an article with this negative slant on Eliot. Against Christine's advice, I called Danny and registered my heated, annotated and verifiable objections to his assumptions, and this had changed the story. The article ran under the headline "Spitzer and Aide Differ on Presidential Race, But It's a Free Country." Instead of portraying Eliot as a weak supporter of the state's junior senator, the article reported that Eliot would not force his staff to conform to his political choices, which was the truth and evidenced one of Eliot's many unorthodox and admirable qualities.

But back in 2006, already understanding how this particular dynamic could be mischievously spun, instead of working hard to inoculate Eliot as I did two years later with the Obama article, I crudely attempted to nudge Eliot toward my point of view about who the next AG should not be. By the time *Daily News* reporter Ben Smith approached me in July 2006 for comment on my financial support for two Democratic AG primary candidates, Denise O'Donnell and Mark Green, the field had narrowed. O'Donnell had dropped out, and Andrew Cuomo, former U.S. Secretary of Housing and Urban Development, and son of former Governor Mario Cuomo, had emerged as the clear and seemingly prohibitive favorite.

The reporter was less interested in my support of Green than he was in my opinion of Cuomo and how he could link that negative point of view to Eliot. It was rumored that Eliot and Andrew disliked each other. In 2000, they had fought a nasty public turf war involving gun control issues. Up to that moment in July, 2006 had been a year with no real drama about the identity of the next governor. The press was looking for storylines, especially those with a controversy involving Eliot. Instead of just praising Green, I had given Ben Smith a very negative assessment of Cuomo. I said that Spitzer's staff in the Office of the Attorney General disliked the prospect of Cuomo becoming their boss, and while disclaiming knowledge of Eliot's opinion (which was not true), I observed that since Eliot and I were so close and similar in our views, it wouldn't surprise me if he shared my opinion of Andrew. This was a stupid thing to do. On July 24, 2006, *The Daily News* ran the story under the headline "Cuomo's AG-ony of Defeat, Eliot Leans to Green?"

My motive was to push Eliot toward opposing Cuomo, who could only be stopped by Eliot, if at all. Having lived through nine years of nastiness and recriminations between my former boss, Attorney General Bob Abrams, and Andrew's father, Governor Mario Cuomo, I knew how destructive of the public interest a bad relationship between these two offices can be. I also knew how good the Cuomos were at infighting. I did not want this for the state, or for Eliot. I did not want the governor to have an enemy with lots of legal tools and prerogatives ready to attack at the first sign of vulnerability. I had argued this case to Eliot many times, but he pushed back and said that he would have the upper hand as governor, that he was tougher than Bob Abrams or Andrew Cuomo and that if he tried to take out Andrew and failed, he would look weak and have an enemy for life. To which I had responded, Andrew was already that enemy. So this interview with Ben Smith was an act of defiance and confirmed the worst of the worries about me at Eliot's campaign headquarters. Eliot never said a word about the article to me, but Rich Baum, the head of the campaign, called to complain.

In this fall 2006 timeframe, Eliot and I began to discuss what my job in the new administration would be. It became an awkward and prolonged discussion, beginning with Eliot expressing surprise that I wanted to leave the law firm and join him in Albany. My desire might have come as a surprise to just about anyone else. I was at the top of my profession. The firm and my career were riding a wave of spectacular and financially lucrative victories. I was on the shortlist of road warriors whom major CEOs called when confronted with a make-or-break antitrust case. But Eliot knew better, we had talked about this moment for years.

I showed him an article published in the *American Banker* newspaper from 2003, where the reporter predicted that he would become governor and noted my intention to join him. Eliot knew that my recent financial success made the decision to leave my firm easier, not harder. He knew my finances intimately. He was my executor. He and Jan "owned" my life insurance policy, and he was the custodian of sensitive instructions to be executed should Jan and I die together—as I always hoped we would, but not quite yet. Eliot knew everything but seemed to have forgotten the part about working together again, despite years of unambiguous discussion.

Finally, a week before the election, we shook hands on what my role would be in the expected new administration. I would report directly to Eliot, troubleshoot sensitive policy matters as they arose, insinuate myself into others at his or my option, and directly supervise a few initiatives for the administration. The most important of these would be an effort to prioritize higher education and elevate New York State's SUNY and CUNY systems into the first tier of U.S. and world public universities. Eliot, however, did not communicate any of this to his staff or even make clear to them that I was joining the administration, not for at least two additional months. This period was filled with strained discussions, as the worried staffers, principally Rich Baum, Darren Dopp and Marlene Turner, respectively the incoming secretary to the governor, communications director, and chief of staff, expressed their concerns about me to Eliot.

Silda the Seer

SILDA MAY HAVE been another important source of opposition to my joining Eliot. During the transition, Silda grabbed me for a cup of coffee and pleaded that I not go to work for Eliot, becoming so emotional that she began to cry. In twenty years I had seen Silda cry only once before, and that had been at Isaac's wedding. She said that my working for Eliot would deprive him of the only intimate outside voice that he respected. Bernie, Eliot's father, was very sick, and Silda believed that other close male friends had receded as outside influences, which left only me. "If you work for Eliot, there won't be anybody he will listen to." I asked Silda why Eliot would stop listening to me if I went to work for him. *"He just would,"* and *"it might also destroy the friendship."* She cited Eliot's estrangement from Carl Meyer, formerly a very close friend who had experienced a brief and stormy tenure as Eliot's assistant in the AG's office.

I trusted Silda and valued her opinion and her loyalty to both Eliot and me. In 1998, she had advised me not to take a position in the AG's office, saying that I was "past all that" and that any position there was "beneath" me, but now, eight years later, a similar recommendation was tinged with sadness and motivated by fear. It was hard for me to understand what Silda was afraid of, but in hindsight, she obviously was prescient. She seemed to know that something was out of kilter, just not what.

Eliot's ambivalence about me joining the administration, whatever its source, had produced many awkward moments. At the news conference held two days after the election, when I was introduced as co-chair of the transition, a reporter asked whether I would join the Spitzer Administration. I responded that I probably would, and then a number of reporters pointed out that the press release stated that none of the transition co-chairs would actually work in the administration. Christine Anderson, the press secretary, had to issue a correction. At the time, it seemed to be a small, awkward moment caused by an unintentional error, though I now believe that was not the case.

During the transition, Eliot treated our handshake about my role as a "definite maybe." Such vacillation was something new and disturbing in our relationship. At one point, he asked whether I wouldn't prefer having my "own building," referring to the large, antiseptic structures on the outskirts of Albany that housed sprawling agencies like the Department of Transportation. Aware of my interest in higher education policy, he asked whether I wanted to be Chancellor of SUNY, the State University of New York. I wanted to have the advisor's job that we had previously agreed to, I said.

Finally, the announcement of my hiring was scheduled for the first wave of senior executive staff appointments, which began on December 7, 2006. However, Darren Dopp called to say that the announcement of my appointment would be delayed. He did this two more times in the following weeks, each time citing some need to balance upstate with downstate, or women and minorities with old white men. Even more annoyingly, Eliot kept on asking me what was holding up the announcement of my appointment, to which I always responded, "Ask Darren."

On December 29, 2006, while dining with my family at a restaurant called Madeleine's on West 43rd Street, I got a call from David Nocenti, the incoming counsel to the governor, whom I had helped recruit to work for Eliot eight years earlier. He said, "Something screwy is going on with your appointment. Darren tells me that the State Police are holding it up for some reason." At that moment, the proximate cause of the weirdness of the preceding several months became clear. I went home and wrote the withdrawal letter excerpted above, referring to Silda's warning that working for Eliot might destroy the friendship. I decided not to bother Eliot with it until after the Inauguration and the State of the State address, only a few days away.

During the inaugural events, Dopp's games continued. The new governor's biography, printed and distributed for the attendees, expunged Eliot's nearly four years as a partner at C&P, although it had been featured prominently in his previous two inaugural bios. Those years had immediately preceded his election as AG. While this censored biography was being distributed, thousands of copies of a special Inauguration Edition of the *Legislative Gazette* were handed out to the attendees, devoted to a loving portrait of the new governor sketched out by his proud mentor, the managing partner of Eliot's old law firm, C&P.

The delayed announcement of my appointment also kept my picture and bio out of the *New York Times*, which did a prominent article about the incoming senior executive staff. But this, I had thought, was a fortunate sleight orchestrated by Dopp, as I would pull the plug on the imminent announcement after the January 3 State of the State address and before the fourth scheduled announcement date of January 5, 2007. I had confronted Dopp, asking him why he had told Nocenti that my appointment was being held up by the State Police, what the issue was, and what business of his was my vetting by the cops? He didn't answer any of these questions, instead shifting the discussion to whether my law firm intended, or ever had intended, to open a branch in Albany, invoking his right and duty to protect Eliot. To this day, I don't know whether Dopp played his first, but certainly not last, State Police game at my expense or merely told David Nocenti that.

Most of this nastiness and game playing occurred during the Spitzer gubernatorial transition. Before the general election, but only a few weeks before, Eliot told me I would chair the transition. Given the size and scope of the transition required in a state with a $120 billion budget, employing almost 200,000 people, and confronting numerous crucial and time-sensitive decisions, there had to be a bad explanation for why I was given this task so late. Either the position of transition chair would be primarily ceremonial, in a process where most of the work had already been done, or worse, we would actually attempt to transition in less than two months. I soon learned that both of these bad explanations applied to the Spitzer gubernatorial transition.

My role as transition chair, and ultimately co-chair, along with five others, was apparently intended by Rich Baum, the incoming secretary to the governor, to be mostly for show. When Eliot first spoke with me, he had said there might be one co-chair, Dick Parsons, chairman and CEO of Time Warner. But every few days in the two weeks before the election, another co-chair was identified, resulting in six announced two days after the election. They were Hunter Rawlings, president emeritus of Cornell; Elizabeth Moore, former counsel to Governor Mario Cuomo; Peter Goldmark, formerly state budget director; Rosanna Rosado, the publisher of *El Diario*, the state's leading Spanish-language newspaper; Dick Parsons; and me.

Two of the transition's co-chairs did not attend a single transition meeting. Two others were confined to a single policy area. Peter Goldmark and I tried our best to put out fires and do something useful in the short time we had. Having largely ceremonial chairs would not have been a problem if the crucial transition projects had been well underway or well executed, but that wasn't the case. A big, impressive, but largely symbolic transition structure had been erected. Part of this gaudy façade were 14 Policy Advisory Committees, loaded with world-class experts. These PACs, in areas such as energy, education, transportation, and arts and culture produced excellent recommendations after spirited and freewheeling meetings.

The transition process culminated in sessions with Eliot, where he demonstrated that he could more than hold his own with the experts in all 14 areas. Eliot's performance was awe inspiring and rivaled the spectacular performances given by President-Elect Clinton when he publicly met with his transition committees in 1992–93. However, to the extent that these experts got involved in the recruitment and vetting of the people who would be hired to direct these policy areas, they found out that they were wasting their time. Their recommendations about hiring staff were, by and large, ignored. They interviewed and checked the references of candidates only to find out that a job had already been promised to someone else before the process had begun. They complained about all this to me and Goldmark and also complained about the insularity of the talent searches, largely limited to locals, AG staff, and the usual suspects.

At that magic moment in late 2006, Eliot could have had his pick of national stars in most areas. Two years before the formation of a Democratic national government, Eliot was widely viewed as a future president, and was the best game in the country for a progressive. This opportunity was largely ignored by the transition, which in reality was being run by Rich Baum. The administration arrived at Inauguration Day without filling many key positions. There was no director of State Operations, the person to whom all executive branch agencies report. There was no director of ops because Paul Francis, the man who was supposed to have this position, and a year later did, was shifted to another unfilled crucial position, that of director of the Division of the Budget. When I arrived at the transition's headquarters on November 8, 2006, I found out that there was no budget director-designee and that we were not even close to choosing one. I was alarmed because the governor's budget and his budget message to the Legislature were scheduled for delivery on January 31. Nearly very day of the transition, I annoyingly prodded Eliot to name a director. At the end, Paul Francis, a brilliant and hardworking guy who had been the campaign's issues director, had to be parachuted in.

Eliot didn't have a full-time professional speechwriter. Instead, this task was primarily delegated to talented but inexperienced general staffers, mostly in their twenties. Even worse, major speeches were being written by a committee of the whole senior executive staff. After I participated in the January 2, 2007, chaotic group drafting of Eliot's mediocre State of the State address, delivered on January 3, I grabbed Eliot and incredulously asked him why he had no experienced full-time speechwriter. I told him that we had collectively produced a poor State of the State speech salvaged by his good delivery and the halo around his every utterance. How, I asked, could this have happened when it had been known for months that he had to deliver this speech on his third day as governor? I told him that the job of being Eliot Spitzer's speechwriter was the best available job in the country for a Democrat in that line of work. His only response was that a job writing speeches for him was only second best; writing speeches for Barack Obama was the best. Given the timing, well before the Obama candidacy was being taken seriously, Eliot's observation had been extraordinarily prescient.

Many substantive transition tasks had been performed badly and much too slowly. There certainly had been a lot of stuff going on all the time, but it had been mostly for show. Of course, ceremony is important in a transition, as the elected starts to symbolically govern prior to actually taking office. However, our transition was also deficient in some of the most crucial areas where ceremony and symbolism would have helped. The single biggest problem awaiting Eliot was the decline of the upstate, and principally Western New York, economy. This is the area from Rochester to Buffalo and south from Erie and Niagara counties to Chautauqua County on the Pennsylvania border. Western New York badly needed our help, after decades of steady economic decline and failed government policies. The transition did not hold a single event in Western New York and certainly none in Buffalo, the epicenter of this major problem. I could not get an answer from anybody as to why not.

At my own expense, I went up to Buffalo for a week and, using my transition title, waved the Spitzer flag. I met with everyone, all dying to meet with someone perceived to be close to Eliot. I held meetings with Mayor Byron Brown, Congressman Brian Higgins, the presidents of the University of Buffalo and Buffalo State, the heads of several Industrial Development Agencies, architects, developers and executives from major employers and sports teams, including the Buffalo Sabres and Buffalo Bills. Upon my return, I gave Eliot a set of recommendations and one clear warning. I strongly advised against hiring someone from outside the region to chair the upstate wing of the Empire State Development Corporation. ESDC, a powerful state authority that dispenses billions of dollars in economic development grants, had always been venued in Manhattan, and then resided a few floors below the governor's own Manhattan office at 633 Third Avenue, near 40th Street. Eliot had wisely campaigned on a promise to establish an upstate component of ESDC, equal in stature to downstate, and to headquarter it in Buffalo.

Everyone I met with in Buffalo mentioned this promise. Whether or not I asked, they had advised that the upstate ESDC chair must come from the region, and preferably from Buffalo. I reported this unanimous request and indeed made some recommendations on whom to hire based upon informal "interviews" I conducted during my trip. I also placed myself on the formal interview committee for these positions, meaning the upstate and downstate ESDC Chairs. For the downstate position, Eliot made the excellent choice of Pat Foye, a master deal lawyer from Skadden, who had mentored Silda during her years at that powerful firm. However, ignoring the advice I had collected empirically, Eliot chose a guy from Pennsylvania to be upstate ESDC chair. He was a good and talented guy, who never moved his family to Buffalo and really never moved there himself. In a *Where's Waldo* manner, the Buffalo press eventually started to report on Dan Gundersen's whereabouts, constantly pointing out that he had not moved to Buffalo and didn't seem to be planning to.

The transition ended with me in a rage over how it had been run and over the "rope-a-dope" that Darren Dopp was attempting to pull on me. I then wrote my letter of withdrawal. However, following the series of pranks and my own lack of resolve, I wound up inadvertently and reluctantly taking my seat as a knight at Eliot's Roundtable.

■ ■ ■

Eliot's Roundtable

I BELIEVE THAT AN altered and impaired Eliot made the mistakes chronicled in this book. I believe that a healthy Eliot, not one being poisoned by constant awareness that his private conduct would come to light and destroy everything, would not have done these things. Eliot, though flawed and fallible like all of us, had performed spectacularly as attorney general, consistently demonstrating the intelligence, integrity, decisiveness and, yes, restraint, that produced his unparalleled achievements and historic electoral plurality. By the time he became governor, however, Eliot was a different man and began making all the mistakes chronicled here. In fairness, he didn't do this all by himself; he was assisted by the people he chose to help him govern New York State, including me.

The transition substantially squandered the opportunity to recruit the best and brightest to fill the top spots on the executive staff and in the agencies. Instead, we settled for some poor, some good, and some great local talent, dominated by people who moved with Eliot from the Office of the Attorney General. Some key AG staff who would have helped the situation did not come along, including the former Solicitor General Caitlin Halligan and Eliot's top two lawyers in the AG's office, Michelle Hirshman and Dieter Snell. Michelle and Dieter had brilliantly managed more than 500 lawyers on the AG's staff. These two were later retained as outside counsel to help represent Eliot and the "Executive Chamber" (the formal statutory name for the governor's office) in the Troopergate investigations and the final conflagration in early March 2008.

From the AG staff that did move with Eliot, and a few outsiders, Eliot assembled an inner group that worked most closely and consistently with him. The group had no structure and little discipline. Over the course of the Plague Year, this dysfunction made things a lot worse. The chaotic January 2, 2007, group drafting of Eliot's State of the State address was an early indicator of the way this undisciplined inner circle—no, inner amoeba—would function throughout Eliot's tenure as governor. That inner group, whatever its shape, comprised the following people:

Rich Baum was secretary to the Governor, the number-two person in state government. He was the person responsible for directing the inner group and the flow of information and directives to and from Eliot. The secretary's status and certain specific responsibilities are enshrined in statute. Based upon prior practice, the Albany establishment had come to expect a strong secretary functioning as a gatekeeper for people inside and outside government seeking to gain access to the governor. Rich, 37 years old when Eliot was sworn in as governor, had served as his chief of staff in the Office of the Attorney General. However, since Rich is not a lawyer, and the business of the AG is to practice law on behalf of the State and its people, there was very little staff for him to have been chief of. He had spent those eight years skillfully serving as Eliot's senior political advisor, translating Eliot's enormous legal victories into political clout. Baum was appointed secretary by Eliot despite his lack of experience in managing a large group of talented and high-octane people. In fact, Rich had shown little desire to do the job, which came with a title that he clearly coveted.

Until he resigned on October 9, 2007, while on indefinite disciplinary suspension for his leading role in Troopergate, Darren Dopp was Eliot's communications director, to whom the Press Office and public information officers of the many executive branch agencies reported. This reporting structure does not give the communications director any authority over the investigative or security functions of the State Police, Darren's Plague Year activities notwithstanding. Darren had been the communications director in Eliot's AG's office. Prior to that, Darren had been a deputy in Governor Mario Cuomo's press office. Darren comes off as a self-effacing American boy next door. His looks and demeanor reminded me of Kevin Bacon, and especially his incarnation as Jack Brennan, Richard Nixon's loyal retainer in life and in the movie *Frost/Nixon*.

When Darren was indefinitely suspended by Eliot in July 2007, press secretary Christine Anderson was elevated to the position of communications director. Christine is a very pretty 30-something blonde who could become drop-dead gorgeous whenever she chose to, as she did about once a month, in order to lift her spirits and ours as well. One of Christine's previous jobs had been in the Clinton Administration's Press Office during the Monica Lewinsky scandal. Christine assumed our top press job in the midst of Troopergate, because her boss, Darren Dopp, had been exposed as the primary evildoer in that affair. Later, of course, she handled the press onslaught during the 61 hours culminating in Eliot's resignation. If it is true that a person is fortunate to live in challenging and interesting times, Christine has been incredibly blessed.

David Nocenti was counsel to the governor, the person most directly responsible for advancing his legislative objectives and for ensuring the administration's and executive branch agencies' compliance with the law. David was the person on the senior executive staff with the best credentials and skills for the post he held. He had textbook demeanor and bearing for the governor's counsel—that of a Jesuit. David had also been Eliot's counsel in the Office of the Attorney General and had served as one of the assistants under Elizabeth Moore when she was Governor Mario Cuomo's counsel. More than any other person on the senior executive staff, the counsel, who leads a small and elite group, stands apart and projects a distinct personality and institutional identity. One of the many minor tragedies of the Plague Year, overshadowed by the big one, is that David Nocenti did not get to be the truly great counsel that he was destined to be and capable of being.

Olivia Golden was the state's Director of Operations, to whom all executive branch agencies reported. She exercised those responsibilities when she finally began full-time work in mid-February 2007 and until she was forced to resign at the end of that year. Olivia, a very smart bureaucrat who was as typical of the Kennedy School assembly line as the Malibu was for the one at GM, was never able to get Eliot's or her senior colleagues' attention. Some of that was due to her late arrival. She started work when the administration was already at war with the Legislature over the comptroller vacancy created by Alan Hevesi's resignation, and when our legislative priorities were overshadowing the more important work of the agencies that reported to her. For these and other reasons, it never happened for Olivia as Director of State Operations, an absolutely crucial post for the success of any New York governor.

When Olivia resigned in December 2007, she was replaced as director of ops by Paul Francis, the person originally intended to have the position, and the person best suited for it. Paul had been the issues director of Eliot's campaign and had spent the better part of two years mastering the intricacies of the state's agencies and public authorities. By virtue of his last-minute appointment to the equally important job of Director of the Division of the Budget, Paul developed an even deeper understanding of how the agencies functioned and how they were funded. During the Plague Year, Paul and I sometimes clashed on specific issues of policy and, most notably, about the importance and funding of public higher education in New York State. Paul performed brilliantly in both of his roles as budget director and later as director of ops.

Peter Pope was the Director of Policy and I was Eliot's senior policy advisor, although my formal title did not have that middle descriptor. That meant that Peter and I effectively had the same job. This overlap never bothered us, and we quickly joined forces. We recruited and jointly supervised a small staff of talented young operatives, including three angels of mercy, Julieta Lozano, Dan Doktori and Haley Plourde-Cole. We brainstormed and helped each other with major forward-looking policy initiatives, such as workers' compensation reform; a higher education commission; a multi-state greenhouse gas–reduction initiative; and a commission to consolidate, coordinate and make more efficient the endless layers of New York State's 4,760 local governments.

Peter and I agreed about most things. We both deluged Eliot with complaints about the workings of the administration. Most of this carping would not have occurred had Rich Baum exercised the kind of authority and leadership expected of the secretary. When that lack of managerial control spawned problems, such as the Troopergate fiasco, Peter and I became part of a five-person team of senior lawyers who represented and defended the Second Floor in the eight Troopergate investigations commenced prior to Eliot's resignation.

Marty Mack was the Director of Intergovernmental Relations. A former mayor of the city of Cortland, "at the door to the Finger Lakes," Marty was the person most knowledgeable about the villages, towns, cities, and counties of the state—the places where the impact of our initiatives were most directly felt and critiqued. Since I ran the governor's commission designed to reduce and streamline those local governments, Marty and I had a lot of interplay during the Plague Year. He was a steady hand who accompanied Eliot on most of his grueling trips around the state. Because of this, when you wanted to know what was going on with the governor, Marty was the best and most reliable source of information.

Marlene Turner's title was chief of staff, but Eliot had once described her function as our "Den Mother." Marlene attempted to control Eliot's schedule and access to his person. This was hard, because Rich was not the gatekeeper he should have been and because Eliot wound up being his own Secretary. Marlene and I were the oldest members of the senior executive staff. Unlike me, Marlene acted her age and was a calming presence in the midst of the constant turmoil that characterized the Plague Year.

I was the senior advisor, the "Monster Man" as I had described my job in a profile published in the *New York Sun* on January 12, 2007. That self-description had been a mistake, since few recognized the football terminology for a roving linebacker. In any event, my job had several specific portfolios plus license from Eliot to get involved in virtually any initiative or problem as I saw fit. I asked for this job description and flexibility but now realize that it exacerbated the dysfunction in the inner group created by Rich Baum's lack of managerial and leadership skills. Other people, including Sean Maloney and David Paterson, were key players and spent a lot of time with Eliot. They generally did their important jobs well, but they were not consistently members of the dysfunctional inner group.

Despite the turmoil in the inner group and the many errors that I dwell on, a lot of very good work was done by Eliot and his administration. The very good and some great work done in those 15 months may usefully be the subject of another book. I have been strongly urged to write it, but doubt I will. It would be even sadder than this one, a chronicle of unfulfilled possibilities and lost opportunities. Some of these come along only once in a generation, or only once in a lifetime, as was true for me.

Grading those 15 months objectively, the administration would have earned a B–/C+ by March 9, 2008. A fairer grade perhaps, and one more accurate, would assign the administration an "incomplete." The weeks just before the scandal broke were among the very best, suggesting that the administration may have been headed toward excellence. The problem was that this range of high C to low B jangled with the extravagant expectations Eliot had created of an A+ performance, symbolized in his campaign slogan *"On day one everything changes."*

The gap between *"On day one everything changes"* and *"You don't turn a battleship in a bathtub,"* a phrase the administration was using by March 2007 to explain why everything had not changed overnight, produced disappointment among the electorate and an explicit violent reaction in the media. We were flogged in the newspapers that had supported Eliot's election, like the *New York Times* and the *New York Daily News,* and also in those that had opposed him, like the *Wall Street Journal* and the *New York Post.*

■ ■ ■

....

Eliot's Inaugural Taunt

THE QUESTION I was most frequently asked in the run-up to the 2006 election was whether I thought Eliot could and would successfully make the transition from attorney general to governor. Although posed in a variety of ways, the question always embodied some amount of skepticism. How could a man so naturally aggressive and prosecutorial successfully run the state without his preferred weapons of accusation, investigation, litigation and criminal prosecution? Even the most ambitious and favorable journalistic analyses of Eliot's career, including Brooke Master's admiring biography *"Spoiling for a Fight* and Peter Elkind's *Satan or Savior?"*, a long and well-documented article for *Fortune* in 2005, reflected these concerns about Eliot's temperament and ability to adapt. I just didn't see it, or didn't want to. My completely candid reply each time was to wax rhapsodic about Eliot's awe-inspiring intellect and energy; how he successfully surmounted each new challenge in his life and career; and how I expected the same or better from him not if, but rather when, he was elected governor.

Eliot had won the love and devotion of Silda Wall, a top-shelf woman who could not be bluffed, bullied or trifled with. Everyplace he went, he exuded confidence, comfort and adaptability. How could such an A+ student of government fail to recognize that success as governor required skill in, and respect for, consensus building, conciliation and compromise?

As Jan and I took our front-row seats for Eliot's Inauguration at 1:00 P.M. on January 1, 2007, nothing that had recently transpired changed my opinion that he would easily adapt to his new job. I had doubts about some of the executive staff who would accompany him, a staff that on that morning at least would not include me, as I would pull the plug after the January 3 State of the State and before the scheduled January 5 announcement of my appointment. The recently concluded transition had pointed to some rocky moments in the first year or so. I had also begun to like Eliot less because of the way he had allowed me to be treated. However, setting aside my own considerable arrogance, I knew that my absence from Eliot's staff would not make a big difference. My basic assessment remained that Eliot had a great skill set to be governor. As I watched Bob Sweet, the federal judge for whom Eliot had clerked more than two decades before, redundantly administer the oath already taken by Eliot the previous midnight, I believed that Eliot had already made the necessary adjustments in demeanor and attitude.

I recalled watching a similar metamorphosis occur in 1998 as part of a small group of intimates huddled in Eliot's tiny rented weekend home in Columbia County, New York. The Justice of the Peace of the town of Gallatin had presided, and after the oath, Eliot and I ran outside into the frigid air in our shirtsleeves and, employing a wrench, pried out the massive cork from a "Jeroboam" of Perrier-Jouët champagne, which I had purchased for the occasion. There were a round of toasts and a brief speech by Eliot delivered with a new and gently formal demeanor, in recognition of his new status. When my turn came, I pointedly did not make a toast to Eliot, who I predicted would be constantly saluted by everyone forever, preferring instead to toast his parents, Bernie and Anne. I said their love would give him the strength to get up when life or his own failings caused him to fall, as they inevitably would. With the aid of a quote supplied by Ethel Kennedy, Eliot invoked the metaphor of the fallen man rising as he announced his resignation as governor, 111 months later, on March 12, 2008.

It was comforting to me that the celebratory dinner on December 31, 2006, had been as small as the one held eight years before at the Stissing House, a country restaurant in Pine Plains, New York, and smaller than the 2002 party for Eliot's second inauguration as AG, when he and I had opened a "Methusaleh" of champagne. It was also reassuring that the invitees for the intimate 1998 and 2006 parties were substantially identical.

When the small New Year's Eve dinner in the formal dining room of the Governor's Mansion in Albany ended and merged with a huge and raucous party in the public rooms of the residence, I did not take it as a sleight that on this occasion I was left to open the much larger "Balthazar" of Veuve Clicquot by myself, nor think it an evil omen that I slashed my hand pretty badly opening this vessel, the equivalent of 16 bottles. It sported custom-made labels, front and back. The front label simply proclaimed the date and occasion. On the back label I "whispered" to Eliot that there was an even larger bottle, a "Nebuchadnezzar," reserved for a future occasion. Unlike the previous mega-bottles, the empty 2007 Balthazar was discarded, leaving only the picture I retained as proof that it ever existed — much like the Spitzer Administration itself.

On New Year's Day, as we waited for Eliot's speech to begin, one discordant note was struck. As he had the night before, Eliot gave the honor of administering the oath to United States District Judge Bob Sweet. It had been OK to do that at the large, but private, New Year's Eve party. It was a mistake to do it in a public ceremony witnessed by hundreds of thousands of New Yorkers live or watching television. The honor should have been given to Judith Kaye, the chief judge of the Court of Appeals, New York's highest court. Judith, a regal woman who bears herself like the state's empress, had recently eulogized her beloved husband, Stephen Kaye, at a funeral that Eliot and I had attended. She came into 2007 a seriously wounded woman, personally and professionally. The 1,300 state judges had not received a pay increase in eight years, and she was bearing the brunt of their anger. As the clock struck one, Judith administered the oaths to Lieutenant Governor David Paterson and Attorney General Andrew Cuomo but was visibly annoyed as Judge Sweet performed the function customarily reserved for her.

Then, in the first minute of his speech, Eliot insulted many of those he called his "partners in government" as they sat close to where he stood. Most foolishly, he dissed the previous administration's "three men in a room" as the governor, Assembly speaker and Senate Majority leader are called in New York. He took an unambiguous and widely reported shot at outgoing Governor George Pataki and the other two, who would inhabit "the room" with him, Republican Senate Majority Leader Joe Bruno and Democratic Assembly Speaker Shelly Silver.

After politely thanking Pataki for his 12 years of service, the sparseness of the thanks making it seem like Eliot was saying to new parents, "Wow, that really is a baby," he had heaped criticism on Pataki, Bruno and Silver by saying:

> Over the last decade, we have seen what can happen when our government stands still in the face of great challenge and inevitable change. We've seen it in the burdensome property taxes and the healthcare we can't afford; in the jobs disappeared from our upstate cities and the schools that keep failing our children; in a government that works for those who hold office — not those who put them there. Like Rip Van Winkle, the legendary character created by the New York author Washington Irving, New York has slept through much of the past decade while the rest of the world has passed us by. Today is the day when all of that changes — when we stop standing still and start moving forward once more.

Jan and I watched the uncomfortable reactions register in the faces, body language and gestures of these three men as they listened to Eliot's speech. The Rip Van Winkle line evoked an angry leer from Bruno, who turned to the person sitting next to him and said, "He's talking about us." Battle was joined right then and right there, if it had not already been well before.

Unless Eliot took seriously what nobody else had, Pataki's exploration of a presidential bid, going after his predecessor had no possible upside. Pataki was leaving the public stage. He hadn't been a great governor, but he had his strengths, including a very good environmental record. He was a nice guy and had many friends in the audience and the state. The Rip Van Winkle line evoked the image of a sleepy Pataki, bandied about by the press for weeks after the governor had hosted a theater party to the Broadway hit *The Drowsy Chaperone*.

Going after Shelly was worse. Eliot would need him almost immediately to achieve the objective of filling the powerful office of state comptroller with a strong and qualified person acceptable to Eliot and in accord with his plans for revamping the state's finances. The office had become vacant due to the conviction and resignation of Alan Hevesi after it had been revealed that Hevesi had habitually used a state vehicle and driver to chauffeur and accompany the comptroller's lonely and ailing wife. The choice of Hevesi's replacement was the Legislature's, not the governor's. In this "election," each state senator and member of the Assembly would have one vote. This gave control to the lower house, with 150 members to the Senate's 62, and therefore ultimate control to Shelly. When interviewed about Eliot's speech and the Rip Van Winkle reference, Shelly nervously said that he hadn't been offended, as he had thought the comments had been directed at Pataki and Bruno. Bruno was deeply offended by Eliot's speech and pushed back hard in the press, defending the former governor and himself and more or less saying, "We'll see." But hadn't the battle lines been drawn well before that, and hadn't the war already commenced?

My sense of Joe Bruno began forming eight years before the 2007 inauguration, at the second Pataki inaugural, on January 1, 1999, a day when Eliot was being sworn in as the new attorney general. The inauguration was held indoors, like all those in memory until Eliot's bold and wonderful 2007 event, held outdoors in the dead of Albany winter. At the 1999 inauguration, my family and I were seated up front with the Spitzer clan. While we were waiting for the ceremonies to begin, I excused myself to use the men's room. When I tried to reenter the auditorium, I realized that I had left my credentials at my seat. The State Police were not willing to allow me back in. Joe Bruno, whom I had never met, spotted the little drama and came over to offer help. After I explained my predicament, he vouched for me with the police and personally escorted me back to my seat and shook the hands of my wife and kids and the Spitzer parents and siblings. It was the grand gesture of a handsome older politician who possessed considerable charm.

Eight years later, at 77, Joe was still handsome. Bobbie, his wife of 57 years, was suffering with advanced Alzheimer's disease and would die a year later. His position as Majority leader had become extremely precarious as his majority had been reduced to just six seats in the 2006 election. That slim majority seemed very likely to disappear in the 2008 election because of a pronounced statewide shift in the electorate toward registered Democrats, and also because of Eliot's then enormous popularity. There was no reason for Eliot to go after Bruno, especially at the Inauguration. On the contrary, there was every reason to publicly embrace and stroke him. He was on the way out, in every sense of the phrase, and in fact was on the verge of being indicted by a grand jury convened by a Republican Department of Justice in 2006.

As I sat there incredulous, listening to Eliot's taunt and watching Bruno's angry "We'll see" reaction, I turned to my wife, Jan, who also recalled and had been touched by Bruno's courtesy eight years earlier and said, "He's on his way out—all Eliot has to do is show him some respect, and he will behave." While I still think that is what Eliot should have done and that it would have worked, I now believe that Joe was plotting and planning for battle before the inaugural speech, perhaps well before.

After Eliot's resignation in 2008, I continued to get scores of press calls inquiring about Eliot's frame of mind, activities and plans. Out of courtesy, reporters would also ask me about how I was doing. Soon after the resignation, a young reporter named Jacob Gershman met me for coffee and asked the standard questions. I liked Gershman, because he worked hard on his stories, which were meticulously researched, though usually registering skepticism about the Spitzer Administration's initiatives. After failing to extract anything to base a new story on, Jacob said, "Hey, I have something for you, which I'm pretty sure you will be interested in seeing."

"Yeah, and what might that be"? I sarcastically responded.

"I have a dossier of more than two hundred pages on you that was given to me by Roger Stone."

I coyly replied, "Yes, that might be of some interest." In August 2007, it had been revealed that Stone, a notorious political tricks operative, had been hired by Bruno as a consultant for the GOP campaign office. Stone had been quickly redeployed on special projects related to the Troopergate scandal, which had begun with truthful assertions that Bruno was using state aircraft for travel to personal and political events.

I skimmed the report delivered to me a week later by Gershman and was shocked, not by its contents, which consisted mainly of newspaper articles followed by nasty, caustic comments about me, my activities and my character, but by the date on the cover, February 15, 2007. The report's "introduction" said that it was just a "first cut" and could be broadened or supplemented as the unknown client directed. I found the report comical in a way. If an article contained in the report was critical, or commented on some asserted negative characteristic of mine, such as aggressiveness, greed or arrogance, the report highlighted the negative quote and embellished it with the unknown author's commentary. Any article that could be negatively spun, was. Any favorable article was derided as a nauseating puff piece.

It was all oddly humorous, even a little flattering I'll admit, but the February 15, 2007, date on the cover amazed me. Reports of this length require weeks of work, at the very least. I was closely associated with Eliot and likely to be part of the governor's inner circle, but I was not alone. There had to have been similar reports about Rich Baum, Paul Francis, David Nocenti, Peter Pope and Darren Dopp, as well as others. There would also have been even more massive reports on David Paterson and Eliot himself. To do such lengthy reports on all these people would have taken months to research and compile. The work on these reports must have been commissioned and begun some time in the fall of 2006, if not before.

Who ordered this? And who compiled this dossier? Who was the intended audience? I do not know. What I do know is that Roger Stone gave my dossier to Jacob Gershman, the *New York Sun*'s Albany reporter. Stone had been hired by Bruno and later fired by him, after it was revealed in July 2007 that while working for the GOP campaign office, he had made an obscene and threatening phone call to Bernie Spitzer, Eliot's gravely ill 84-year-old father. After Eliot's resignation, Stone bragged about and marketed his self-declared role in uncovering Eliot's patronage of prostitutes. So, as I said, bitter battle lines may have been drawn by Bruno before Eliot chose to publicly taunt him. If so, whether Bruno was merely arming for a potential war or had begun a clandestine preemptive war is not known.

Despite the inaugural taunts, Eliot pushed through several major initiatives in the first few months of his term, including ethics reforms and an entire revamping of New York's Workers' Compensation system. These were important measures that had evaded substantial reform and improvement for decades. For almost any other governor, the things accomplished in the first three months of the Spitzer term would have been judged as a year's work and a good one at that. In these victories, Joe Bruno and Shelly Silver had cooperated, seemingly unwilling or unable to get in the path of the enormous popular support that Eliot wielded. In the midst of this rapid initial progress, which matched the rhetoric of everything changing on Day One, Eliot confronted the issue of the imminent legislative vote to fill the office of New York comptroller. However, the choice of a comptroller was the Legislature's prerogative.

■ ■ ■

....

An Early War
with the Assembly and
Attempt to Seize the Senate

THEODORE ROOSEVELT WAS the role model Eliot had frequently pointed to during his campaign and in numerous public pronouncements. Eliot had taken a scholarly interest in the man and truly admired him. Abraham Lincoln is the Republican most Democratic politicians admire and invoke when attempting to appear nonpartisan. However, for Eliot, Teddy Roosevelt was better. He was a New York City kid who had become New York governor and later a great president, with his head right next to Lincoln's in the granite of South Dakota's Black Hills.

As Eliot's term began, it would have been wise to remember and internalize T.R.'s most famous utterance—because in the matter of picking a replacement for Alan Hevesi, Eliot screamed at the top of his lungs but had no real weapon to wield. That is, none other than the enormous popularity that he enjoyed with the voters. Ironically, that popularity began to dissipate in this very early contest, once it became clear that Eliot had picked a fight that he could win only if his opponents, Shelly Silver and Joe Bruno, let him win.

The Legislature had the sole constitutional authority to fill the vacancy created when Alan Hevesi had been convicted of a felony and resigned. In this "election" of a comptroller, each senator and member of the Assembly would cast one vote. That meant that the Democrats in the Assembly, with more members than the total number of Republicans in both houses, would control the election. The last time a similar vacancy had occurred was 1993, when both Comptroller Ned Reagan and Attorney General Bob Abrams had resigned their long-held offices to take private-sector jobs.

In both of those 1993 contests, then Assembly Speaker Saul Weprin, Shelly Silver's predecessor, had decided whom he wanted and herded his obedient members into rubber-stamping the selections. Weprin had backed Carl McCall for comptroller and Oliver Koppel for attorney general. The 1993 election of McCall contradicted one of Eliot's assertions, that without his intervention the Assembly would mechanically elevate one of their own, without regard to whether the chosen member would make a good comptroller. McCall had never served in the Assembly, nor had Carol Bellamy, the runner-up in that 1993 election. As it turned out, it was Eliot's strident suggestion that ultimately ensured the election of Tom DiNapoli, an assembly-man from Nassau County.

In January 2007, at the height of his popularity, Eliot had pressured Silver and Bruno to agree that a screening panel comprising

three former comptrollers would choose a slate of "up to five candidates" from which the Legislature would elect Alan Hevesi's
successor. By forcing Shelly to make this deal, Eliot had weakened
him in the eyes of his conference, the Democratic members of the
Assembly. Joe Bruno could feign statesmanship and go along with
the arrangement without losing stature in his conference, because
the Democrats in the Assembly controlled the election.

Shelly underestimated the revulsion of his members, as
it became clear to them that he had not only surrendered an
important constitutional prerogative of the Legislature, but that
the governor viewed membership in the Assembly as a virtual
disqualification for the office of comptroller. Silver's control over
his conference was waning. Eliot had resoundingly supplanted
him as the most powerful Democrat in state government. Even
Shelly's distant second-place position had become tenuous,
because the upper house was likely to pass into Democratic
hands in 2008, and through Eliot's conversion of Republican
senators into Spitzer cabinet members, possibly sooner. Then
Shelly had cut the screening panel deal with its implicit double
insult to his Assembly colleagues.

Shelly's conference started to revolt and publicly denounce
the deal. This uprising might have been stopped had the screening panel produced a slate of five comptroller candidates that
included two, or even three, of the five members of the Assembly who had been actively campaigning for the position. Eliot
had offered cabinet positions to two of these members, Tom
DiNapoli and Pete Grannis, making it harder for him to claim
that they were not qualified.

During the transition, Eliot had interviewed a number of potential candidates, even though he had no constitutional authority in the matter of whom the Legislature would elect. The fact of these interviews had leaked out, and after the inauguration, it was rumored that Eliot was lobbying the independent panel to deliver a slate devoid of Assembly members. Then the independent screening panel had done just that, and worse, they had reported only three names despite having the authority to name five. It was a slap in the face of the Legislature, effectively announcing that not one of their 212 members was qualified to be comptroller. Indeed, they were so unworthy that the panel had left two slots empty rather than filling them with legislators. The two empty slots gave Shelly the pretext for reneging on his public commitment, by arguing counterfactually and dishonestly that the agreement required the panel to report five qualified candidates, rather than the "up to five" that had been agreed to. Joe Bruno, for his part, played statesman by agreeing that the deal had indeed been "up to five." Barely suppressing his glee, Bruno publicly asked what he was to do when the two Democrats who were parties to the deal couldn't agree.

As the comptroller deal fell apart, two more factors came into play. The first was the stature of the leading and consensus candidate from the Assembly, Tom DiNapoli. Although less credentialed for the position than Richard Brodsky, a Westchester Democratic assemblyman, who was also seeking the job, DiNapoli was more popular among his colleagues. He had been a serious candidate for the powerful position of Nassau County

Executive and initially had also sought the Democratic nomination for lieutenant governor in the 2006 election. He had quietly backed off at Eliot's request. That widely known favor to the governor, and the fact that DiNapoli had been offered several positions in the new cabinet, caused resentment when Eliot attacked the group of candidates from the Assembly (including Tom) before the legislative vote and specifically attacked DiNapoli after he was elected.

The second aggravating factor was the late-January revelation by Assembly Minority Leader Jim Tedisco. Jim had complained to Eliot about being excluded from the negotiation of a major ethics bill, to which Eliot's reported response was, "Listen, I'm a fucking steamroller, and I'll roll over you and anybody else." Perhaps this was not the best thing to say to Tedisco, but it was also fairly typical of the way politicians privately express themselves. In this case, it was a mock serious echo of the line in the song "Steamroller" performed by James Taylor weeks before at a free inaugural concert held at the Times Union Center in Albany. Under traditional "rules of engagement," politicians like Tedisco and Eliot could use such hard language in private exchanges without fear of later reading their words in the glaring headlines of the *New York Post*. However, when your first speech as governor indicts the Legislature for a decade of Rip Van Winkle slumber, for putting its own interests above the public's, you've got to anticipate that the old rules among elected officials will change on you.

The widely reported "fucking steamroller" comment (not actually reported that way, but simply with an "f" and hyphens whose contents were unambiguous) was grafted on to the comptroller debate just as Silver and the Assembly were getting ready to break their promise. When they reneged, it made their actions seem less treacherous. They were just standing up to a bully.

Eliot had to attack Shelly and the Legislature for violating a solemn public agreement in the comptroller contest. He did not have to attack DiNapoli once Tom had been elected. When we spoke about it, I pointed out that his own reasoning for staying neutral in the recent attorney general primary should have applied. How much worse to make an enemy out of DiNapoli, who, unlike Andrew Cuomo, was actually a friend and had already won the election? And, like the attorney general, the comptroller possessed powerful weapons that could be used to make the governor's job much more difficult.

After attacking DiNapoli, Eliot went on the road in February attacking Democratic members of the Assembly in their own districts, threatening to throw his enormous weight against them in the next election, less than two years away. At one point during this period, Marlene Turner, Eliot's chief of staff, turned to me and asked, "How did we get here? It's only February, and we have no friends left to defend us." That same week, I had lunch with Silda, who asked me, "Who is this guy?" I responded with the hopeful prediction that it was just "the intoxication of the moment" and that the guy we knew and loved would soon return.

Flipping the Senate

WHILE ELIOT'S BATTLE with Shelly and the Assembly was playing out, a simultaneous war on a second front, with Joe Bruno and the Republican-controlled Senate, raged on. Eliot and Rich Baum had decided that it was important to wrest control of the Senate from Republican hands before the 2008 elections, when the Democrats were likely to gain control, especially if the Spitzer Administration achieved a modest number of the objectives it had set for itself. The effort to flip the Senate became an obsession throughout Eliot's short tenure, contributing to and exacerbating all of the other problems of the Plague Year.

Since 1939, and with only one exception, in 1965, Republicans had controlled the New York State Senate. Throughout most of this same period, the Democrats had controlled the New York State Assembly. Political giants from both parties, including Thomas Dewey, Averill Harriman, Nelson Rockefeller and Mario Cuomo, governed, and virtually always with one house of the Legislature in the hands of the opposing party, either dominated by a Republican Senate Majority Leader or a Democratic Speaker of the Assembly. The Brennan Center for Justice, in a report issued in 2004, concluded that New York's Legislature was the most dysfunctional in the country, asserting further that this largely one-man rule of each house was a major cause and attribute of the malady. Even powerful governors like Republican Nelson Rockefeller and Democrat Herbert Lehman had often been prevented from having their way by the Assembly Speaker or Senate Majority Leader of the opposite party, until a price for acquiescence had been exacted. Only Rockefeller, with his 15-year reign and commanding presence, was able frequently to, though not always, push through his big initiatives. These had included the draconian Rockefeller drug laws and construction of the monstrous Empire State Plaza in Albany, whose architectural style is a cross between Brasilia and the set of *The Martian Chronicles*, a 1970s TV mini-series starring Rock Hudson.

Eliot was in a hurry to enact his ambitious agenda. He didn't want to wait and apparently felt that his landslide victory meant that he didn't have to wait until the November 2008 elections, when the Senate would likely pass into Democratic hands. He resisted cutting the kind of deals that would induce Joe Bruno to go along with major Spitzer initiatives, while waiting for control of the Senate to change hands. Over the years, Eliot and I had frequently discussed the meaning of Mario Cuomo's failure, his virtual refusal to take the State Senate in 1986, when the opportunity had existed to do so. That year, a number of Republicans seeking reelection had been vulnerable. Cuomo was at the apex of his popularity, still riding the wave of his celebrated keynote address at the 1984 Democratic National Convention. Had he thrown his considerable weight against the vulnerable Republicans, control of the Senate likely would have passed to the Democrats, and Cuomo would have had the support he needed to push through his ambitious but vague agenda.

Mario Cuomo's agenda had included the things that never got done because, he said, the Republican-controlled senate, led by Senate Majority Leader Warren Anderson, always blocked them. These were the big-picture items that involved the New York "family" Cuomo frequently talked about. Nevertheless, Cuomo decided to stay out of the contested Senate races and allowed the upper house to stay Republican. In return for the favor, the Republicans fielded a weak candidate for governor, Westchester County Executive Andrew O'Rourke, and gave him shockingly little funding. In the 1986 election campaign, Cuomo had spent $6.8 million to O'Rourke's $1.3 million. As a result, Cuomo, who would have won anyway, triumphed by the lopsided margin of 65 to 35 (a record margin, until Eliot). This, in turn, added fuel to the Cuomo-for-President groundswell, which seemed likely to produce the 1988 Democratic presidential nominee.

Eliot understood that 1986 had been a watershed lost opportunity. In my view, Cuomo's 1986 tacit deal with the Republicans spoke volumes about his true character. To me, it said that Cuomo hadn't really wanted to realize his agenda, because, in truth, he had none—just his speech about New York being one big family.

Eliot knew this history well and, unlike Cuomo, had more than his own platitude of "One New York." Eliot had a real agenda, an extraordinarily detailed one at that. It called for revitalization of the upstate economy. It halted and reversed the growth of Medicaid, whose voracious appetite for funds foreclosed substantial progress in other areas, while delivering mediocre healthcare to the state's poor. It included funding primary and secondary education on a more equitable basis and for massive investments in public higher education. It detailed plans to repair the state's crumbling infrastructure and to refocus its workforce on high-tech industries. In these and all other areas of major concern, Eliot's plan was well thought out and specific—in details that Eliot had mastered. Eliot was ready for his moment but had miscalculated when it would arrive.

Instead of using the first two years of his term to sharpen the skills of his new team in Albany and take the substantial early successes that even Senate Republicans were willing to give him, Eliot tried to flip the Senate in the first two months. Even before the inauguration, Rich Baum was hunting for Republican senators who might switch parties or create vacancies by accepting Spitzer cabinet positions. It was an obsession for Baum, who talked, and seemingly thought, about little else. Baum did this at a time when the transition had failed to hire a director of State Operations to coordinate the agencies. On "Day One," communication and direction from the governor to his army of agencies, employing tens of thousands of people, was unstructured and difficult. That problem continued through mid-February, when Olivia Golden began full-time work as director of ops. To some extent, the problem continued throughout 2007.

Baum's plan to flip the Senate almost worked. Senate Republicans, sensing their likely loss of control in the 2008 elections, had little appetite for the severe reduction in stature and relevance they would soon suffer. So switching parties or taking cabinet positions, which paid much more than their senate salaries and brought immediate power, were enticing options. Eliot was a new and muscular Democrat. He was closer to their views than he was to those of Assembly Democrats on issues such as the death penalty, civil commitment of sex offenders, tax credits for private school tuition, charter schools and tax policy.

Mike Balboni, a popular Nassau Republican senator, vacated his seat and became our deputy secretary for Homeland Security. Mike's vacant seat was won by Democrat Craig Johnson in one of the most expensive legislative elections in New York State history. Baum and the administration also courted Assemblymen Joseph Robach and James Alesi from Rochester, George Maziarz representing Niagara and Orleans counties, John DeFrancesco from Syracuse, John Bonacic from the Catskill region and James Wright of Watertown.

The plan almost worked, but didn't, and it eventually backfired. As Eliot went to war with the Legislature, a close association with the new governor became less enticing to wavering Republicans. Moreover, as the stories of the administration's efforts to convert Republicans leaked and were embellished by the recently receptive but now born-again Republicans, the souring relationship between the Second Floor and Third Floor (where the Senate resides) became toxic. As the early Senate flip strategy and the arrangement for selection of a comptroller began to encounter resistance in late January, Eliot prepared to deliver his first budget message on January 31, 2007.

■ ■ ■

....

The Battleship in the Bathtub

T HE FISCAL 2007–08 budget was, for me, a barometer of all that went wrong during the Plague Year and of the wide gap between expectation and delivery. On January 30, 2007, a too-large group of people from Eliot's executive staff and the Division of the Budget were putting him through dry runs of the budget messages he would deliver the next day. I was worried. While Eliot was well prepared for publicly presenting an A- budget proposal, he was wounded because of the building rancor with the Legislature. The *New York Post* had already called our press office for confirmation of the nasty "Steamroller" exchange between Eliot and Assembly Minority Leader Jim Tedisco. I suspected that the *Post* would publish the story at the worst possible moment for us. The comptroller dispute was building. Moreover, the budget was really where the rubber would hit the road, fulfilling, or not, promises made and the lavish expectations about how fast reform would occur.

The proposed budget was, by any measure, damn good. Among its many virtues was that it boldly confronted and attacked the cancerous growth of Medicaid, which cost the state more than an astounding $45 billion annually. Medicaid spending substantially foreclosed the possibility of progress in education, infrastructure construction and repair and numerous environmental and social programs, all the while delivering mediocre healthcare to a minority of the state's population. Medicaid was the most important reason that the Empire State's budget was 85 percent of California's, even though New York had only 53 percent of the Golden State's population. In the proposed budget, the annual growth rate for Medicaid, which consistently had been 8 percent, was reduced to less than 1 percent and saved some $1.35 billion.

The proposed budget also fulfilled a campaign promise, and a court mandate, by providing New York City schools with greatly increased funding. It went even farther, increasing funding for all public schools in the state and directing the lion's share of the increase to poorly funded districts, where the money was most needed. It attacked a "share" system more favorable to wealthier suburban school districts and replaced it with a "foundation formula" based upon need and conditioned upon school districts entering into so-called Contracts for Excellence. These contracts required the recipient districts to reduce class size, lengthen the school day and year and demonstrate improvement in educational outcomes, such as tests and graduation rates. Educators knew that those proposals contained all the elements necessary to commence a hundred-year war.

The proposed budget projected $6 billion in property tax reductions over three years and increased aid to local governments, especially to less-affluent municipalities. It purported to neither raise a single tax rate nor erect any new taxes. Nevertheless, the proposed closing of various tax loopholes and some higher fees would inevitably trigger a dispute about the definition of new and higher taxes. The budget also thrust deeply into social, educational and environmental policy. It doubled the state's acceptance of, or tolerance for, charter schools, a holy grail for some and a bête-noir for others. The proposal vastly expanded the state's container deposit law and earmarked the revenues for environmental projects. Also included were bold initiatives in high-technology areas that New York was well positioned to lead in, such as stem cell research, nanotechnology and bioinformatics. For vision, audacity and detail, including the specificity of funding, it was a world-class proposal.

But there were also problems in our budget proposal, and the prep questions we hurled at Eliot focused on them. Even the billions assigned to increased educational aid and property tax relief would be less than many had expected. The reallocation of funding to needy schools and municipalities under Eliot's rallying cry of "One New York" would provoke resistance and cause some to promote class warfare. I also had my own little nits to pick.

Despite my Monster Man license, I had not been able to insinuate myself into the budget-making process in any substantial way, and my trivial input had produced small results. Eliot had promised that the state would, for the first time, help fund the various programs providing legal services for the poor. This was one of my portfolios, and, as a veteran of the Legal Services Program, the issue was important to me. In a short pitched battle with the Division of the Budget, I had gotten a tiny $3 million to back this campaign promise, which I had also inserted into Eliot's State of the State speech. I defended another $5 million for legal services, which we took credit for, but in truth was Chief Judge Judith Kaye's money, earmarked by her for these programs. I thought I was so tricky and smart—inserting promises into the State of the State speech during that chaotic last-minute drafting session, thinking that this would guarantee at least some modest delivery on the rhetoric. In other areas, however, I was not successful, such as a $15 million promise to the state's academic libraries, which I stuck into Eliot's speech, but the budget division veterans ignored.

I had also argued directly to Eliot for more funding for public higher education. He pointed to his State of the State promise to convene a Commission on Higher Education. The Commission would propose vastly increased funding and how it should be used. Increased resources for higher education would begin in the 2008–09 budget. Eliot had also directed me to formulate and assemble the higher education commission. The next year and the next budget would be the time and place for higher ed. to become a major pillar of New York State's bright future.

It was a bold, visionary budget, but the bottom-line tab for the total package was a big problem. We had tried to do too much and at too high a price. Depending on how you counted, the increase in the budget was double or triple the rate of inflation. In an attempt to avoid that comparative metric, we had adopted another benchmark, New York's "estimated rate of long-term personal income growth." The problem with that alternative measure was that our rate of increase exceeded that metric as well. Since it was certain that the Legislature would insist on adding to our budget proposal, the absolute number proposed at $120.6 billion would likely grow. Furthermore, storm clouds in the national economy were also building, due to the cascading sub-prime mortgage crisis, suggesting that our predictions of future budget deficits would likely understate the problem. And so I was worried as we prepped Eliot on January 30, 2007, the day before he was to deliver his two budget messages, and the next morning as we took our seats with members of the Legislature for the governor's first speech of the day. There was one matter not subject to any doubt. Every senator and member of the Assembly had either read or heard about that morning's *New York Post* coverage of Eliot's boast to Assembly Minority Leader Jim Tedisco that "I'm a fucking steamroller, and I'll roll over you and anybody else who gets in my way."

Eliot delivered a polished and solid budget address to the hostile legislators. His command of the arcania of this massive document, with thousands of line items totaling $120.6 billion, was inspiring, at least to me. The legislators, however, seemed less impressed and were clearly pissed off. For the first time, of what would become routine, I watched people recently in awe of the man take him on publicly. Assemblyman Harvey Weisenberg from Nassau County, dressed in a bright red sweatshirt, an obvious act of disrespect, pelted Eliot with questions and criticisms about the Executive Budget's treatment of his district. Eliot handled this gracefully, but the shift in attitude and demeanor was apparent to everyone.

The skill Eliot had shown in handling Harvey Sweatshirt and the other aggressive interrogators from the Legislature highlighted the Jekyll-and-Hyde shifts that occurred in Eliot's demeanor throughout the Plague Year. At times Eliot was supremely in control, and at other times seemingly emotionally unhinged. A pattern could not be discerned. I couldn't correlate Eliot's shifting mood to the severity of a current problem or where the administration was in the process of solving it or making it worse. This visible emotional rollercoaster contributed to my belief that during the unhinged moments, a toxic intravenous drip had been at work. A voice in the back of Eliot's head had been chanting a particularly nasty and accelerated version of *Sic Transit Gloria*.

Barely an hour after addressing the Legislature, Eliot delivered a similar, but more theatrical and expanded, version of the budget message to the public. His performance was equally impressive, and the audience, though principally composed of the skeptical press, was more polite.

Over the course of the next two months, the budget proposal, which, had it been enacted without major alteration, would have deserved the A– grade I initially assigned, was transformed into the B/B– budget that emerged at the other end of the sausage factory. It was enacted on April 2, 2007. That was one day beyond the April 1 statutory deadline for an "on-time" budget. That tiny gap had no practical significance. What mattered were the tactics employed to deliver this almost on-time budget. Eliot had drawn a line in the sand about elevating the importance of a good budget over an on-time budget. He had said:

I, in no way, will regret having a late budget if it is the only way we can tame the rapid spending that has too often been the story up here in Albany.

However, at the very end of the process, Eliot had chosen a Lake Wobegon budget so it would be on time. And that "better than average" budget wasn't even technically on time. The modus operandi was to ignore that fact and say it was on time rather than to say it was a day late but that it didn't matter, which was the truth.

The two-month slippage in the quality of the budget from "damn good" to "not bad" occurred while the war with the Legislature was escalating. The "Steamroller" comment, reported the morning of Eliot's budget messages, certainly intensified the hostility. Six days later, Democrat Craig Johnson won the obscenely expensive and bitterly contested special election to fill the Senate seat vacated by Republican Mike Balboni. The Republicans' hold on the Senate became more precarious and deepened Joe Bruno's strong conviction that Eliot was out to get, not just the Senate, but him personally. Abe Lackman, Bruno's confidante and former chief of staff, assured me that Bruno really believed that.

Two days after the special election, the Legislature elected Tom DiNapoli as comptroller. Eliot immediately attacked Tom and the Democratic members of the assembly who had voted for him, doing so while making appearances in their legislative districts. I made two very small attempts at peacemaking or, at least, ratcheting down the level of hostility with the Legislature.

First, I had lunch with Mark Weprin, a Democratic member of the Assembly from Queens, in a dining room within the underground concourse that links the Capitol with the other buildings of the Empire State Plaza. This was a place where members and the press frequently dined. Mark is the son of the late Assembly Speaker Saul Weprin and, more importantly, was my friend and Eliot's from our former lives as partners at C&P. The small gesture seemed to work in a small way, or at least was noticed as I'd hoped. In a February 13, 2007, *New York Times* article headlined "On Tour to Talk Up Budget Plan, Spitzer Stays on Attack," it was noted that:

> [P]olitical observers [were] wondering if the governor, even given his popularity in the polls, can sell an ambitious agenda by burning bridges with the legislature. That may explain why the governor's aides have been reaching out to legislators in recent days. Not long after Mr. Spitzer's morning appearance in Mamaroneck, [where Eliot had attacked a Democratic Assemblyman] one of his top advisers, Lloyd Constantine, was seen having lunch with Assemblyman Mark Weprin, a Democrat who seconded the nomination of Mr. DiNapoli to be comptroller.

Rich Baum called me the day this article appeared in the *Times*, one of the five or so times he called me during the entire Plague Year. He complained about me allowing myself to be seen publicly with Weprin. Baum was sure that Mark had fed the "story" to the *Times* to show he was still tight with the governor.

I would have laughed at the stupidity of Baum's implicit reasoning if I had not been on a speeding train headed for a wall because of it. So, instead I simply told Rich that it was a lunch involving old friends and that the Spitzer Administration needed friends.

My second small conciliatory effort involved reaching out directly to Tom DiNapoli. At the time, I was putting together the Commission on Local Government Efficiency and Competitiveness (LGEC), whose formation Eliot had heralded in the State of the State. Realizing that the comptroller's office had extensive expertise in the finances of New York's local governments, I scheduled a meeting with DiNapoli to seek his advice in structuring the commission and to ask him to designate one member from his senior staff to become a commission member. I told DiNapoli that the executive order I was drafting for Eliot's signature would incorporate his advice and his appointee ex-officio and acknowledge the comptroller's key role in improving the efficiency of local government.

That was the text of our meeting. The subtext, however, was that I was there to pay my respects. Being so closely linked to Eliot, I thought that my deferential courtesy call might slightly take the edge off Eliot's recent attacks on Tom's qualifications. Tom's designee to the LGEC, Mark Pattison, became a particularly strong, articulate and hardworking member of the commission. So the text of the meeting worked well. The subtext was another matter. As I expected, and had predicted to Eliot, DiNapoli soon attacked.

Aside from the legislators themselves, the major combatants in the battle to radically alter Eliot's budget proposal and take him down a notch were the Greater New York Hospital Association and SEIU 1199, a healthcare workers union, which is the largest local in the world. They were the major defenders of the miserable Medicaid and overall healthcare status quo. They launched a multimillion-dollar ad campaign targeting the Executive Budget's proposed cuts in Medicaid spending and accused Eliot of trying to deprive old people and needy children of medical care, when in fact the opposite was the truth. The 1199/GNHA coalition put the interests of its members before the needs of patients. Eliot's proposals shifted the emphasis of funding toward patients' needs. We countered the coalition's ads with our own, which, while based on the facts, were not as skillful or effective. More decisively, 1199/GNHA had a majority of the Legislature beholden to, and united with, them in the desire to show the crusading governor a thing or two.

There had never been any question that Eliot's budget proposal would change in the process of negotiation. All budget proposals do. The questions were, by how much, and for Eliot's first budget, how open and visible to the public the process would be. Eliot had properly emphasized, with much passion and sound reasoning, the importance of eliminating budget-making by the "three men in a room." For decades, the budget had been negotiated by the governor, speaker and Majority leader behind closed doors. Most of the other members of the Legislature knew little about the substance of those meetings until they were concluded, with no time to even read the budget they would vote upon, let alone help shape it. They discovered, simultaneously with the public, most of the details of the budget after it was enacted.

I had not been involved with the February–March 2007 budget negotiations and had little more than a general understanding of most line items, drilling down only on those few I had championed and largely failed to advance. My input, if any, was to get progress reports from Eliot and respond with advice. As we headed into the last week before the April 1 deadline, I was worried about whether Eliot would hang tough enough to enact a budget that would enable him to substantially achieve his objectives.

My worries notwithstanding, I did something of which I am not proud. When the going got tough, the tough went to Paris; I left with my family on March 30, 2007, insincerely telling myself that I was confident that Eliot would get what we needed or stand by his promise to tolerate a late budget if that was the only way to get a good one. He told me he would, and I selfishly chose to believe him. The trip had been planned a year in advance, and like most things in my family's life at the time, it had involved Eliot and Silda. At a charity auction in the spring of 2006, I had bid for and "won" a luxury vacation in Paris for my family. I had even outbid Eliot's mother, Anne, who was bidding on Eliot's behalf and in response to his hand signals.

The charity auction at Christie's was held by Silda's wonderful Children for Children Foundation, and we were bidding well above the level that the trip would have cost in the open market. That's the idea of a charity auction. The trip to Paris was scheduled for a year later, and by then tension and weirdness had invaded my relationship with Eliot. Instead of doing what I should have done—cancelled my trip or joined my family in France later after the budget endgame had played out—I boarded a plane for Paris. I had asked Eliot if I should stay—knowing full well that he would not allow me to disappoint Jan and our kids. At the time, I rationalized, focusing on my de minimis role in the budget. Maybe the symbolic sacrifice would have helped a bit by strengthening Eliot's resolve. More likely, nothing that I or anyone else might have done would have blasted through the chaos in Eliot's mind. Certainly nothing would have altered the fact that a fuse was burning, and the only question was its length.

The final budget was negotiated by five, not three, men in a closed room in the Executive Chamber. The usual three were joined by the Assembly and Senate Minority leaders, Jim Tedisco and Malcolm Smith. The enacted budget was an impersonation of the governor's January 31, 2007, proposal. The budget reduced previously scheduled Medicaid spending by roughly $1 billion, holding the growth rate in that program to below 2 percent, while it had previously grown at roughly 8 percent annually. The absolute gap between that final agreement and Eliot's proposal of $1.35 billion in savings was modest, but that $350 million restored slightly more than half of the proposed Medicaid cuts to hospitals and nursing homes, who had waged the TV ad campaign along with 1199 and GNHA.

The budget also arguably ended the time-honored "share" system that allocated educational aid on the basis of school population rather than need, resulting in much less overall funding for poor school districts in inner cities and rural areas than for affluent suburban school districts. With property values and property tax revenues so much higher in places like Nassau, Westchester, Suffolk and Rockland counties, poor school districts had fallen farther and farther behind in funding and educational performance.

Officially ending this system, and replacing it with a new "foundation" school aid formula, based upon need and conditioned upon objectively measurable improvements in educational outcomes, was, in addition to the Medicaid reforms, one of the two most important victories in the budget. Next to the school funding victory, however, was a significant asterisk, variously estimated in the range of $330 million to $400 million. That amount was given to the wealthier school districts outside of the foundation formula to partially make up for what they would have gotten under the old share system. Even worse, the sum was not spread evenly among the affluent districts according to their former shares. Instead, most of it was sent to Long Island school districts, the lynchpin of the Republicans' tenuous control over the Senate. Westchester school districts, who demographically were very similar to those on Long Island, got little of the substantial side money. This left Westchester Democrats bitter and Long Island Republicans bragging, not only that they had gotten as much as under the old share system, but that, contrary to the governor's talk about permanent reform, they would get their share the next and every succeeding year as well. The truth was toward the middle of these boasts and Eliot's contrary claim that he had substantially succeeded in ending the share system. Still the half-loaf truth was a significant achievement.

Another achievement was approximately $1.3 billion in additional property tax relief flowing directly to taxpayers. That was $200 million less than proposed, not much of a concession and possibly a helpful one given the overall size and growth in the budget. A more mischievous change pushed most of the added tax rebates to wealthier taxpayers, in a fashion generically similar to the way the Senate Republicans had sent most of the additional school aid, departing from the new foundation formula, to affluent school districts.

In the pull-and-tug over property tax rebates, both sides failed to confront the very sound argument that property tax is a bad way to finance education. Property tax, an inherently regressive levy, because it treats rich and poor homeowners equally, becomes even more regressive when poor people are living in homes whose prices have skyrocketed—as virtually all homes had before the housing bubble burst in 2007. Eliot would not confront that basic flaw of property tax and begin to press for shifting some of the burden of school financing to progressive income taxation. He could not have gotten such a radical, but sensible, reform in his first budget but might have during the successful eight- or 12-year run that everyone expected to be Eliot's lot; that is, everyone except Eliot. Or so I believe, because to think otherwise would mean believing that Eliot was delusional.

In February 2008, when I shared my views on this subject with Nassau County Executive Tom Suozzi, in what I had thought was a private conversation, it was overheard and reported in *Newsday*. The Press Office was quick to distance itself from my suggestion and restate Eliot's commitment not to raise income taxes. That day, I ran into Rich Baum, who was gleeful about my fuck-up. I was embarrassed by my carelessness, but happy that the world knew that at least one person in the administration had understood that funding schools through property taxes was a dead end.

Another flaw had been introduced into the otherwise good property tax rebates. They would be sent in rebate checks. The rebates should have been automatically deducted from tax bills. This procedure would have saved time, money, and lots of mis-directed and uncashed checks. I had advocated it to everyone on our side of the budget negotiations, including Eliot. The wisdom came not from me, but real experts, such as Nassau Comptroller Howard Weitzman, one of the three candidates for state comptroller reported by the independent panel. Weitzman had been offered a position in our cabinet. The legislators wanted rebate checks as gaudy physical manifestations of the bacon they had brought home to their constituents. It is a wonder that they hadn't insisted that their pictures be engraved on the checks. This was a small point, but to me, it was another sign that the 2007–08 budget represented business as usual to a greater degree than Eliot had wanted or was willing to admit.

The enacted budget did not have the $1,000 tax credit for private school tuition Eliot had proposed. When asked why it had been deleted, he responded, "Because there's a legislature." That legislature was pretty consistent. Where Eliot proposed additional spending, they went along, as with expanded health insurance coverage, a major stem cell initiative and funding for various high-tech projects. The Legislature was far less accommodating to Eliot's revenue proposals, stripping out an expansion of the state's bottle-deposit law, rejecting the closure of five out of seven tax loopholes, and exacting a business tax cut in return for the two loopholes they agreed to plug.

Despite Eliot's promise to open the endgame to public scrutiny and more extensive participation by rank-and-file legislators, the process had ended as an agreement among Eliot and the four legislative leaders. He even issued a "message of necessity" eliminating the statutory three-day "aging" process, which would have allowed the public and the other 207 legislators three days to read, consider and "have at" the proposed budget. The obvious countervailing factor was that in those three days, the deal might have fallen apart for any number of good or bad reasons. Democracy and open government are very messy. Another countervailing factor was that three days of aging would not have allowed us to make the counterfactual and irrelevant claim that we had delivered an on-time budget.

While Eliot could assign blame for the loss of the private school tuition tax credit and other proposals to the fact that "there's a legislature," the message of necessity had been his. The very negative reaction to the vintage-Albany closed process was predictable and justified. More than the loss of, or alteration in, any of Eliot's proposals, the shrouded conclusion stunned and disillusioned leaders and institutions in Eliot's base. His response to their criticisms included wisecracks, such as "Rome wasn't built in a day" and variations on that platitude.

The tab for our proposed budget had been $120.6 billion, representing a growth rate twice that of inflation. The cost of the enacted budget was $120.9 billion according to the Division of the Budget. The Associated Press put the tab at $121.6 billion, and the *New York Times* put it at $121.8 billion. Because of the secretive ending negotiation, the details of the budget did not completely emerge for days. That made it hard for us to argue persuasively that our numbers were correct. When Comptroller Tom DiNapoli attacked, as had been inevitable, his calculation was a whopping $123.6 billion. This provoked a debate between Tom and our budget director, Paul Francis, about what should and should not have been counted in the total. Of course, Paul was correct that DiNapoli had included items that had traditionally been reflected in "other state fiscal documents." But DiNapoli correctly pointed out that this numbers magic was a bad practice employed to obscure the real cost of state government. Behind all this was Tom's obvious motive to show Eliot that he, too, was a reformer and not only qualified to be comptroller but capable of making Eliot's life a lot more difficult.

Regardless of whose calculation was more valid, it was a higher price tag for a budget that, in many respects, delivered less than our original proposal. It provided less reform of Medicaid and of a regressive public school funding formula, less property tax relief, no tuition tax credits, no expansion of the bottle law and no pay increases for the 1,300 state judges, who by then had not received a raise in eight years.

■ ■ ■

Stiffing the Judges

IN MAY 2008, two months after Eliot's resignation and passage of the ninth consecutive budget without pay raises for the state's judges, a Siena College Poll revealed that 55 percent of New Yorkers opposed such pay increases and only 39 percent favored them. At the time, the salaries of Supreme Court justices, an elite within the roughly 1,300 state judges, was $136,700, well below the starting salary of a first-year associate at many large New York City law firms, without counting the virtually automatic bonuses these rookies received. Lawyers dream, scheme and strive to be elected or appointed to the bench, still the nobility of the legal profession. When they succeed in being elected or appointed New York Supreme Court justices, they exercise vast powers, some beyond any possessed by the governor.

We want judges to do their jobs well. Society expects judges to be among the very smartest, wisest, most scholarly and compassionate people. We want judges to stay on the bench for long tenures and get better at their jobs and, while doing that, be able to live not opulently, but decently. We don't object to having some millionaires on the bench. Whether or not they can get into heaven as easily as a camel fits through the eye of a needle, wealthy people have often made good judges. But we wouldn't want the bench to be dominated by rich men and women capable of stomaching the salary, and declining the type of money paid to seasoned lawyers by big law firms.

In 1999, when the salaries of New York's judges were raised to $136,700, roughly the level of federal judges at the time, judicial pay in New York was barely sufficient to meet the objectives we just discussed. Each year that the judges' pay has remained at that level, New York has moved farther away from a position of sufficiency to a point in 2007, where Chief Judge Judith Kaye was getting stacks and bytes of hate mail from the members of her tribe. She described for me some of the email, including a few laced with obscenities. Unlike the 55 percent of New Yorker's who opposed raising judicial pay, virtually no one in elected state office needed to be convinced that the state's judges badly needed an increase. In his January 3, 2007, State of the State speech, Eliot had called for one. He included a retroactive 21 percent pay-increase line item in the budget he proposed four weeks later.

The legislators didn't need to be convinced that the judges needed a raise, but they were focused on the fact that they also had not gotten a pay increase since 1999, when their salaries had been set at $79,500. New York legislators are part-time employees and, unlike judges, are permitted to hold other jobs and earn substantial outside income. This arrangement may have made sense a long time ago, but no longer does. If New York were a country, its economy would rank among the largest in the world.

New York would be a member of the G20. It needs a full-time Legislature, despite Eliot's sarcastic comment suggesting his desire to have none at all, and despite the banal opinion that with the extra time, legislators would just make more mischief and spend more taxpayer money. It is also said that their additional pay would cost too much.

Making the job of New York's 212 legislators full-time and doubling their pay would cost less than $20 million annually and produce massive benefits. For one, it would substantially eliminate the ubiquitous conflicts of interest that exist when a legislator confronts a bill impacting a legal or consulting client. Legislators would also do more work, and having more time to do it insist on a lot more power than they get under the three- or five-men-in-a-room arrangement. That arrangement is ultimately the choice of the legislators and one easier to make when they are part-timers, scrambling to make a living elsewhere. It must be said that many good senators and members of the Assembly already treat their jobs as full-time. Betty Little, a Republican senator from the North Country, whom I came to admire during the Plague Year, spent her out-of-session time endlessly traveling around a district encompassing 7,800 square miles, 121 municipalities and 53 school districts.

In 2007, the Legislature also wanted a pay increase and really needed one, whether or not it had been "earned" on any particular scale of merit. However, because a majority of the public also opposed both legislative and judicial pay increases, they were treated like live grenades. Linking their proposed raises to the judges' made the legislators feel more secure and made it impossible for Eliot to increase one without the other. If Eliot had been possessed by any illusion that he could shame the Legislature into decoupling the two sets of proposed raises, it should have been dispelled by the comptroller fiasco.

Joe Bruno had little shame, and Shelly Silver had none. Certainly not of this variety. In truth, they really hadn't needed to be ashamed of seeking a pay increase for their members, who hadn't received one in eight years. Nevertheless, Eliot was not deterred from attempting to decouple, with the result being a 2007–08 budget devoid of pay increases for both judges and the Legislature. That is where it lay in the hangover period after the April 2, 2007, budget enactment, when I got a phone call from Chief Judge Judith Kaye. She asked me to find a place where we could have dinner alone and unobserved. I had responded that we should eat at my place in Chatham, 31 miles from the Capitol. I offered to cook her a great dinner and pair it with fine wine.

We made a date for a few days later and, anticipating the evening, I was both excited and anxious. I wasn't worried about whether my cooking would be good enough. I am a decent chef. Instead, my anxiety arose from the obvious topic to be discussed during dinner, and whether I had any ability to help her judges get the pay increases they had been demanding with increasing anger. During the transition, I had met with numerous judges who were livid about this issue and had backed their anger with detailed salary comparisons and charts plotting their decline in inflation-adjusted compensation. I knew that the recently enacted budget, which spent so much money, but not a cent on a pay raise for them, had made all this much worse.

On the other hand, I was excited about this private and intimate visit. Judith, as I've noted, is New York royalty. When she gives you her undivided attention, it feels like the sun is shining just for you. I would have that experience for several hours. Our dinner was wonderful except for the prime beef, which I overcooked. She graciously observed that it reminded her of the way her mother would have prepared it. We told stories and reminisced, and I tried in some small way to comfort the recently widowed chief by speaking lovingly about Steve, a master litigator who had always been generous with his time and advice for younger lawyers, like me. We talked about the hate mail she was getting, and she told me what I already knew—that her inability to deliver pay increases for the judges was killing her. Coming on the heels of Steve's death, it was a horrible way to spend her scheduled last year as chief judge of New York—a job she had loved so much that she had declined Bill Clinton's offer to become attorney general of the United States and likely after that a United States Supreme Court Justice. At dinner, I promised Judith that I would ask Eliot to assign me the judicial pay project. I did not tell her exactly what tools I would employ to break the stalemate.

My plan involved approaching Joe and Shelly for separate man-to-man meetings. I had clear and distinct impressions of these two guys. Bruno was an old-fashioned politician, who at his stage of life wanted to be stroked and given a graceful exit. In the first few months, I had tried to cultivate him and his staff. He had been scheduled to attend two small meetings I had set up just for this purpose. I even lined up former Lieutenant Governor Stan Lundine to attend and make the introductions; as

Lundine is among the very few people in state government liked and respected by members of both political parties. Following blow-ups with Eliot, Bruno had instead sent his surrogates, Jeff Lovell and Mike Avella. So I stroked them. Then I went to Shelly Silver and some of his key aides, soliciting their advice on the two gubernatorial commissions I was putting together and acceded to their request that they appoint two members to the Higher Education Commission, while relegating the minority leaders to just one. When a Silver deputy had made this seemingly petty request, I discovered how put off Silver's camp was by Eliot's insistence that the minority leaders be included in key deals. Eliot was right to do this and to begin to lay the foundation for even broader participation of rank-and-file members. That was one reason why the endgame closed-door budget deal, with Eliot's message of necessity, had been so bad and so contrary to the direction he had wanted to go and had promised the voters.

I paid several courtesy calls to Shelly, and we played an advanced game of Jewish Geography. I recognized his delight when he discovered that I, an apparent Gentile, was in fact not only a Jew, but one with a solid education and strong Jewish awareness. For Shelly, I was a happy contrast to Eliot, whose relative lack of Jewish identity clearly annoyed the speaker.

So with all that nice groundwork and good feeling already in place, my pitch to Joe and Shelly would have been the same, though delivered to Shelly with a Jewish accent. The pitch would have relied heavily on my very personal knowledge of Judith's distress as a widow and on their male chivalry. It would also have involved a pinch of Buddhist philosophy. I would have strongly suggested, without promising, that if they allowed uncoupled judicial pay increases to happen, good things would soon happen for their members as well.

I advised Eliot that there was absolutely no downside to this strategy. It might not work, but at worst it would result in a few futile meetings involving a high official in the administration stroking Joe and Shelly. Nothing bad could come of it, yet Eliot condescendingly dismissed my plea to make this effort. On this, as on many other occasions during the Plague Year, Eliot seemed more concerned about being right than being successful. I am a very persuasive guy, having convinced all sorts of people to do things they had no desire to do until I showed them that the idea had been theirs all along. But I could not persuade Eliot to allow me to make this risk-free attempt. I apologized to Judith. Her discomfort deepened, but not as much as after the next incident in the judicial pay saga.

Throughout 2007, working with Bob Hermann, the head of the Governor's Office of Regulatory Reform, or GORR, I had been looking for ways to increase state funding for civil legal services programs, serving the needs of the state's poor. Bob, formerly New York State's solicitor general, had left a lucrative law firm partnership to head GORR, a small, funky and underutilized agency. Increasing the funding of legal services programs was a labor close to both our hearts, as our legal careers had included cherished stints there. We had secured a direct state appropriation in the budget for the first time and defended Judith Kaye's $5 million budgetary earmark for legal services. But a far more quantitatively significant contribution could be made through IOLA, the Interest On Lawyer Accounts Fund.

IOLA bank accounts are repositories for relatively small sums of client money, which lawyers hold in escrow until being disbursed to their clients. All of these small sums of money from all the lawyers in the state amount to a very large pot, and the interest paid on that can also be very large. By law, the interest on these IOLA accounts primarily goes to help fund legal services. The IOLA law says that the interest rate paid on IOLA accounts must be comparable to that paid on similar bank accounts. The banks had taken the position that IOLA accounts were not like any other accounts. So they paid one-quarter to one-fifth the rate of interest on IOLA accounts, benefiting poor people, as they did on the functionally identical accounts of their commercial customers. Don't you love big banks, and don't you know that despite the clear statutory language requiring parity, the Pataki administration had acquiesced?

Bob Hermann and I invaded IOLA, a quasi-independent state entity. We forced it to begin a rulemaking that resulted in the banks agreeing to at least quadruple the amount of interest paid on IOLA accounts. It was a modest but very sweet victory and one whose significance was clear to Eliot, who cared deeply about the plight of the state's poor and believed in the mission of legal services. Right after our victory on IOLA, Judge Kaye called Eliot in another attempt at convincing him to do whatever was necessary to get pay increases for her judges. That would have required Eliot to agree to the linkage of judge and legislator pay without demanding campaign finance reform as a quid pro quo. Eliot had even been given a fig leaf. Under a proposed compromise, the judges' pay increases would have been explicit, whereas the legislators' raises would have been attenuated by going through a special commission.

When Judith called, Eliot was in a car with David Paterson. Eliot screamed at her, reducing her to tears. He berated her for not calling him or me to congratulate us for this great thing we had just done with IOLA. Judith then called to congratulate me and related the rest of the story. It was the second time in 2007 that Eliot had screamed at Judith, a woman no one I knew (except for Eliot) would dare scream at.

Judges acquire little fiefdoms. Each has a clerk or two and a bailiff and other staff. Most judges have families and become pillars of their communities. Even without robes, their pronouncements count for a lot. Within these 1,300 modern feudal manors throughout the state, the continuing pay nightmare caused ill will toward the Spitzer Administration. Eliot wanted the judges to get pay increases and indeed to get them retroactively. Initially, he hadn't been willing to give legislators a raise as a price for the judges getting theirs. Then, to counter the Legislature's linkage strategy, he employed his own, tying them to campaign finance reform. That further complicated the game theory. Eliot wasn't willing to let me try a different approach. While the judges and those in their orbit were mad at everybody, they were more angry with us, expecting the worst from the Legislature but better from their hero, the bold new governor. Not for one second did they take any satisfaction from the fact that Eliot had rhetorically championed their cause. That and $2.50 would buy them a cup of coffee at Starbucks—something they could no longer afford.

Toward the end of the 2007 legislative session, Eliot quietly told Joe and Shelly that if they would allow the judicial pay increases to go through, he would accept legislative pay increases late in 2007 or in early 2008. But by that time, there was little good feeling or trust to tap and to permit those two to take the six-month leap of faith. Eliot would have honored his promise, but men who are used to breaking their word have difficulty believing that others won't. Eliot's offer was made as Troopergate was about to unfold. If there had been any chance that Joe would take that leap, Troopergate eliminated it.

■ ■ ■

····

The Recent Unpleasantness

A S OF JUNE 2009, Troopergate had resulted in ten separate investigations. Only the last of these attempted to
deal with a problem far more serious than the facts underlying
Troopergate, the failure of the first nine to conduct a simple and
straightforward inquiry of bad conduct by state officials.

As the facts of, and fanciful assertions about, this scandal
started circulating, and I was conscripted by Eliot to become one
of the lawyers representing the Executive Chamber in the various probes, I refused to use the term "Troopergate." It is beyond
annoying that since the 1972 break-in at the Democratic headquarters in Washington, D.C., all political scandals must bear
the "gate" suffix. A Gibbons or Toynbee would say that a key
moment in the decline of Western Civilization had occurred
when that naming convention began. So I called Troopergate
"The Recent Unpleasantness," borrowing the phrase and irony
from the term used to describe several great wars. I anonymously referred to it that way in Nick Paumgarten's long 2007
New Yorker article, written when the building disillusionment
with the Spitzer Administration had started to spawn "serious"

articles, attempting to analyze, "What the fuck had happened to a man and a regime of which so much had been expected?"

My crankiness has been validated. There has already been a subsequent "Troopergate"—the one where Sarah Palin is presumed by me to have wondered out loud, "Who will rid me of this insolent state trooper–ex-brother-in-law?" and spawning several investigations in Alaska and a major topic in the 2008 presidential campaign. So it's The Recent Unpleasantness or "TRU" here.

The essential truth about TRU is that, like Watergate, the precipitating facts were not very compelling, although in Watergate there was an actual illegal break-in. TRU involved no clear violation of any law, civil or criminal. Think of TRU as you would think of that dead or barely live bird that your dog carries home clenched in its mouth and drops at your feet, hoping to be loved and rewarded by you, even though you are somewhat revolted by what the dog has done. While you may feign gratitude, you sure want the dog to take the bounty out of your sight and never bring you a gift like that again. The drooling creature that brought TRU to an annoyed governor in 2007 was Communications Director Darren Dopp.

There is a prehistory to TRU that must be told. These antecedents are well known by Albany types, and there is no one more knowledgeable about the facts than Darren himself. The press, at least, believes that there is an insatiable and longstanding fascination with the use of private aircraft by the wealthy and the powerful—especially if the powerful are public officials. In recent years, Jane Swift, the first female governor of

Massachusetts, lost her job because she was using a state helicopter to ferry her newborns and a babysitter. Indeed, the gist of the Hevesi scandal in New York was the misuse of a state-owned vehicle and "pilot," albeit in performing terrestrial chores for the comptroller's wife.

Until TRU, the biggest and most notorious travel scandal in New York history had been "Air Cuomo," the term George Pataki used to describe the persistent use of state aircraft for personal travel by Governor Mario Cuomo and his family. In 1994, Pataki defeated Cuomo's bid for a fourth term, in part by railing against Air Cuomo and using it as a metaphor for what he claimed was a broader pattern of waste and abuse in his opponent's administration. In 1995, ex-Governor Cuomo actually reimbursed the state $29,000 for a small number of the many more trips that members of his family had taken on state aircraft. One of those family members was young Andrew Cuomo, who had worked for the governor for part of that period. A playmate of Andrew's at the time was a young guy in the Cuomo press office, Darren Dopp. Darren had responded to some of the press inquiries concerning Air Cuomo.

Many years later, when Andrew became Secretary of Housing and Urban Development (HUD) in the Clinton cabinet, he was criticized for taking 24 trips to New York State at the federal government's expense. He travelled to no other state under his jurisdiction more than four times. This gave credence to the charge that he was travelling so often to New York for reasons other than HUD business. Andrew's travel to New York had coincided with the planning stages of his unsuccessful bid for governor in 2002.

After George Pataki was elected governor, he seemingly forgot about his campaign pledges to sell the state's fleet of aircraft and to use commercial flights. Some aircraft were sold, but others were purchased, and the helicopter fleet was upgraded. The Pataki family, like the Cuomos, were frequent flyers in travel tenuously connected to any service to New York State. The fact that George liked to lay his head each night on a pillow in his own bed—that bed being in Garrison, New York, some 81 miles from Albany—ensured that the governor himself was a very heavy user of state aircraft. This was his choice, as the Governor's Mansion in Albany had many comfortable beds suitable for George's 6′4½″ frame. All this had spawned a spate of "Air Pataki" articles, reaching a crescendo toward the end of the 12-year Pataki Administration. Coming in, we (the Spitzer people) worried that the Air Pataki issue might have to be dealt with, and that it would become an unwelcome distraction.

The state air fleet is not used exclusively by the governor and family. When the governor says, "OK," it can be used by other state officials. He can deny approval for a good reason, or a bad one, or for no reason at all. I had flown in state planes and helicopters many times during the Mario Cuomo years, always with my boss, Attorney General Bob Abrams. A few times, we had been accompanied by members of the Cuomo family. I hated these flights, especially those on state helicopters, which were so noisy as to preclude productive work sessions. Toward the end of my tenure, I refused to ride along, meeting Bob in Albany or New York City and always beating him there by taking a train or my car. For trips of, say, 150 miles or less, the productivity and efficiency rationale for using the state aircraft holds little, if any, water.

But unlike me and Eliot (who also disliked using the fleet, especially for short trips), Joe Bruno loved to use the state aircraft. He liked the trappings of power, the perceived convenience, and he especially liked the price. During the final Pataki years, Bruno and the governor had frequently been at odds over various policies. Pataki's people also suspected that Joe had been misusing the state fleet, and had begun to restrict his access. In a private conversation, Joe had complained to Eliot that Pataki's people had become difficult and asked Eliot to assure him that there would be no similar problem in the new regime. Eliot assured him that he could use the aircraft when available and when the travel was for official business.

So, as we took over, Communications Director Darren Dopp understood one thing, if nothing else. The press would be all over the use of the state aircraft, past and present, especially on days when they had nothing better to write about. In the spring of 2007, Darren enlisted two administration officials, Bill Howard and Preston Felton, to collect documents and information about Joe Bruno's trips to New York City using state aircraft and State Police escorts. Bruno's trips involved predominantly political or private business, although some small amount of work for the state was done during each trip. In some instances, the state work was inconsequential and clearly used as a pretext for taking a trip paid for by the state. Preston Felton and Bill Howard, Darren's accomplices, were then, respectively, the acting superintendent of the State Police and the assistant secretary for Homeland Security, serving as the Executive Chamber's liaison to the police.

Dopp ordered Howard, who in turn ordered Felton, to provide information on several trips Bruno made to New York City in May 2007. The information included details of the various stops Bruno made on each trip, and showed that most of the stops were for political and personal business. Because some of those details were re-created after the trips, an error was made in at least one instance.

Immediately prior to Dopp's enterprise, information of this specific type had not been maintained by the State Police, although it may have been in an earlier period. While compiling this intelligence on Joe's trips, the State Police did not collect or re-create similar information for trips taken by Eliot or Lieutenant Governor David Paterson. The format for compiling this information had been established for Darren's special project. In one instance, Dopp directed that the information be reformatted so that the details of each Bruno trip would stand out clearly for public consumption.

After this embarrassing information about Bruno had been compiled, re-created, formatted and reformatted, it was summarized by Darren in a late June 2007 internal memo "to the file." Darren transmitted information about Bruno's trips to Albany *Times Union* reporter James Odato on June 28, 2007. TRU's public phase began with the *TU*'s publication of Odato's July 1, 2007, article titled "State Flies Bruno to Fundraisers, Taxpayers Finance Trips of Senate Majority Leader to New York

City Political Events." Odato's exposé was strikingly similar in numerous factual details and inferences to the late June memo that Darren had written about Bruno's trips. At that time, Dopp had sought the assistance of several Executive Chamber attorneys in evaluating whether Bruno's conduct violated the law, and if so, which, if any, of the state's investigative and prosecutorial bodies had the authority to "torture" Bruno, already the subject of an unrelated federal grand jury probe.

Odato made a Freedom of Information Law (or FOIL) request for information about Bruno's trips on July 10, 2007. That was nine days after his article in the *TU*, and 13 days after he had received the information from Dopp. Dopp's explanation, that the information had previously been orally requested by Odato pursuant to FOIL, was later rejected by both the attorney general and the state's Commission on Public Integrity as being false and/or pretextual.

In part because of Darren's sloppiness in doing these things, but probably more because he was infuriated that Darren had snubbed him and chosen Odato and the *TU* for an exclusive leak in this project, Fred Dicker of the *New York Post* did some nice investigative work. He quickly discovered most of what Darren had done and the glaring inconsistencies in Darren's shifting explanation of how the *TU* story had come into being. By July 5, 2007, the trophy head of Joe Bruno in Darren's mouth had been replaced by Dicker's story of a conspiracy in the governor's office: to use the State Police to spy on Joe Bruno and release embarrassing information about him—some which arguably compromised the Majority leader's safety.

While that speedy and spectacular turnaround in the press was underway, two investigations concerning Senator Bruno's travel morphed into hybrids, now investigating both the legality of the trips and the propriety and legality of what Darren, Howard, Felton and suspected others in the governor's office had done to poor old Joe Bruno.

Attorney General Andrew Cuomo began an investigation in early July 2007, as had State Inspector General Kris Hamann, or so she said. A third investigation had apparently been opened by Albany District Attorney David Soares, who at the end of the three-week rush to judgment made a pronouncement on the legality of Bruno's use of the aircraft, while expressing no view about the actions of Darren and his co-conspirators.

The public drumbeat became "What did the governor know about all this, and when did he know it?" Though this Watergate artifact was as trite and annoying as the "gate" naming convention itself, it was a natural and appropriate question to ask. As it was being asked with steadily increasing frequency, Eliot directed me to become part of the small team of senior lawyers on the Second Floor who had been quickly cobbled together to deal with the investigations.

That team initially had comprised David Nocenti, the governor's counsel; Peter Pope, our director of Policy; and Sean Maloney, Rich Baum's first deputy secretary. This task fell squarely within Nocenti's expertise and title, but not so for the other two. Pope and Maloney, like me, were experienced litigators, but their jobs on the Second Floor, like mine, were not lawyers' jobs. Pope had recently pulled off the minor miracles of the legislative session by successfully shepherding enactment of a landmark worker's compensation reform and a major expansion and toughening of the state's criminal penalties for sex trafficking—one of the Spitzer Administration's legislative priorities.

Maloney had run for attorney general the previous year, the first openly gay candidate for statewide office in New York. The handsome, well-spoken and quick-witted former White House staffer looked like a GQ model. Sean had done extremely well in introducing himself to the public in the 2006 AG primary debates, while finishing third to the eventual primary and general election victor Andrew Cuomo.

Rich Baum had hired Sean late to be his first deputy. He had been given little to do, both because Rich didn't know how to delegate authority in the Executive Chamber and because he didn't seem to trust Sean, for reasons neither Sean nor I ever discovered. Before being pressed into duty in the TRU investigations, Sean's major initiatives had involved expediting two actions that Eliot would have taken eventually, but had been criticized for moving too slowly on. Sean had pushed Eliot to expedite the delivery of his campaign promise to back legislation for same-sex marriage in New York. Sean had also coordinated Eliot's endorsement of Hillary for president, which the Clinton people had complained was too late in coming.

I had joined the senior lawyer team handling the TRU investigations at Eliot's direction during the week of July 16, 2007, and was briefed by David and Peter about the contents and stunningly fast pace of the only real investigation, the one being conducted by Cuomo's staff. Kris Hamman, the state inspector general, had begun an investigation at about the same time as Andrew, but within days she started to fade and defer to the attorney general. Like a deer in the headlights, Kris, a smart veteran of Manhattan DA Bob Morgenthau's prosecutor/politician factory, seemed to forget that her jurisdiction to investigate these facts was clearly superior to Andrew's. As Cuomo rushed to make a splash, Kris seemed incapable of asserting herself and taking the time to do a thorough and professional job. When Cuomo prematurely announced the results of his incomplete probe, she effectively whispered, "Me too." It was neither the first nor the last time during the Plague Year that Kris experienced stage fright. She was another product of our bad transition, and our penchant to hire convenient and usual suspects.

After being briefed by Nocenti and Pope, I met with Eliot, who told me flat out that he hadn't known that Darren had been using the State Police in collecting information about Bruno's trips. Eliot, I and everyone else had understood that there were always FOIL requests seeking information about the use of state aircraft by him and others. We also understood that there would be news articles. The State Police involvement was a different matter, which Eliot hadn't known about. I told him that the venality, if there had been any, resided in the State Police's involvement. So he had nothing to fear and every reason to expedite the full disclosure of information that would properly assign blame and make clear his lack of knowledge and involvement. My first job would be to read through several months of all of Eliot's email with all the people possibly involved in TRU. I reviewed this email, amounting to hundreds with Darren, Bill Howard, Preston Felton and Rich Baum. Because Rich had received email from Darren and Bill Howard referring to their activities, the Eliot/Rich email was within the "must review" zone.

Eliot wanted me, and me alone, to read through all of this arguably relevant email whether he was the author, the recipient, or merely copied. I would confirm or contradict his recollection of what he had known or at least would have known had he read the email. He had said that he had never known nor heard the details of Darren's activities and certainly not about the State Police angle. But he and I were both concerned that in one or more of the hundreds of email there might be some vague reference to this stuff, and maybe only in one where he was not the author or recipient but merely copied. I said I would read all this email carefully, but quickly, and cull and reread any with even the slightest bit of ambiguity. Before leaving Eliot to begin my work, I rendered my second verdict on TRU, one that has never changed. The "crime," Darren's primarily but everyone's, was wasting any time battling Joe Bruno—an old man—who soon would lose his majority or even sooner be indicted by the Republican United States Attorney in Albany.

My first verdict on TRU had been harshly delivered to Eliot on July 10, 2007, before I'd been drafted to defend the Executive Chamber and to read Eliot's email. I pummeled him that night for what I still consider the worst, and in retrospect the most revealing, interview he gave during the Plague Year. In a

July 10 *New York Times* article by Nick Confessore and Danny Hakim, Eliot revealed ambivalence about being governor and had shoved Silda in front of him like a human shield:

> You know what she's [Silda] been telling me? She looks at me and says: "Do you really want this stuff? And do you want them [Eliot's three daughters] to see this stuff?"
>
> [and]
>
> She says, you know, "What was wrong with going into the family business? That wouldn't have been so bad."
>
> [and]
>
> I'm happy with the choice [becoming Governor], but that's what makes it hard.... Trust me, I'm not complaining. You get the downside risk that you become a target. Fine by me, you're a grown-up. You know this going in, but it's the collateral effect on other people that you worry about. Is it worth it for them? ...Look, I don't challenge my judgments about getting in, but that's Silda's view.

I plowed into him for this atrocious interview, but to Eliot the article wasn't "that bad" and was maybe even "pretty good" because it mentioned Bruno's air travel and demonstrated to Eliot that Bruno was in trouble in the press over his trips. I told him that it looked to me like we were in trouble over Joe's trips and that the more time we spent on Joe and the Legislature, the more difficult things would get, that it would consume energy better spent in numerous projects involving our vast array of executive branch agencies.

A week later, I was immersed in Eliot's email. I read each twice and then reread any that raised the slightest concern, completing the assignment in several heavily caffeinated days and nights. I then went to Eliot and said, "You're clean." I was relieved and a bit surprised that Eliot's huge stack of email revealed nothing of concern with respect to TRU.

The Executive Chamber existed more in cyberspace than on Mother Earth. It had been off-putting to walk down the halls to my beloved secretaries Kathy Schanz and Jennica Hawkins seeking some information and have them tell me, "I will email it to you." Eventually I would understand the reasons why they would say and do that. The absence of a trace, or as lawyers say, a "scintilla" of information about the State Police involvement or anything else improper in any email with Eliot was not just comforting, but surprising, given the enormous volume of cyber-intercourse during those months. The email showed that Eliot thought that there was a FOIL request for Bruno's, David Paterson's, and his own travel stuff. Darren had told everybody that there was such a request, although it had actually been made after Odato's story. The knowledge that sooner or later there would be stories was not only reflected in the email but common knowledge to everyone.

The documents revealed that Eliot not only was unaware of the State Police involvement in monitoring Bruno's movements, but specifically told Darren not to issue a press release that he'd drafted, questioning the propriety of Bruno's use of state aircraft for a trip on May 17, 2007. Eliot instructed him to stand down, saying that it "was an unnecessary distraction."

While Eliot's initial resistance to Dopp's desire to publicize Bruno's travel abuses and his stand-down order were followed by his acceptance of the fact that stories would appear, that was merely a function of his belief that a FOIL request had been received. FOIL mandates disclosure whether or not the government wants to make such information public.

As hostilities between Eliot and Bruno intensified, the governor's recognition of the inevitability of disclosure changed to mild interest and, eventually, to eager anticipation. However, that progression had nothing to do with any knowledge by Eliot of the State Police gambit. Eliot possessed none. Instead, it reflected Eliot's accurate understanding of the way FOIL works. There had been a FOIL request for records involving Joe's, David Paterson's and Eliot's trips, or so Eliot had been told by Dopp. There would be newspaper stories, and with Joe, there would be blood.

Once I confirmed that Eliot was clean, the real task was to remember the third lesson from the gates: "Don't stonewall, don't cover up, and punish those who were culpable, and do it swiftly and severely, but fairly." The Cuomo investigation was cooperating with one of those objectives, the desire for speed, but taking that to an unhealthy extreme. In his desire to make a big splash and avoid sharing the limelight with the inspector general and the Albany County DA, Cuomo's staff was proceeding with reckless speed. They were not simply cutting corners, but failing to do many things essential for the investigation to be definitive and respected and to provide closure.

The 53-page Cuomo Report was issued on Monday, July 23, 2007, only 22 days after Jim Odato's first article in the

Times Union. The Cuomo Report purportedly covered both aspects of TRU, Bruno's use of state aircraft and Darren Dopp's use of the State Police in his inept effort to discredit Bruno. In the frenzied week that preceded the release of the Cuomo Report, the team of senior Executive Chamber lawyers had to make decisions in haste and with a gun to our heads. The weapon had been Cuomo's stated intention to release his findings on July 23, with or without the Executive Chamber's full cooperation. The bullet in the gun had been the attorney general's promise that unless we accommodated his haste, the report would prominently complain about the governor's refusal to cooperate in the very investigation that he had sought.

There simply was no way in this timeframe for either our senior lawyer team or Cuomo's team to do the things needed to make the investigation thorough. Our side had been acting without outside counsel and without the infrastructure of a law office. We had to review thousands of email and other documents, assess whether any privileges should be asserted and deal with the live witnesses whom the Office of the Attorney General (OAG) might want to question under oath.

As this played out, we were showered with irony. The time pressure used by Cuomo's people was similar to that which many Spitzer corporate targets had complained about during his years as AG. A similar comparison applied to Cuomo's threat to scream that we had not cooperated with his investigation. Cuomo's campaign for AG had prominently featured commercials that promised he would be an attorney general just like Eliot

Spitzer. Andrew's tactics in TRU were a caricature of Eliot's as AG, but a clever one.

The grandest irony of all was that Andrew, a frequent passenger of Air Cuomo and alleged frequent abuser of his federal flight privileges while secretary of HUD, was about to clobber the senior staff of his old rival, the one who had taken the title of Governor, which Andrew believed was his birthright. This particular irony, no doubt joyful for Andrew, might have been slightly tempered by yet another—the starring role of villain played by Darren Dopp, Andrew's pal from the Governor Mario and Air Cuomo days.

During the week of July 16, 2007, our team and Cuomo's worked around the clock to produce and digest all the information that could be handled under the impossibly short deadline that the AG had imposed. Much, but not everything, got done. We produced virtually everything they asked for, but Cuomo's people failed to ask for certain categories of documents they should have. We tried not to be cute and actually gave them some, but not all, of the pertinent stuff they had failed to ask for. As it became clear who the culprits were, another issue to be resolved was who else would testify. Cuomo's staff had already questioned Bill Howard and Preston Felton under oath.

The Cuomo Report could not possibly be complete or respected without sworn oral testimony from Darren Dopp. Once Darren's role in TRU had become clear to us, he was informed that his and the Executive Chamber's interests diverged and that he should retain his own lawyer. Darren retained a lawyer named Terence Kindlon. Terry ultimately refused Cuomo's request that Darren testify, despite Darren's sincere desire to do so. We didn't want Darren to testify and might have sought to block his testimony on various legal grounds, including attorney-client privilege, had Kindlon not already made a decision that Darren would not voluntarily submit to questioning by Cuomo's staff. Although we never had to reach that point, our consensus opinion, after much debate, was that it was better that Darren not testify and instead submit a brief written statement admitting certain errors.

The basis of our consensus opinion about whether or not Darren should testify had been a unanimous concern about and for him. We all were concerned that if Darren testified he might not tell the truth—and subject himself to further peril, including a perjury charge. Darren might have thought that whatever he said at the moment was true, but we feared it would not be. Just reading Darren's email from the spring of 2007 had revealed him telling Eliot, other Second Floor colleagues, and reporters a constantly shifting story. Fred Dicker had quickly figured out how Darren had changed the story when pressed to justify certain actions. After the weekend of July 20–22, 2007, we would all witness Darren shifting, changing and flatly contradicting his own previous versions of "the truth." At several moments during that period, Darren's indictment for perjury or false swearing by the Albany County district attorney seemed imminent. I went into DA Soares' office on December 19, 2007, to argue against him seeking Darren's indictment, invoking the so-called "interests of justice." I did this despite the fact that the Executive Chamber was not representing Darren.

In July 2007, when Darren's private lawyer decided that Dopp would not testify, it was Cuomo's colossal error to accept that decision yet still issue a report pretending to be comprehensive. At the time, Cuomo said that he did not have the power to force anyone to testify. That claim was disingenuous at best. An aggressive prosecutor, knowledgeable of his own jurisdiction, would have used the subpoena power available in tax investigations. There was an obvious tax angle in this affair, as clearly stated in Cuomo's own report. Moreover, Eliot could have conferred subpoena power on Andrew, especially if the AG had asked to become a "Special Prosecutor" for this investigation.

Later on, when Darren's diary was discovered, there were glimpses of a continuing friendship between Andrew and Darren and discussions about the toxic relationship between Eliot and Joe Bruno and about Darren's role in that dynamic. Indeed, the diary reflects Andrew giving Darren advice on how to comport himself. Much later, Darren testified that he discussed Bruno's use of state aircraft with Andrew in May 2007, well before TRU's public phase.

Another person who should have testified in Andrew Cuomo's investigation was Rich Baum. That failure was equally ours and Andrew's. A review of Rich's email showed that he had not been an active participant in Darren's co-option of the State Police. However, at various points in time, Rich had received email from both Darren and Bill Howard, which should have sounded alarms and caused him to ask some tough questions. Given the expanse of his responsibilities and the mindboggling number of email he received, his culpability for TRU was of a much lower order than Dopp's, Howard's, or Felton's. Nevertheless, Rich bore some responsibility, and it was obvious to Cuomo's staff, who requested, but didn't demand, that Baum testify.

We were equally to blame in Rich's failure to testify. To his credit, Rich, like Darren, wanted to testify. It's as simple as that. The issue is always that simple. You must testify, tell the complete truth, tell it quickly and do it without compulsion. It is the ultimate lesson of all the "gates." Rich's testimony, given months later to the Commission on Public Integrity, would have placed the major responsibility for TRU where it belonged, with Dopp and Howard. Baum's testimony would have confirmed the relatively minor sins of omission that he had committed, and it would have truthfully cleared Eliot.

I came into the debate over whether Rich should testify both late and with a significant disability. I joined the Nocenti/Maloncy/Pope team two weeks after they began their work. For the first few days, I did nothing but read and report on Eliot's email. By the time I was fully integrated into the team, we had reached the weekend of July 20–22, 2007. I found, to my horror, that in various discussions of our strategy, Rich was present. This was bad for him and made it difficult for us to do our work properly. Though Rich's level of culpability for TRU was clearly much lower than Darren's, he, too, should have been directed to get his own lawyer. He later was told to do so, and did. However, on that crucial weekend Peter Pope's and my suggestions in that regard were not heeded. Had Baum been separately represented, he probably would have testified, as he wanted to. My handicap in this debate was the widespread knowledge that I assigned major blame for the errors of the administration to Rich. Some also knew that I had advised Eliot to remove him from his position as secretary and redeploy him as a political advisor.

In 1998, while I was running the Spitzer AG transition, I had witnessed Rich's masterful direction of the attorney general election recount, a consequence of Dennis Vacco's refusal to concede. Rich was then still in his twenties but showed the poise and judgment of a seasoned politico. Politics, not policy, leadership and organization, were Rich's strong suits. My broaching the subjects of Rich getting his own lawyer, of him testifying, and of his culpability, was being heard by suspicious ears who thought I had an axe to grind. Worst of all, during some of these discussions, Rich was present. This was intolerable and dangerous both for him and for the Executive Chamber. At one point, I finally ordered him to leave the room and thereafter became infamous for demanding his removal whenever he reappeared in such discussions in the days, weeks and months ahead. The only exceptions were a few occasions when Eliot was present and allowed Rich to sit in, over my protest. At one such meeting at the Mansion on July 22, 2007, Rich apologized to the group for missing the red flags that clearly had been waved in his face, and he again expressed his willingness to testify.

I was viewed as an asshole for demanding that Baum be excluded from our legal and strategy discussions, for assigning him some degree of culpability for TRU and for urging that he be disciplined. But I should have been an even bigger asshole and demanded that he testify to Cuomo, as he had desired. In failing to do that, I had been much more guilty than the others in making a crucial mistake. My judgment had not been clouded by friendship or eight years of kinship in the AG's office.

Eliot also should have testified in Andrew's investigation. Incredibly, Cuomo didn't seek his testimony. We should have insisted on it. Eliot had nothing to hide and everything to gain by giving an early and full statement under oath. The failure of Dopp and Baum to testify would then have seemed inconsequential. Their testimony had been necessary to inculpate or exculpate Eliot. The entire complexion of TRU would have changed with the simple act of Eliot testifying. None among us advocated that. Instead of testimony from Darren, Rich and Eliot, Cuomo accepted short written statements from Rich and Darren and asked nothing of Eliot. Darren's statement, purportedly given under oath, was inadvertently not actually sworn, setting up a bizarre twist in TRU months later.

Finally, Cuomo failed to interview Joe Bruno. This failure was even more egregious than the failure to interrogate Dopp. Cuomo's staff had hundreds of Darren's email. This evidence had allowed them to piece together Darren's project, with a decent degree of accuracy. Not so with Bruno, because Cuomo hadn't asked for email, relying almost exclusively on unsworn statements of Bruno's subordinates and friends. Andrew hadn't even gotten a cursory written statement from Bruno like the one secured from Dopp. The last 13 pages of the Cuomo Report were devoted to a finding that there had been no violation of law by the Majority leader. This conclusion had been reached without asking Joe Bruno a single question. The report, however, contained factual findings that strongly argued that Bruno may have committed violations of New York's Penal and Public Officers laws.

Andrew had concluded that it did not violate a longstanding ethics ruling to use state aircraft for trips where only a minor part of the business conducted was for the state and most was personal or political. However, Andrew never followed two other trails begun in his own report. The report stated that an old ethics ruling permitting so-called "mixed use" of the aircraft had resulted in Bruno's "abuse of state resources." It went on to say that in "extreme instances" use of state aircraft for private purposes might be illegal. The report did not explain why these facts did not constitute such "extreme instances." Evidence that these abuses had been "extreme" abounded. Bruno had never reported the value of the transportation used for non-state business as income. The fact that mixed use was permitted and that the state did not require reimbursement did not change the tax issue. This tax angle was referred to in the Cuomo Report as the "imputed income" issue but then just ignored.

Following any of these obvious investigative paths would have taken Andrew Cuomo to places he apparently had not wanted to go. It would have interfered with his intention to hastily release the half-baked report on Monday, July 23. Monday is the best day for a story designed to achieve maximum exposure and permit a full week of follow-up stories, as occurred here. Another undesirable destination for Andrew may have been any finding that mixed use of state aircraft had serious Penal Law, Public Officers Law and tax implications. It had been reported that in just seven of the 12 Governor Mario Cuomo years, the first family had travelled on state aircraft 762 times, with and without the governor. Comparisons between Bruno's abuses and this ancient, but well-known, Air Cuomo history would have been inconvenient for Andrew.

It is arguable whether any of Bruno's abusive practices violated the law. What is not seriously debatable is that the failure to ask Bruno any questions about them deprived the Cuomo Report of any pretense to regularity and comprehensiveness. These glaring deficiencies built on the inadequacies arising from the lack of oral testimony from Darren, Rich and Eliot. The report, which was initially praised by Bruno, because it trashed the governor's office, and by Eliot, because we had agreed to do so, was within days appropriately treated as an inadequate and badly flawed exercise.

The Cuomo Report described Dopp's scheme and fixed blame on three people, Darren, Bill Howard and Preston Felton. While concluding that no law, civil or criminal, had been violated, the report strongly and appropriately criticized the conduct. The report also rejected Bruno's assertion that he had been placed under surveillance by the State Police on the Executive Chamber's order. This conclusion was an exercise in legal semantics. The chronicling of Bruno's movements would not have met the legal definition of "surveillance" or have been viewed as such by law enforcement professionals. However, the specificity with which Bruno's movements were detailed by the State Police looked, smelled and tasted like surveillance to a lay person. The Cuomo Report called upon Eliot to punish Dopp, Howard and Felton.

We had prepared for the issue of punishment and debated the sanctions throughout the preceding weekend. Of the three men to be sanctioned, Bill Howard presented the easiest case. Bill was a rock-ribbed Republican holdover from the Pataki Administration. From our review of the documents, it was easy to see that he had fallen victim to his desire to dispel a non-existent suspicion about his loyalty to the Democratic governor. Bill had been asked to stay and work for us because he was considered to be among the most, if not the most, knowledgeable person in the state during an emergency or disaster. In the first few months, Bill had proven his worth when terror threats and crises, such as serious flooding upstate, had arisen. We had retained or hired a number of Pataki loyalists. Among them were some of our very best hires, including Dennis Whalen, the deputy secretary for Healthcare, and Mike Balboni, the Republican Senator from Long Island who became deputy secretary for Homeland Security.

Even before his Inauguration, Eliot had ordered that no inquiry into party affiliation be made in hiring or in any other substantive decision. Bill never got this message and was trying to overcome a non-existent prejudice against Republicans. In response to a May 2007 *New York Post* article, entitled, "CREW 'CHAOS' CRISIS CRIPPLING SPITZER," written by Fred Dicker, which divided the Executive Chamber into two non-existent warring camps, a Baum/Dopp faction and a Constantine/Paul Francis one, Bill Howard had sent an email to Rich stroking him and saying, "Consider me on Team Baum." What better way for Howard to overcome a non-existent prejudice against Republicans than to help Dopp discredit Joe Bruno, the state's top Republican?

In one email exchange between Howard and Baum, Bill had commented on the federal investigation of Bruno and the imminent Bruno travel story, saying, "The impending travel stuff implies more problems, particularly in the tax area I think. I think timing right for that move." Howard was referring to the imputation of income Bruno had received by taking flights for non-state business and the tax problems that might ensue for Bruno if the IRS were to find out.

Bill Howard had to go. He had to be banished from the Second Floor and probably just fired outright. Two facts had made that difficult to accomplish immediately. First, Howard's superior expertise in how to handle disasters needed to be replaced before cutting him loose. Second, Bill, like some other high-level appointees in the Executive Chamber, had a reserve civil service appointment he could fall back on. It's not impossible to fire a civil servant in New York, but it's pretty damn hard and takes a long time. So we decided to remove Howard from the Chamber and send him to another agency where his expertise could be tapped in the event of an emergency, while we built some healthy redundancy into our emergency-response capacity.

The disciplining of Preston Felton was a more difficult issue. Preston had been dissuaded from retiring to become acting superintendent of the State Police, with the likelihood of Eliot making that appointment permanent. The appointment would require senate confirmation, meaning Joe Bruno's blessing. Preston was the first African-American to head the

State Police. That added to the tension around the issue of disciplining him.

Our unanimous point of view was that Felton had behaved badly but had been unfairly put into this position by high-level staffers in the Executive Chamber. The State Police serve the governor. An order from the governor or his representative is akin to the president's order to the military. An illegal or improper order can be disobeyed, but it is very, very hard to do that. It was clear that Eliot would not nominate Felton to become permanent head of the State Police after Preston's major lapse in judgment. If Eliot had, Bruno would have made sure that the Senate would block the appointment in the confirmation process. The decision was made not to formally discipline Felton, and truthfully say that he had been put in an untenable position by the Executive Chamber.

The sanctions discussed for Darren ranged from outright dismissal to a 30-day suspension. I was a known detractor of Darren's. Others had worked with Darren for eight triumphant years and had close personal relationships with him. The Eliot factor also affected our decision making about Darren. Eliot had been wise enough to delegate authority on this issue but would have vetoed a penalty unacceptable to him. Eliot was extremely loyal to his staff, manifesting that good trait with an unhealthy reluctance to fire people who needed to be fired. When Eliot got up and took full responsibility for a mistake that his staff had made, a standard politician's tactic often devoid of sincerity, Eliot actually meant it. He emotionally punished himself for the errors of others. When he did this during the Plague Year, as he had to more than once, his acceptance of responsibility for the misconduct of others looked and felt acutely painful and sincere. Not until later did I understand that was also because of his guilt-ridden conscience.

Trying to separate my own negative feelings about Darren from my job, I had still argued for him to be fired. It was hard to see how he could ever return to his position as communications director. It had become clear that he was dissembling with various reporters. Leaving aside his misuse of the State Police, a suspicious and adversarial relationship with the press would have destroyed his effectiveness. In the end, we decided to suspend him indefinitely without pay, but for a minimum of 30 days. I was worried that the press would call it a "30-day suspension," when in fact it had been "indefinite" with the first consideration of whether to end it, extend or make it permanent coming after 30 days. My fears were immediately realized. The announcement was either badly communicated or misinterpreted to mean just a 30-day "slap on the wrist."

Of course, Darren never came back. Throughout the Plague Year, we failed to see the inevitability of certain outcomes and to preempt the destructive process by acting swiftly and decisively. Eliot knew that TRU was bad stuff, but had thought it would be newsworthy for a few days, or a week at most. The lawyer team thought differently. A memo summarizing the entire affair, written primarily by Peter Pope, and constantly updated, had in its earliest iterations the prediction that TRU would make national headlines. Those headlines appeared, but the story lingered much longer than a week, through and beyond the day eight months later when Eliot Spitzer resigned.

The longevity of the story resulted in part from Eliot's July 23, 2007, shamefaced mea culpa. We had agreed to accept the Cuomo Report's findings on Sunday, July 22, after the major points had been summarized for us by Cuomo's staff and they threatened to scream that we had obstructed their investigation. In our desire to avoid opening a second front in the imminent war, we caved in to Cuomo's demand. In turn, Cuomo's staff agreed to accept written sworn statements from Baum and Dopp in lieu of live testimony, though they would not reference these statements in the report. Andrew's staff reneged on that agreement at the first opportunity.

Acceptance of the Cuomo Report's findings had been agreed to, but the nature of Eliot's public response and his demeanor were a different story. On the morning of July 23, 2007, we gathered over breakfast at the Governor's Mansion and later at the Capitol, for the last-minute chores before release of the Cuomo Report and Eliot's response.

We read the report, which had been accurately summarized for us the previous day, and worked on Eliot's statement. As I listened, Eliot called Bruno and delivered a short and sincere apology. After that, Eliot's inner circle met in his private conference room, and he apologized to us. This apology was awkward because Rich Baum had been present, and this group knew that Baum, not Eliot, bore significant responsibility for the coming circus. After that, we rounded up a larger group of senior executive staff and those agency heads who could be quickly collected for a meeting in the beautiful ceremonial Red Room of the Capitol. Eliot apologized to this group and prepared them for what they were about to experience. When the governor publicly admits error, his agencies and subordinates suffer.

Finally, Eliot addressed the press, who later assembled in the Red Room. Eliot played his role well, as I later told him. The problem was that he was acting skillfully in a badly written play. In this instance, it was his senior lawyers who were primarily to blame for the rotten script.

In the very first Q and A, Eliot defended Rich Baum, placing him on the "innocent" side of the fence and saying that Rich had acted in reliance on the misinformation that Dopp and Howard had purveyed. Because Eliot defended Rich, the record released by Cuomo was carefully examined to determine whether Eliot's defense made sense. It provoked reporters to question why Rich had not testified and whether the governor's refusal to discipline Baum had been part of an effort to protect himself. Rich was counterfactually assumed to be the link between Eliot and all others in the administration. The secretary to the governor had been the gatekeeper in previous administrations. The Albany press corps had assumed that Rich played that role. That misunderstanding was incorporated into their questions on July 23 and into their implicit skepticism about Eliot's answers.

Eliot need not have disciplined Rich but could have simply chastised him. Eliot was criticizing himself for stuff he had known nothing about. Why not administer some public reprimand to Baum, who had been warned that something improper had been going on, as became clear from the email released along with Cuomo's report? President Ronald Reagan had famously not fired his budget director, David Stockman, when he had taken him "in back of the woodshed" for a whipping after Stockman had publicly explained the fallacy in "trickle-down economics." In 2009, President-Elect Obama would not dismiss Treasury Secretary-designate Tim Geithner, but still criticized the future supervisor of the IRS for his cavalier and opportunistic approach to his federal tax obligations. Such public criticism that falls short of dismissal is comforting to the public, giving them the message that the Big Guy "gets it."

The second part of the rotten script, quickly exposed in a question from a reporter, was the failure to fire Darren. It was inconceivable to me that Dopp could ever resume his duties. The "indefinite suspension" that Eliot announced, which quickly became the "30-day suspension" because of a glitch in our press release, begged the question implicit in my conclusion: Darren could not and would not return.

The biggest problem at the press conference was Eliot's tone and demeanor. His embrace of the Cuomo Report had been total, unconditional and shamefaced. It should have been technical, lawyerly and aggressive. Eliot should have responded to Cuomo's report in an entirely different way.

The report had found that there had been no "surveillance" of Senator Bruno and no violation of any law. Emphasizing these two crucial conclusions, Eliot could have politely thanked Andrew and gone on to emphasize certain other parts of Cuomo's report. Eliot should have recited a key finding of the report, which said:

The various documents and information collected by the Superintendent at the request of Howard were all highly pertinent to whether Senator Bruno's use of state aircraft was, in fact, in connection with legislative business in New York City as Senator Bruno certified.

Eliot should have pointed out that his administration had instituted the procedure requiring these "certifications" concerning the purpose of trips using state aircraft, in an effort to protect taxpayer money. While accepting Cuomo's conclusion that Bruno's use of the aircraft had not violated one seemingly controlling, but old, state policy, Eliot should have emphasized Cuomo's finding that this policy was unwise and in need of repair. Eliot should also have quoted Cuomo's finding that Bruno's use of the state aircraft resulted in the "abuse of state resources." That key phrase was the flip side of the *governor's office did bad things but broke no laws and conducted no surveillance* conclusion in the report. We had totally missed this potential sound bite and failed to show the obvious moral equivalency. Emphasizing it might have resulted in a much more balanced response from the press and public. That response should have been, "These guys have both been naughty — no laws violated — both learned their lesson — let's get back to work."

While embracing and aggressively emphasizing all these things, Eliot could have announced the same disciplinary decisions concerning Dopp, Howard and Felton plus some discipline or reprimand for Baum, noting that their desire to protect state resources and to disseminate truthful information had gone too far. These disciplinary measures and new procedures on use of the aircraft, FOIL and insulation of the State Police from the governor's political agenda would prevent conduct like this in the future.

That type of response would have shown Eliot to be more honest and decisive than Andrew, especially with regard to Baum, whom Cuomo had suspiciously exempted from his recommendations for discipline. It would have tempered the swift outrage directed at Eliot, not Andrew, when it became clear that Baum bore some responsibility and that neither Rich nor Darren had actually been questioned.

A first press conference like that would have framed the debate in an entirely different way. But for that to have happened, we needed things we didn't have at the time. We needed better advice from his lawyer team, including me. We also needed a more confident and unashamed governor. The man who delivered the mea culpa on July 23, 2007, was a man full of shame. At the time, I had thought the shame noble and Christlike, with Eliot suffering for the sins of others. Indeed, I complimented him for the manner in which he had conducted that news conference. However, Eliot's demeanor at that first press conference helped create the atmosphere for the second one, held four days later.

By July 27, 2007, the Cuomo Report had been analyzed and picked apart. After that careful scrutiny, the failure of Dopp and Baum to testify had been seized upon by the press and Bruno. Initially, Bruno had applauded the Cuomo Report because it trashed the governor's office and exonerated him. Joe's first response was, "The Attorney General did an excellent job on this investigation...it is imperative that we move forward so that we can address the people's business." However, he quickly recognized the story's staying power and realized that the easiest way to support the charge that the Cuomo probe was incomplete, if not a whitewash, was to focus on the absence of live testimony from Dopp and Baum.

The press did the same. By July 2007, the subject of what constituted a thorough investigation was hardly new. At that very moment, the Bush Administration was refusing the demands of congressional Democrats for the president's aides and Justice Department officials to submit to questioning under oath about the politically motivated mass firing of a group of United States Attorneys. Similar disputes about who would or would not testify, on what basis and under oath or not, had also arisen in the Valerie Plame affair, leading to the indictment and conviction of I. Lewis "Scooter" Libby, Vice President Cheney's chief of staff. Scooter had been sentenced just a month before the TRU press conferences, held in late July 2007.

New Yorkers had also recently experienced eight years of an enormously successful attorney general, who had frequently and publicly pilloried corporate targets for their failure to fully cooperate with the investigative demands of his office. At some earlier, more innocent, time, the intricacies of an investigation done with or without subpoenae, leading to written or oral statements, given under oath or unsworn, would have been far too abstruse for the public to understand or care about. However, the press and public who "consumed" the Cuomo Report understood all this esoterica too well. They relished the irony that Eliot, the Grand Inquisitor, was the one now being pressured to answer the questions.

The second press conference was held after four days of mounting outrage about the Cuomo Report's inadequacies, outrage directed at Eliot, not Andrew, the report's father. Not a peep had been heard about Cuomo's failure to put Bruno under oath, although this and Andrew's entire approach to that part of his investigation was worse than his clearly deficient inquiry into Dopp's special project. With this backdrop, Eliot attempted to hold a news conference on the morning of July 27, 2007, one of two scheduled for the governor that day. The first was supposed to be devoted to a discussion of the bills Eliot had recently signed into law, symbolically demonstrating that he was already back doing the "people's business" after the brief dust-up four days earlier. A second news conference had been scheduled for later that day, so Eliot could address any residual questions about TRU. That plan fell apart immediately.

Led by Fred Dicker of the *New York Post,* who at one point stood on a table and interrupted the proceedings with his shouted questions, the Albany press corps essentially gang-raped Eliot as he tried to respond to the only question they wanted to have answered. Their question had nothing to do with Eliot's opening comments but instead the failure/refusal of Dopp and Baum to testify. Eliot tried to talk about recent legislation, such as a law increasing public vessel safety, another facilitating state contracts with not-for-profits and a third protecting consumers from toxic wood preservatives. Dicker ignored all that and began the assault with a question repeated by various reporters in 12 variations.

> How can you have told us on Monday that you cooperated fully with the Cuomo investigation when you are aware that two of your top aides...had refused to testify under oath?

Before Eliot could finish his response that this was Cuomo's decision with which he would not "quibble," Dicker cut him off. "That version of the facts does not jibe with what Cuomo said...." This went on for several more rounds, with Eliot twice attempting to calm Dicker with "Fred, Fred, Fred — that is sufficient — a little decorum."

Then the other reporters jumped in and shouted questions over each other — but the questions were all essentially the same, and put most incisively by Bill Lambdin of New York City's public television station.

> As a former prosecutor, would you be satisfied with an investigation that failed to talk to two of the principal witnesses involved in what you are investigating?

The response, "I will not second-guess what the attorney general has done," repeated several times and coming from Eliot, a skillful prosecutor, and world-class second-guesser, sounded false and hollow. After 12 minutes of this, which to me felt like 12 years, Eliot ignored the last shouted question, said he would be back for his 2:30 P.M. news conference and walked out. The afternoon press event was promptly cancelled.

Andrew did not hold a news conference to defend his own work product, either on July 23, when the report was released, or later, when it came under attack. His staff reneged on the bad agreement forged Sunday night, July 22, that they would accept Dopp's and Baum's written statements and we would accept the conclusions of his sloppy, incomplete and rushed report. When pressed to explain acceptance of these two brief and relatively opaque written statements, Cuomo's staff had just cited the refusal of Dopp and Baum to testify. They also claimed to lack subpoena power, failing to mention their authority when conducting a tax investigation or the subpoena power that comes with the special prosecutor status they hadn't sought from the governor. Eliot would have been hard pressed to withhold the special prosecutor designation if Cuomo had publicly requested it, as Andrew well knew from his experience in his father's administration. As the press conference and week ended, it was abundantly clear that Eliot's prediction that TRU would be a one-week story had been wildly optimistic and proven inaccurate.

■ ■ ■

····

TRU Drags Us Down

B Y THE CONCLUSION of the July 27, 2007, chaotic press conference, it became clear that more investigation would be,
and indeed should be, done. In the following month, three new
TRU investigations were commenced. Albany District Attorney David Soares began the second of his three separate investigations. The Republican majority in the Senate also began
an investigation through the Senate's Investigation Committee. The third new investigation was commenced by the state's
Ethics Commission a day or two before the disastrous July 27
news conference. That investigation was later continued by the
Commission on Public Integrity, a new body that assumed the
powers of both the Ethics Commission and the state's Lobbying Commission on September 22, 2007. Although this Ethics/
Integrity Commission investigation was badly flawed, it turned
out to be the closest to a definitive probe of TRU, among the
ten attempted.

Although the Commission on Public Integrity's investigation
was necessary, due to the Cuomo Report's glaring inadequacies,
I dreaded it from the get-go. A thorough investigation ultimately

would help Eliot, nevertheless I feared that this one would be conducted badly, because of the commission's leadership. One of Eliot's significant legislative victories in the early part of 2007 had involved toughening the state's ethics-in-government laws and the merger of the separate ethics and lobbying commissions into the unified Commission on Public Integrity, with expanded powers. The governor had the authority to appoint the chair and a majority of the members of the new commission. When in April 2007 Eliot told me he was likely to appoint John Feerick as chair of the Ethics Commission, who later would become chair of the Commission on Public Integrity, I had tried to dissuade him. Eliot thinks he knows everybody. In this case, however, my knowledge of, and experience with, John Feerick had been much more extensive than Eliot's.

John Feerick is almost universally respected, revered and liked. It's hard not to feel that way about him. If Santa Claus were both a lawyer and an Irishman, he would be John Feerick. John, 71 years old when Eliot appointed him, had amassed a career full of apparent achievement, including substantial credit for the formulation of the 25th Amendment to the United States Constitution, which deals with transfer of executive authority during periods when the president is incapacitated. Among the many other highlights were Feerick's long and prominent partnership in the Skadden Arps law firm, the deanship of Fordham University Law School and chairmanship of the Special New York State Commission on Government Integrity, which sat from 1987 through 1990. This earlier integrity effort is usually referred to as the "Feerick Commission."

The 1987 Feerick Commission's mandate was to broadly investigate and make recommendations for reducing corruption in state government. After more than two years of investigation, Feerick issued a report, titled "The Midas Touch," finding substantial ethical lapses in the fundraising practices used in the campaigns of Governor Mario Cuomo, Comptroller Edward ("Ned") Regan and Attorney General Robert Abrams.

A careful reading of the 1989 Feerick Commission Report, which I would not recommend to anyone other than a public policy student looking for an arcane topic for a master's thesis, shows that the Feerick Commission found that the Cuomo, Abrams and Regan campaigns had all engaged in activity that created appearances of impropriety, particularly with respect to the relationship between campaign contributions and access to the officeholder for state business. The pervasive ethical breaches of the Cuomo fundraising machine had been found to be roughly equivalent with the minor and occasional ethical lapses in the efforts of Bob Abrams' campaign. Having worked for Bob for more than a decade, I can attest to how scrupulous he was and his sensitivity to even the slightest appearance of impropriety. He once refused my gift of a set of silver collar stays because I was a state employee, and the gift might have been construed as an attempt to court favor with my superior.

The Feerick Commission's investigation apparently had been influenced by two former Abrams' employees, who served on Feerick's staff, each of whom had felt unfairly treated by Bob in promotions and status. They used their insider knowledge about Bob's virtually, but not absolutely, spotless fundraising practices.

John Feerick had allowed all this to happen. Years later, the Feerick Commission Report sprang to a second nasty life when it was used by Al D'Amato to equate his own monumental ethical failings with the exaggerated findings about Bob in the Feerick Commission Report.

John Feerick had been dean of Fordham Law School during the seven years I taught the basic antitrust law course as an adjunct professor. My skill in the endeavor is for my former students to judge. Objectively, I had taken the course from 20 or so students in the first year to roughly 100 in the last few. I declined to accept compensation for teaching during my last five years. Not once in those seven years had John Feerick thanked me for teaching the course, for donating my salary back to the law school or for plugging the gaping hole in his school's offerings caused when the "regular" antitrust professor left for a "one-year" tour of duty in Skadden Arps Brussels office, which stretched into many years. The only times I heard from Dean Feerick in those seven years were when my grades were late and he called to complain. After seven years, John let one of his associate deans thank me and inform me that my services were no longer needed, whereupon I was replaced by an old pal of John's from Skadden who wanted to teach a course.

The Skadden/Feerick connection was of particular interest to me. The fascinating part was the reverence that virtually everyone at Skadden had for Feerick and the frequency with which his name and connection were invoked, years after he had departed. Given my own high estimation of the typical Skadden skill set, and my somewhat lower calculation of John's, because of the Feerick Commission and our limited interaction at Fordham, I believed something other than his legal skills accounted for this constant dropping of John's name.

Skadden was one of the great "Jewish" law firms that came of age back when the "white shoe" law firms had few or no spots for very talented Jewish lawyers. For some of these firms, the "Jewish" designation had been a badge of honor, as they ate the lunch of the old, decaying and inbred firms. As Jewish firms like Skadden and Weil Gotshal rose to the top of the heap, and as Jews found their way to, and eventually into the leadership of, the old WASPy firms, these lines of demarcation began to blur. Now they are of mainly historical interest. But at Skadden, as it began to grow from 18 lawyers to the more than 2,000 today, that firm wanted to have it both ways. It was a Jewish firm but wanted to be seen as just a great firm. What better way than to put a big, jolly Irishman front and center, even well after he had left the firm? It was the affirmative version of the involuntary branding of the Corleone Family as the "Irish Gang" in Mario Puzo's *The Godfather*, because the otherwise all-Sicilian family had adopted the Irish orphan Tom Hagen. If John Feerick did not realize his special role in Skadden, he wasn't very perceptive. If he did and acquiesced, I respected him less, deducting from a modest initial level of respect.

There were further trivial counts in my subjective indictment of John Feerick that, taken together, compelled me to try to dissuade Eliot from appointing Feerick to head the new Commission on Public Integrity. Sooner or later, this new body would have something important to investigate, and I didn't want Feerick there when that happened. I related all these experiences and impressions to Eliot, and said, "Don't appoint him."

Eliot dismissively responded, "Maybe you're right about him, but it doesn't matter — everyone knows him, everyone likes him and he will be a popular choice."

Back in June, several weeks before TRU came to light, Feerick appointed Herbert Teitelbaum as the executive director of the Commission. I was more disturbed by this appointment than by Feerick's, since the executive director actually runs the investigations. The governor appointed the commission's chair but had no control over his appointments to staff the commission. So, I initially stayed quiet. My skepticism about Teitelbaum had an even less objective basis than my negative opinion of Feerick.

Teitelbaum had been with Feerick at Skadden. Nothing there. Later he had been a partner of two good friends of mine in a litigation boutique, not unlike my own. Herb and I had been adversaries in investigations that I had conducted for the AG's office in the early 1980s. I didn't like his condescending demeanor and ceaseless name-dropping, especially coming from someone representing clients whose legal fates were more or less in my hands. My bias against Herb came more from an impression than from any firsthand experience. It was merely a hunch, one as insubstantial as the hunch that motivated Sister Aloysius Beauvier in the play/movie *Doubt* to hound Father Flynn out of St. Nicholas School. Like Sister Aloysius, I was certain about my hunch, while doubtful it was proper to act upon it.

Herb's nice legal career had not included any great accomplishment. He had run a nice firm, made lots of money, but had never landed a whale, let alone Moby-Dick. My impression was that this gnawed at him and increasingly so as the years went by and the opportunities for real achievement had dwindled. His father-in-law had been a powerhouse in the profession and the greater world, the legendary Morris Abram, whose slogan in an unsuccessful U.S. senatorial campaign had been "Who is Morris Abram?" The voters didn't know or elect him, but he was a legal and intellectual giant who had been president of Brandeis University in the days when that school was a haven for Jewish intellectuals, unwelcome in the halls of Ivy, not unlike Skadden and Weil provided a home for talented Jewish lawyers excluded from Ivy League law firms. The incredibly accomplished parent is a problem for the aspiring child. But the renowned father-in-law is even worse for a man. As he is comparing his own accomplishments to "Dad's," he fears that his wife is comparing him to her father as well.

The Ethics Commission chaired by Feerick and directed by Teitelbaum began their investigation on July 26, 2007, the day before Eliot's chaotic press conference. Two days later, Rick Karlin, a reporter for the Albany *Times Union*, counterfactually and illogically suggested that Teitelbaum's "ties" to Eliot called into question his ability to fairly conduct the investigation. In the article titled, "Ethics Panel Has Ties to Spitzer: Committee [sic] May Have Conflict In Probing Governor's Conduct," Karlin cited the fact that $117,000-plus of the roughly $118,000 that Teitelbaum's former law firm had given to political campaigns in the previous four years had gone to Eliot's 2006 and 2010 campaign committees. That Teitelbaum himself had not contributed to Eliot and had made a $1,000 contribution to the quixotic campaign of Eliot's Republican opponent, John Faso, were deemed irrelevant in the *TU*'s attempt to invent a story.

Regardless of the illogic of the charge, the *TU*'s silly story had given me what I needed to go to Eliot in an attempt to get Teitelbaum out of this incipient probe. I told Eliot that he should publicly disagree with the charge that Teitelbaum's "ties" to him created a conflict, but invoking the need to avoid even the "appearance of impropriety," ask for Teitelbaum to recuse himself from this investigation. I told him that I feared that the governor's head on a plate might be viewed by Teitelbaum as the "big one" that had eluded him during his legal career. However, I admitted that these concerns had little basis other than a very definite bad feeling. If we were going to play this card, it had to be played immediately. As he had with my recommendation about Feerick, Eliot dismissed my suggestion, focusing more on the lack of substance in the charge that Teitelbaum was biased toward him, than on the crazy atmosphere surrounding TRU and its many offshoots. Soon after, when Teitelbaum began acting erratically, and the commission began leaking information to the press about its highly confidential investigation, both Eliot and I sought the advice of a trusted mutual friend.

Eliot's and my friend had been a Skadden partner and a colleague of both Teitelbaum's and Feerick's. His pronouncement on Teitelbaum, delivered without prompting, was, "He goes to sleep every night dreaming about how he will take down the governor." The basis of that speculation was the same as mine. As I've said, Herb struck me as a frustrated man who never had landed the big one, and my hunch was that now, late in his career, this investigation offered him just that chance. By the time we got that assessment, it was too late to do anything about Herb or Feerick or the Ethics, soon to be Integrity, Commission, careening out of control.

The Commission on Public Integrity report issued a year later, on July 24, 2008, was delivered after a shoddy and unprofessional process and one in which the commission itself violated the law numerous times. In doing its job so sloppily and slowly, the commission never projected the power nor engendered the respect necessary to get the other investigators to defer. That lack of respect was exacerbated by the baseless charge, constantly heard in the press, that Feerick, Teitelbaum and the commission were trying to protect Eliot.

As Feerick/Teitelbaum began their investigation, Albany District Attorney David Soares began his second distinct probe. Soares II, as I call it, surfaced on July 27, 2007. The DA's apparent motivations were the publicity surrounding TRU, the competitive atmosphere among potential prosecutors and his lack of respect for the shoddy Cuomo Report. Soares II concluded with a report issued on September 21, 2007. Soares III, the district attorney's third investigation, concluded with a report conveniently issued on March 29, 2008, two weeks after Eliot's resignation. The Soares trilogy is the most bizarre, unprofessional and frightening government probe I have encountered in 37 years of legal practice. As one of the lawyers representing the Second Floor, and later as a witness called by Soares to testify, I thought about the classic *Twilight Zone* episode, one of four reprised in *Twilight Zone: The Movie*, where a six-year-old-boy rules, tortures and toys with an isolated American town using God-like powers, which are contrasted with his juvenile temperament and moral sensibility.

The third competing investigation in this three-ring circus was the New York State Senate's, under the dubious and partisan powers possessed by the Bruno-controlled Senate Investigations Committee. This investigation, which by law had to be connected to, and in aid of, some legislative proposal, managed to kill a few trees. It also enriched a few lawyers brought in by both sides from private law firms. Otherwise, it produced nothing worthy of note. The Senate Investigations Committee folded its tent when Eliot abandoned office, unlike the district attorney and the Commission on Public Integrity, which properly felt constrained to conclude their efforts with formal reports.

Constant leaking of information from the confidential investigation being conducted by Feerick/Teitelbaum began the day it was commenced, July 26, 2007. On that day, I received an email from a friend of Herb's showing that Teitelbaum was already having conversations about his commission's confidential proceedings with this "outsider."

While this defective process began in Feerick/Teitelbaum's offices in the Alfred E. Smith building in Albany, a few blocks away, the DA's office began to leak the workings and details of their own probe even more frequently than the Commission on Public Integrity. The leaking became so bad that, one autumn 2007 day while I was walking down the hill from the Capitol to meet with Soares, I was called on my cell phone by a reporter who said, "Hey, I know you are going over to talk with Soares — can you tell me what you are going to talk about with him?"

The constant leaking from these two separate, competing and ultimately antagonistic probes (Soares eventually investigated Teitelbaum for potential criminal violations) helped lead Eliot's senior lawyer team into a serious error in the way we responded to the investigations. By the end of the third week of July 2007, we had gotten our arms around the email and other documents and interviewed people with relevant information. Our team, led by David Nocenti, had a choice of two paths in responding to the investigations. One had been to quickly produce all the documents, offer, or even insist, that everyone testify under oath and then make all of that documentation and testimony public.

The alternative path, which we unfortunately took, was to deal with the investigations in a traditional lawyerly way. We produced all of the documents requested, except those subject to well-established privilege, such as "attorney-client" communications. For such withheld documents, we explained the basis for claiming privilege and allowed the investigators to challenge the privilege, with a court potentially making the decision of whether the document had to be produced. The vast majority of such disputes over privilege are resolved among the parties without court intervention, as were virtually all of the disputes that arose during TRU.

Once Eliot's email had been reviewed, and I had been satisfied that he was clean, we should have loaded up a truck and dumped all of the documents on Feerick/Teitelbaum and Soares, contemporaneously provided them to the press and put the "witnesses" onto a bus and parked them in front of the DA's and Commission on Public Integrity's offices with a neon sign flashing, "We want to testify—now!" Some witnesses, like Dopp, were not under our control, as they had retained their own counsel. For those people, the clear and public directive should have been, "Testify now, or your employment in the Executive Chamber is terminated, forthwith." Eliot would have testified quickly, and his testimony would have been promptly made public. After constant debate, we chose the second path, which, though reasonable, was not the wise path.

We were following conventional lawyer's practice. You deal with things in an orderly and traditional way. Established privileges are there for a reason. While we had never given serious consideration to invoking "executive privilege" (inaccurate press reports to the contrary), the attorney-client privilege was another matter. The governor has a "counsel" for a reason. Simply waiving the privilege that exists for communications between the governor and his counsel, without careful deliberation, might have served Eliot's interests but done harm to future governors who would need to invoke the privilege for good and valid reasons. Amazingly, we hid from ourselves the simple fact that one of Eliot's set plays as attorney general had been to demand that targets of his investigations waive attorney-client privilege or suffer the consequences of a withering and highly publicized investigation, culminating in civil suit, indictment or both. Eventually, but too late to get the benefit, we waived attorney-client privilege, produced the email that might have been shielded and these were made public when the various investigative reports were released.

Another mistake was our attempt to avoid the disclosure of harmless, but very embarrassing, documents, primarily email. By July 2007, everyone knew that Joe Bruno and Eliot Spitzer were not fond of each other. Even if Eliot's silly statements that he considered Joe a "good friend" were to be believed, the public had already heard and read many salty and nasty descriptions of the opposite "good friend" from both Eliot and Joe. The downside of disclosing a few more unflattering descriptions of Joe by Eliot in the email was far outweighed by the benefits of speedy disclosure. There were also some innocent, but ambiguous, references in the email that would have needed explanation, and which when later disclosed were explained with no bad effect. However, when the decision about how to respond to the investigations was made, the consensus had been that wholesale public disclosure of all the email would set us on a course of months of embarrassment and explanation, at a time when some, including Eliot, still naively thought that TRU would have no legs.

The third reason we adopted a traditional, and somewhat adversarial, posture in responding to Feerick/Teitelbaum and Soares was the simple fact that we didn't trust them. The distrust had built steadily. Government investigations, especially those involving conduct that may result in serious civil or criminal penalties, are supposed to be conducted under a cloak of confidentiality. When this goes according to the book, the public may hear confirmation that an investigation has begun and some time later the announcement of findings, perhaps accompanied by a settlement, fines and/or an indictment or guilty plea. Little or nothing should be disclosed between these opening and concluding statements other than an occasional confirmation that the investigation is ongoing.

Despite the public's desire to know everything, there are good reasons for the details of a government investigation to remain secret while in progress. The pursuit of truth and justice will be seriously impaired if people and institutions under investigation, or those simply providing evidence, expect or fear that their identities, documents and testimony will be leaked to the press. These witnesses are always free to disclose their own testimony, at any time, should they so choose. Another important reason for confidentiality is to avoid damaging the reputations of targets, subjects and witnesses in investigations who are never charged. Investigations conducted by the Commission on Public Integrity and the district attorney are cloaked in secrecy by law.

Even before the press and public became aware of the Ethics Commission investigation, Teitelbaum began to disclose details of the commission's confidential work. On July 26, 2007, I received a fax from Bob Hermann, who was working with me on the IOLA project and was a close friend and former law partner of Herb's. The fax revealed the conversations Herb was already having with Bob about the Ethics Commission's imminent revision of an old interpretation that seemingly allowed Joe Bruno to use state aircraft for trips when most of his business was private or political.

In the next 13 days, Hermann approached me five of six more times with information and advice from "Herb" about the investigation and how the Second Floor should respond. One of the consistent messages was a warning not to withhold any documents on the basis of privilege. Inasmuch as Teitelbaum was already communicating with the senior lawyer team, actually representing the Executive Chamber, I was annoyed and concerned. Hermann was outside the Executive Chamber and had no role in responding to the various TRU probes. These "back channel" communications, as Teitelbaum described them to his assistant Maeve Tooher, were not helpful. They were just careless bantering and boasting of the type that government investigators are required to avoid.

I approached Richard Rifkin and asked him whether these communications from Herb to Bob were "kosher." Richard, the governor's "special counsel" had been added to our senior lawyer team in large measure because he had served as executive director of the Ethics Commission a decade earlier. Rifkin quickly pointed to provisions in the Public Officers Law, which showed that Herb's actions were illegal. When Hermann called me again, as he did on August 8, as I was driving around Skaneateles, one of New York's Finger Lakes, during my visits to that region's SUNY campuses, he again started to tell me what Herb was saying concerning the Second Floor's response to his probe. I stopped him mid-sentence. I told Bob that Herb (not he) was violating the law and directed him to cease having any conversations with Teitelbaum on the subject. My assistant Dan Doktori was seated next to me while this conversation occurred. Teitelbaum's actions in July and August 2007 and at least one subsequent breach of confidentiality in October would later become the subject of a criminal investigation by Soares and a second inspector general's investigation.

After I had scolded and ordered Hermann to cease receiving Teitelbaum's improper disclosures, I stopped hearing from him about this for almost three months. Nevertheless, other leaks from the commission started to occur on a regular basis. In August 2007, Rifkin wrote to Feerick complaining about these leaks and later received a perfunctory denial from Feerick. It was not gratifying for me to watch Feerick and Teitelbaum so quickly conform to the harsh portraits I had drawn for Eliot a few months before. Despite his denial, Feerick attempted to create a mechanism to stop the leaks, at least those not directly attributable to Herb. Feerick did this in late September 2007 when the Ethics Commission morphed into the Commission on Public Integrity. At the time, Feerick created a so-called Working Group comprising five among the Commission on Public Integrity's 13 commissioners plus Teitelbaum. The Working Group commissioners were Feerick, former New York Court of Appeals Judge Howard Levine, former United States Attorney Loretta Lynch, former prosecutor Robert Giuffra and another former government lawyer, John Mitchell.

These Working Group commissioners had been considered trustworthy by Feerick. However, in taking this legally dubious step, vital information was withheld from the other eight commissioners, who had then rubberstamped decisions without important information. One such decision was a unanimous vote of confidence in Teitelbaum after DA Soares had provided

Feerick with evidence that his executive director had improperly disclosed confidential information.

From the moment the Commission on Public Integrity came into being on September 22, 2007 until the day it issued its report on July 24, 2008, it was a sieve, constantly feeding the details of its "confidential" investigation to the press. Down the hill, David Soares' competing TRU investigation matched, and indeed overmatched, Feerick/Teitelbaum, leak for leak. Leaks sourced to Soares' office and/or the Commission on Public Integrity, replete with verbatim quotes, appeared on September 24, October 8, October 22 and October 29 in the *New York Post* and *New York Daily News*. The press was quite properly willing to report these leaks, but also often reassembled facts, innuendo and leaks into a Picasso-like Cubist rendering.

During the course of TRU, the Albany press corps frequently mischaracterized facts simply because it made for a sexier story. I woke up one morning to read a *Daily News* article written by Liz Benjamin which said that Constantine was "*caught* on tape *admitting* that a key member of the panel probing Troopergate improperly tried to pass him information on the investigation...." So I called Liz, whom I knew a bit. I confirmed that she knew the real story, that I wasn't "caught admitting" this, but had voluntarily come forward with the information and later voluntarily went into David Soares' office without counsel to testify about it. Liz assured me that she knew all that but said, "Lloyd, I work for a tabloid—understand."

One of the documents that we tried to withhold from the investigators, on the basis of privilege, was a July 28, 2007, email from Rich Baum to Eliot pleading that he not be fired and lashing out at other Second Floor residents, including me. The wasted and destructive effort to shield this embarrassing, but innocent, email was a microcosm of the folly in our entire approach to the TRU investigations.

On Saturday, July 28, 2007, Eliot called to give me a heads-up that Rich Baum would be forced out of his position as secretary the next day. I was relieved but not joyful, as I told him. There was little joy on the Second Floor at that time and certainly none to be found in the firing or demotion of a colleague, who, despite his failings, was working his ass off for New York and its governor.

After Rich's limited culpability for TRU came to light, I assumed that Eliot would take care of the situation himself, and I discontinued my efforts to have Baum removed from his position. Eliot's call on July 28 (telling me that Rich would be removed the next day) confirmed my assumption. However, on that same day, Rich had sent Eliot an email making his argument for remaining secretary:

> Moving me out of the position of Secretary now will have a negative effect on you at a sensitive time. Whatever we or you say, the fact is it will be perceived that I was moved as a response to the recent scandal. Everyone will assume it's either because of some still-hidden culpability on my part or because of my management failure. Either way, this only moves the scandal one step closer to you and defeats our (truthful) effort to cabin it in the communications

office. I know you want to show change, but I truly think the way to do it is through addition not subtraction.

You should do what's best for you and for the state, but I have to note, the unfairness of the situation I've been put in. When David [Nocenti] called me into the office last Saturday to lay out the plan going forward, I said I had nothing for [sic] fear from testifying, that I was willing to do so and that my failure to testify would make my position untenable. Everyone there pushed me very hard to go along with the path that was being laid out. I said that at a minimum I needed to do a sworn statement. At that point Lloyd objected to my presence, and I was ejected. I've lived through a week of attacks on my reputation because of that decision for the team and, ultimately, you. I know you say this move is not as a result of the bad publicity but that [sic] fact is we would not be talking this way now and people would not be focusing in on me if not for the past week. I don't know what to say other than it just doesn't seem right.

The above quotation represents one-third of the email. The other two-thirds were "redacted" and never produced to the Commission on Public Integrity, although Teitelbaum was permitted to read the entire document. No one else read the whole thing, other than the three people to whom it was sent, Eliot, David Nocenti and Avi Shick, an old colleague of Baum's from the Spitzer AG's office, who had become the president of the Empire State Development Corporation.

When the Commission on Public Integrity properly demanded that Baum's withheld email be produced, we wasted a precious week trying to protect it. Eliot did not want anyone to read it because of the apparently embarrassing attacks on me and others in the administration, which comprised the bulk of the email. I say, "apparently" because even Peter Pope, Sean Maloney and I were not permitted to read the redacted portions. The redacted portions were vaguely described to us by David. At that point, I was faced with the choice of going along with Eliot's decision about who could see this document, resigning my position in the administration, or staying on as senior advisor, but ceasing to act as one of the lawyers defending the administration. Exercising the second or third option seemed necessary, because it is untenable for a lawyer to defend a client and vouch for its documents if the lawyer doesn't know the precise contents of those documents.

Nevertheless, I chose to stay and continue in this untenable posture out of misguided loyalty to Eliot—choosing to believe as I did, and still do, that the rest of the document was merely a personal attack on me and others, irrelevant to the facts of TRU. This particular type of loyalty was misguided, not because it hurt me, but because it hurt Eliot, who was implicitly demanding the loyalty to his own detriment. The casualties in this affair were our precious time, a further deterioration of trust between our team and Teitelbaum's, and my lowered opinion of Eliot's judgment and my own. My opinion of Eliot had already taken a hit when he had failed to pull the trigger on Rich, as he said he was about to, during his phone call to me on July 28. Eliot had bought into the perverse logic in Rich's email, that removing him would be viewed by the public as an admission that Rich bore some culpability for TRU and/or had been a failure as a manager. While all three of these things were true (the culpability, the management failure and that these would have been the cause of his removal), acting upon them would have been a sign of strength and sanity.

Baum's email tried to induce fear by suggesting that he was all that stood between TRU and Eliot. The parenthetical "(truthful)" in the sentence where Rich wrote "...this only moves the scandal one step closer to you and defeats our (truthful) effort to cabin it in the communications office" was what the kids in my Long Island neighborhood called a "tell," but Freud called a "slip." There had been an effort to cabin TRU in the "communications office" of Darren Dopp. This wasn't to protect Eliot, who bore no responsibility, but to protect Rich, who did. Therefore, the effort was not entirely "truthful" in Rich's guilty mind and deserved the parentheses he had inserted.

Baum carelessly sent his email outside the Executive Chamber to his pal Avi Schick—who also is a friend of mine. Doing so destroyed the attorney-client privilege that otherwise might have protected it from disclosure, because it had been sent to counsel David Nocenti. This had made our attempts to shield the email from production futile, and was yet another measure of precisely why Baum had to be replaced. That never happened. With the exception of the one moment of resolve that Eliot had shown on July 28, 2007, the worse Rich had performed, the more Eliot had dug in. By February 2008, after more than seven months of TRU corrosively interfering with all of the administration's initiatives, Eliot lost it in a tirade about TRU, directed at me, Nocenti, Christine Anderson and Marlene Turner. Shrieking at the top of his lungs, Eliot assured us that he would fire each and every one of us—the entire executive staff —"except Rich," and he made that reservation three times. This made perfect sense to me, because by then I believed that the guy who made that statement was the Impostor and that we were inhabiting "Bizarro" Second Floor.

On November 1, 2007, I was pulled out of a meeting in the governor's Manhattan offices by an "urgent" request for a face-to-face with Bob Hermann. Bob and I had been working on several projects designed to support legal services for the state's poor. I stepped out to see Hermann, who was visibly shaken. He told me that the Commission on Public Integrity had referred to DA Soares the matter of whether Darren Dopp's sworn testimony before the commission had contradicted his "sworn" written statement to Attorney General Cuomo. The referral invited prosecution of Dopp for perjury and an investigation of Peter Pope, Sean Maloney and David Nocenti for helping to draft Dopp's sworn statement. Hermann also disclosed the names of the Working Group of commissioners that Feerick had designated to deal with this sensitive referral and attempt to stop the leaks from the commission.

Hermann told me that he knew I must disclose this sensitive information to "the governor" but asked me to promise that I would not tell Eliot that he was the source. I refused and told him I was livid that he continued to listen to Herb Teitelbaum's leaks in violation of my clear directive to him over the phone from my car back in August 2007. That October afternoon, I called an ethics lawyer named Hal Lieberman to ask for guidance on how to proceed and then directly marched into Eliot's office, told him exactly what had happened and identified Hermann.

Within days, the fact of the Commission on Public Integrity's ultra-secret and highly sensitive criminal referral to the Albany DA was leaked to the press by both Soares' office and the commission itself. Within weeks, staff at the commission were summoned to testify before a grand jury that Soares had convened. Still later, the circumstances under which we learned about the referral became the subject of yet another investigation by Soares—this time of whether Teitelbaum had violated the law in disclosing information to Hermann.

Leaks from the district attorney's office and the Commission on Public Integrity about these offshoots from TRU were published in the Albany *Times Union*, the *New York Times* and the *Daily News* during the November 8–12, 2007, time period and spotlighted two new problems. First, Eliot's senior lawyer team was being decimated, because we were being called as witnesses in the investigation of these TRU offshoots. This happened to Pope, Maloney and Nocenti and, much later on, to me as well. Once we were considered witnesses, our utility as lawyers representing the Executive Chamber was severely diminished. The second new problem, spotlighted in the leaks, was David Soares' apparent resolve to indict Darren Dopp for perjury. When the fact of this imminent indictment was leaked, neither Nocenti, Pope nor Maloney could meet with Soares and attempt to dissuade him from taking this step. This was because the district attorney had categorized them as witnesses, and possibly subjects, of this new investigative tangent of TRU.

Despite my opinion of Darren Dopp, any criminal charge relating to the alleged inconsistency between his two sworn statements would have been a travesty. Darren was a man with a family who would unfairly suffer grievously. I persuaded Eliot to let me meet with Soares in an attempt to dissuade him from indicting Dopp.

The supposedly indictable inconsistency was Darren's testimony to the Commission on Public Integrity that he did not believe he had done anything wrong, which allegedly conflicted with a mild apology in Darren's "sworn" statement to Cuomo. I had a transcript of the testimony that Darren had given to Soares on August 14, 2007, and found seven places where Darren had similarly told the DA's assistants, as he had told Teitelbaum, that he didn't think he had done anything wrong. Regardless of what I thought of Darren, he sincerely believed he had done nothing wrong, that his actions might have created "an appearance of impropriety," but nothing more than that.

A few days later, on December 4, 2007, as I trudged down the hill from the Capitol to the DA's office with a plea for Darren in my briefcase, I got a call on my cell phone from Jim Odato of the *Times Union*. Odato told me that he knew I was going to meet with Soares and asked me what the meeting was about. I truthfully responded that I wasn't doing any such thing, as I pivoted 180 degrees and returned to the Capitol. Such was the extent of the leaking throughout the fall and winter of the

Plague Year. Another leak reported by Liz Benjamin on December 17, 2007, caused me to reschedule the meeting with Soares. Benjamin reported that Soares was angry and frustrated with our responses to his investigation and would quickly convene a grand jury, of which Eliot himself might be a target.

Soares had been pummeled by the press for allegedly being in bed with Eliot, and most consistently by *New York Daily News* reporter Michael Goodwin, who eventually drew Soares into a name-calling contest. Goodwin called Soares a "coward," Soares dared Goodwin to call him that to his face and Goodwin accepted. On the way to that threatened *boyo a boyo,* Goodwin's December 5, 2007, column ripped Soares for his timidity and deference to Eliot.

Eliot and I were livid because we were cooperating with Soares' every fitful and unfocused request. Eliot himself had never been a target of any of these amateurish investigations. Suggestions to the contrary were false and unacceptable. Eliot directed me to call Soares and meet with him quickly, as I did on December 19, 2007. At the meeting attended by Soares and his assistant Brett Knowles, the DA assured me that there was no dispute with our office or the governor. He confirmed that we had promptly cooperated with all his requests and flatly stated that Eliot was not a target or subject of his investigation. He went on to say that he was as distressed as we were that the contrary was being reported and sourced to his office. I told Soares about the call from the reporter during my aborted visit to his office 15 days earlier. He just shrugged. I demanded that he make a public statement, confirming each of the admissions he had just made to me, saying it was damaging to the state to allow the false impression that the governor was under criminal investigation. Soares agreed and promised to "promptly" inform me whether he would accede to the request.

I then made my plea for Darren, going through the numerous instances where Darren had expressed the same opinion about the propriety of his conduct to Soares' assistants on August 14, as he had to Teitelbaum on October 11. I noted that the DA's staff had reviewed Darren's "sworn" statement for Cuomo before questioning him in August. Any inconsistency was mere nuance. Nothing in that regard had been noted in Soares' September 21, 2007, report. Soares listened politely, and I then departed.

Soares' demeanor gave me little confidence that he would act responsibly. Any doubt about what Soares would do was soon eliminated. Within 15 minutes upon my return to the Capitol, I was given a copy of Michael Goodwin's *Daily News* article of that day. Titled "It's Time To Call in The Feds," Goodwin opined that "The incestuous nature of Albany politics will never permit the truth. It's time to stop kidding ourselves. It's time to call in the Feds." The article was essentially a series of taunts at Soares, about his intelligence, experience, courage, independence and just about everything other than the size of his penis. After reading the article, I knew that Soares wouldn't issue the statement, but still expected that he would honor his promise to "promptly" inform me. After several days without a word, I wrote to Soares reminding him. After several more, I called to make yet another appointment. I was told that the DA would have been pleased to meet with me again, but, "Sorry," he couldn't because I was now (like Nocenti, Maloney and Pope) deemed a "witness." I would be a witness in the DA's new investigation concerning Teitelbaum's alleged leaking of information.

Soares' third investigation was clearly charted by the charges hurled at him by the press and was a desperate attempt to indict someone for something—anything. Soares even considered filing criminal charges against David Nocenti because David had inadvertently failed to properly "swear" Darren Dopp when notarizing Dopp's statement to Cuomo.

Except for constantly breaking the laws concerning confidentiality, fighting with each other and tilting at ludicrous targets such as the Nocenti notarization nonsense, little was done by the Commission on Public Integrity or the district attorney from mid-autumn 2007 through the end of the Spitzer Administration. When they finally announced their findings, virtually nothing new was revealed. The essential facts were as I recited earlier in this book and already known the year before.

At the end, the Commission on Public Integrity charged the same people whom Cuomo had recommended for sanction, namely Dopp, Howard and Felton, and added Rich Baum. Although Rich's culpability was clearly of a lower order, that culpability was implicit in the AG's report. Andrew did not call for Baum to be sanctioned, as he had with the other three, but that omission had nothing to do with the facts or testimony; Andrew had simply done Rich or Eliot, or both, a favor. That type of "favor," however, usually hurts the recipients—as this favor had and was probably intended to.

The Commission on Public Integrity's findings, that Dopp, Howard, Felton and Baum were the people culpable for the malicious and stupid game that Darren played with the State Police, was correct. That this conduct violated any law is questionable. The provisions of the Public Officers Law cited by the commission, with one exception, are so vague and subjective that they would not likely survive a serious constitutional challenge. The commission cited all four men for violating Public Officers Law Section 74(3)(h), which provides:

> An officer or employee of a state agency...should endeavor to pursue a course of conduct which will not raise suspicion among the public that he is likely to be engaged in acts that are in violation of his trust.

I have argued constitutional law cases in the United States District, Circuit and Supreme courts and cannot conceive that a statute as subjective as this one could withstand a challenge that it is void for its vagueness. For some reason, Rich agreed not to contest this charge, of highly dubious validity.

In addition to being charged under the same vague provision, Dopp, Howard and Felton were also charged with violating Public Officers Law Section 74(3)(d), which provides:

> No officer or employee of a state agency...should use or attempt to use his official position to secure unwarranted privileges or exemptions for himself or others.

This provision is almost as vague as the first one and also would require a court to find that Joe Bruno's misery conferred an "unwarranted privilege or exemption[s]" on Dopp, Howard or Felton or upon Eliot, whom these guys were apparently trying to please by making Joe miserable.

In addition to those vague charges, Preston Felton was also charged with violating one other provision of the law, Public Officers Law Section 74(3)(c) which provides:

No officer or employee of a state agency…should disclose confidential information acquired by him in the course of his official duties nor use such information to further his personal interests.

Citing this reasonably clear provision, the Commission on Public Integrity made its strongest case for a violation, finding that when Preston Felton obtained and released itineraries detailing Joe Bruno's movements on the ground, he was acting outside established procedure. This charge also has weaknesses, but it is at least plausible. The provision that Felton was cited for violating is the same provision that Richard Rifkin had pointed me to in August 2007 when I asked him whether it was "kosher" for Teitelbaum to be disclosing confidential information to Bob Hermann. This same provision clearly applied to each and every leak of confidential information emanating from the Commission on Public Integrity during the course of its probe.

Albany District Attorney David Soares' third investigation concluded with a 20-page report issued on March 28, 2008, 11 days after the effective date of Eliot's resignation. Soares III, like Soares II, was premised on the conclusion that no law had been violated when the State Police collected, and Dopp released, Joe Bruno's travel records, regardless of whether those acts involved "political plotting." Soares concluded that Dopp may have committed two crimes involving "false swearing." Soares also concluded that Nocenti, Maloney and Pope did not coerce Dopp to swear falsely, nor was there a viable case against Nocenti for his actions as a notary public.

Soares immunized Dopp from prosecution in order to secure what the DA referred to as Darren's "truthful" February 5, 2008, sworn testimony that supposedly conflicted with Eliot's unsworn statement to Soares in August 2007. Soares concluded that Dopp's belated "truthful" testimony demonstrated that Eliot's statement concerning his role in the release of Bruno's travel records was "not truthful." The report does not present any evidence suggesting that Eliot was aware of the way Dopp and Howard had collected the information from the State Police, the basis for the claims of foul play.

The Soares III report said that the DA "intended" or "considered" presenting Eliot's and Dopp's "conflicting accounts to a grand jury." Of course, the grand jury could not have indicted Eliot, because his August 2007 statement was unsworn. Instead, Soares invoked the power of a grand jury to "examine evidence" concerning any "misconduct, nonfeasance, or neglect in public office" in order to recommend "removal or disciplinary action." The fanciful grand jury presentation that the DA "intended" never actually occurred, because, according to Soares, Eliot's resignation had deprived him of his authority to act.

Now let us consider a few facts retrieved from Planet Earth. First, the "truthful" Dopp testimony of February 5, 2008, conflicts with numerous other versions of the "truth" told by Darren, including Dopp's testimony to the Commission on Public Integrity and his previous testimony to Soares, as well as numerous public statements. Might that be the real reason Soares did not take this conflict to a grand jury that had no power to indict?

While vouching for the veracity of Dopp's last stab at the truth, Soares listed evidence that he said tended to "corroborate" it, including diary entries that Darren wrote in late August 2007, after Eliot had indefinitely suspended him. One such diary entry says, "Releasing public records on public official use of public aircraft? Doing it at direction of boss? Doing it after discussing it to death internally?" These ambiguous, self-serving, question mark–pocked and after-the-fact diary entries contrast with the entries in Darren's diary during the actual period that he belatedly testified he was getting Eliot's OK to release Bruno's travel records. On those days, when the "OK" was purportedly given, there is absolutely nothing in Darren's diary about the issue. Darren's post-suspension account also conflicts with the documented instances when Eliot specifically told him to back off, because Darren's travel gambit was a "distraction."

Soares also pointed to other August and September 2007 irrelevant Dopp diary entries as corroborative. One cited by Soares is Dopp's testimony that he told Andrew Cuomo in May 2007 "that the Executive Chamber was looking into usage of the State Aircraft." Regardless of how Soares viewed this conversation as corroborative, his report incredibly noted that "the Attorney General has stated publicly that he has no recollection of such a conversation with Dopp."

Did David Soares insert this fact into his report in order to sneer at his own assertion that the evidence was corroborative? Was he hinting that his coulda/woulda/shoulda grand jury might have considered reporting that Andrew Cuomo was also lying? Was Soares intending to recommend to his imaginary grand jury, removal or disciplinary action against both the governor and the attorney general? Or is it just that David Soares hasn't the vaguest idea what his job actually entails or how to do it?

Soares' March 28, 2008, report purported to state what the DA's third investigation involved, listing the charges he considered and the names of all the witnesses interviewed. The report says that the only charges considered were those arising from the Dopp statement to Andrew Cuomo on July 22, 2007. Every person purportedly interviewed was listed on page 4 of the report. My name is not there.

On February 25, 2008, I was questioned by Soares' assistants, and the transcript of that interview is now public. I was questioned in the district attorney's investigation of whether Herbert Teitelbaum had committed a crime relative to the Teitelbaum/Hermann conversations. That, in point of fact, is what David Soares was investigating during the period he now claims he "intended" or "considered" asking a grand jury to investigate Eliot, because his unsworn statement conflicted with the testimony of Darren Dopp, who, the DA said, could have been prosecuted for two crimes involving false swearing.

The Soares trilogy thus concluded with neither a bang nor a whimper, but with a mixture of fantasy and lies. Neither the disgraceful Soares III report nor the one issued by the Commission on Public Integrity could possibly give the public the sense that they understood what had actually happened in TRU or that the state's various redundant investigative bodies had properly done their jobs.

In 2009, the second TRU probe conducted by the Office of State Inspector General issued a report severely criticizing the Commission on Public Integrity and called for the firing of Herbert Teitelbaum specifically. Teitelbaum quickly resigned his position as executive director, while professing his innocence. John Feerick had quit his post during the pendency of the inspector general's investigation, but four months before the report was issued. In 2010, Andrew Cuomo will, in all likelihood, run for governor and accredit himself, as he already has, as the intrepid attorney general who left no stone unturned in his investigation of a sitting governor. The facts will testify otherwise.

■ ■ ■

....

Changing Course
or Changing the Subject?

WHEN TRU ERUPTED, and the battle between Eliot and Joe Bruno intensified in July 2007, one casualty was a package of bills embodying the governor's legislative priorities and those of the Senate and Assembly. On our list had been campaign finance reforms; property tax rebates for senior citizens; a law to expedite the siting and construction of clean energy power plants; reform of the Wicks Law, which stifles important public construction projects, and other bills involving public authorities reform; brownfields cleanup; expansion of the State's DNA database; and a "healthy schools" nutritional plan.

The priority for the Legislature had been roughly $1 billion in capital projects, which the members could campaign on in the elections to be held in November 2008. Those contests would involve the Senate Republicans' attempt to maintain tenuous control of their last slice of power in New York State. Democrats already held every statewide office, plus the Assembly and both seats in the U.S. Senate, and they also were picking off formerly safe Republican congressional districts.

A compromise, which would have resulted in the enactment of both sets of bills, those favored by Eliot and others favored by the Legislature, was skillfully crafted by Rich Baum, with the style and assurance of a master chef. After TRU erupted, Bruno and his Senate majority walked out, leaving Rich's banquet in a Dumpster. When that happened, the administration's attention had shifted from enacting new laws to the major progress that could be achieved in the agencies and public authorities directly or effectively under the governor's control.

Even before the Cuomo Report and the Senate's abandonment of the compromise package of bills, I and others in the Executive Chamber had been advising Eliot to shift emphasis from enacting laws to governing through our agencies. Major reform was occurring there. Progress was underway in health, transportation, insurance, energy, the environment, criminal justice and many other areas. Bold new ideas were being advanced even in places where our influence was attenuated, such as education. Primary and secondary education were largely the domain of independent "Regents" appointed by the Legislature. This was one legacy from Eliot's hero Teddy Roosevelt that he was trying to dilute or bypass using force and favors. Our influence over higher education and the state's 87 public colleges, annually enrolling more than 650,000 degree candidates, was less attenuated, but it would take several years for us to assert that control, as governor-appointed trustees were phased in. Stewardship of that effort, and the changes that would make higher education a centerpiece of the state's economic revitalization, was one of my assignments from Eliot, and one I eagerly undertook.

The agencies and authorities were fashioning and pushing reform within existing budgets and without new legislation. In the two months between the July 23, 2007, Cuomo Report and September 21, our press office and those at the agencies heralded scores of these initiatives. Using three state housing agencies, Eliot pumped hundreds of millions into affordable housing projects and a program designed to slow the wave of housing foreclosures beginning to sweep across New York and the nation. The Department of Health (DOH) launched numerous initiatives, including the nation's first program extending supportive services to severely disabled children in foster care and a program to ban toys that posed a serious lead poisoning threat to children. The DOH also fanned out across the state in aggressive outreach to start enrolling the 400,000 uninsured children in the Child Health Plus program.

Upstate economic development became the focus of more than a dozen grant approvals and announcements. These included an expansion of low-cost hydropower to Western New York municipalities and an agreement on the development of a major Catskill region resort, which had been disputed by environmentalists and developers for seven years. There were many primary education announcements, including the extension of universal pre-kindergarten to 134 additional New York school districts and programs designed to make primary education healthier through improved nutrition and exercise. We also announced that a second wave of banks would adopt our new

IOLA regulations in advance of their September 2007 effective date.

Eliot began several programs that confronted the reality of the large and growing immigrant population in the state, both legal and undocumented. Eliot and our Department of Labor announced a "Labor-On-Wheels" program for the DOL to reach out to the state's immigrant workforce, and one with our Bureau of Refugee and Immigrant Assistance to help permanent resident aliens with the process of becoming U.S. citizens. These and other programs that assisted the state's immigrants were important to Eliot, a second-generation American. He understood that New York's economic vitality had always benefitted from the constant influx of immigrants, both lawful, like Eliot's grandparents, and illegal, like my own mother. Eliot had heard about that seven-year-old orphan's brutal 1920 entry, through Boston after she had been turned away from Ellis Island in the custody of a consumptive aunt.

TRU and the near-constant leaking from the three investigations that commenced in late July 2007 drowned out all this positive news coming from our agencies. Eliot's poll numbers steadily declined, and with them the public support that would have assisted these agency initiatives and buttressed the governor's legislative program when the lawmakers returned to work in body, mind and spirit.

With the Legislature out of town, Eliot seemed to settle down a bit. Beginning in June, on an evening with Silda, Jan and me at Café Carlyle to see Judy Collins perform, there was a modest renewal of a social relationship. One mid-summer evening, Eliot and I played tennis together for the first time in more than 18 months and afterward dined alone in the backyard of the mansion. Despite all that had happened, Eliot seemed stoically committed and at peace. Right after Labor Day, Eliot made a television appearance at an evening session of the U.S. Open as a guest commentator along with John McEnroe, his old schoolboy rival on the tennis court and soccer field. In my estimation, it was and is the best TV appearance Eliot ever made. He exuded poise, confidence, and command while chatting about a sport he loves and plays well, and about his then-recent battles with the Legislature. The hopeful image I took away from the appearance was of two men who had conquered their tempers and their inner demons to become dominant world champions.

On September 21, 2007, Eliot announced yet another agency initiative intending to benefit the immigrant population and the state as a whole. Coming from the Department of Motor Vehicles, this initiative required neither legislation nor additional funding and would have saved New York and its residents hundreds of millions annually, making the state safer and more secure in the process. Eliot announced that in December 2007, the DMV would resume issuing driver's licenses in the manner it had until 2002, the year that agency, under Pataki, began requiring Social Security numbers as proof that a license applicant was lawfully residing in New York State. Although this administrative resumption of the pre-2002 practice would also have applied to U.S. citizens and lawful resident aliens, the clear effect and Eliot's purpose was to enable illegal aliens to obtain driver's licenses.

When Eliot announced this in September, New York was hardly alone; at least 11 other states in recent years had similarly licensed illegals. At the time of Eliot's announcement, seven or eight were doing it, including border states like New Mexico and crimson red states like Utah. After Pataki's 2002 change, 3,000 drivers up for renewal lost their licenses each month, but almost all continued to drive without license or insurance. Eliot's announcement was delivery on a campaign promise, in an election he had won by 40 points. Many tangible and quantifiable benefits would accrue. All that seemed to matter—for about four days. Rationality prevailed during that brief period as the program was applauded by police and immigrants' rights groups, which recognized that large numbers of illegals seeking licenses would finally come out of the shadows.

This brief pax of rationality was made possible by the hospitalization of Lou Dobbs, the nation's most rabid immigration fear monger. Moreover, Joe Bruno's first public reaction to the announcement had been sane and concise. Perhaps Joe had recalled his own immigrant heritage or remembered that Eliot's plan was merely the reinstatement of DMV practice during his first seven years as majority leader. Maybe he had remembered that in the following five years, roughly 152,000 formerly licensed drivers had been sent out to roam anonymously on the state's roads. Bruno's first pronouncement on the plan, reported in the *New York Post* on September 25, was:

> **We have hundreds of thousands of aliens here, and I'm not sure if its serves the public good to deprive them of**

the ability to go to school, to go to work to do the kinds of
things you have to do to lead a normal life.

This statement was the calm and considered opinion of a legislator from upstate, where virtually the only way to get around
is to use a private vehicle. The very next day, the *Post* reported
Bruno's change of heart. He apparently had been spoken to by
Republican Party boss Joe Mondello, who already was railing
against the plan. Bruno denounced the license initiative as:

> ...a political move on the part of the governor to get these
> people beholden to him.... They can vote [and] they're not
> even legal.

In exactly one day, Bruno had retreated to the New York
GOP mantra that the margin of many recent Democratic electoral victories had been provided by aliens voting illegally and
in gratitude to the party that made their illicit residency in
New York both possible and cushy — replete with privileges
lawfully reserved to "our people." After that, a heated debate
ensued. It was a debate on our side, with the governor making
a principled and well-documented argument, almost always in
a tone that lacked the stridency of many of his other Plague
Year disputes. On the Bruno/Mondello/Merola side, the last
guy being the leader of a group of county clerks who vowed to
defy the governor and take him to court, the argument was an
ugly shouting match, suffused with racism and appeals to fear
about terrorism.

A few days later, Lou Dobbs got out of the hospital and returned to his show on CNN, and the rant against Eliot became a nightly national event. Most of Dobbs' guests joined in smashing the piñata. One night, however, Jose Serrano, a New York legislator of Puerto Rican descent, appeared as a guest in support of the governor. After his appearance, Serrano was bombarded with hate mail, *including a demand for him to return to Mexico.* "These people" all look and sound alike.

How do we count the ways the license plan would have benefitted the state? One way is simply to chronicle the wildly varying numbers that were thrown about in reporting the uproar that Eliot's plan unleashed. One set of numbers was the head count of illegal aliens in New York State and the nation. New York had been reported to have as few as 500,000 and as many as "several million," at least according to junior U.S. Senator Hillary Clinton. The national figure had been variously reported in the range of 11.9 million to above 17 million. Each of these numbers had been just a guess. We don't have a good handle on this very large and, more or less, permanent component of our population and workforce. We know they are here, and when we allow ourselves, we see them, or at least glance obliquely at them.

In late October 2007, six weeks after the license plan debate went national, I attended a very heated Sunday-morning breakfast meeting along with Eliot, David Paterson, Senator Eric Schneiderman and several Latino legislators. The lawmakers spoke with passion about the practical and symbolic importance of the license plan to their constituents. Their most telling point was to challenge us to look around the restaurant, behind the counter and in the kitchen and to "see" the illegal population. They were preparing and serving our food, washing our dishes, keeping the place nice and clean, so that politicians like Eliot could trumpet a "Fanfare for the Common Man" by dining in such "Regular Joe" establishments. It was a sobering challenge. Since then, I have looked around more carefully in both my Manhattan and upstate communities and seen "these people" everywhere—working for me and making my life more pleasant.

As the debate, fueled nightly by Lou Dobbs, became hysterical, some states that granted licenses seemed to deny they were doing it, and others discussed plans to revoke the policy. The actors in this drama included many national figures, among them leading authorities on immigration and homeland security. New Mexico Governor Bill Richardson stood by his state's policy of licensing illegals, but future Homeland Security Secretary Janet Napolitano, then governor of Arizona, who initially backed the licensing of illegals, changed course after a dispute about border security caused her to put her plan on hold.

The most prominent of the national leaders who got sucked into the debate over Eliot's plan were those seeking nomination as the Democratic Party's presidential candidate in 2008. At the debate held on October 30, 2007, several candidates were drawn into taking a position on Eliot's plan. Senator Christopher Dodd of Connecticut squarely opposed it. Former Senator John Edwards, who generally supported the principle of licensing illegals, did not address the merits of the proposal at the debate but criticized Hillary Clinton for the way she responded to debate moderator Tim Russert's question about the Spitzer plan. By late October 2006, the race was widely viewed as Hillary's to lose, with the most likely beneficiary of a Clinton stumble or collapse being freshman United States Senator Barack Obama.

At the debate, Obama had been clear, concise and firm in his support for Eliot's initiative:

> I think it is the right idea, and I disagree with Chris because there is a public safety concern. We can make sure that drivers who are illegal come out of the shadows, that they can be tracked, that they are properly trained, and that will make our roads safer.

In contrast to Obama's clear "yea" and Dodd's unequivocal "nay," Clinton had been all over the place, seemingly supporting, then opposing, then reacting angrily when the other candidates and Russert had noted her inconsistency on an issue confronting her state and Eliot, her governor — whose immense coattails had added significantly to her margin of victory in the senatorial election that had occurred less than a year earlier.

Russert asked:

> Senator Clinton, Governor of New York Eliot Spitzer has proposed giving drivers licenses to illegal immigrants.... Why does it make a lot of sense to give an illegal immigrant a driver's license?

CLINTON: Well, what Governor Spitzer is trying to do is fill the vacuum left by the failure of this administration to bring about comprehensive immigration reform. We know in New York we have several million at any one time who are in New York illegally. They are undocumented workers. They are driving on our roads....

However, after Dodd attacked the plan, Clinton interjected:

Well, I just want to add, I did not say that it should be done, but I recognize why Governor Spitzer is trying to do—

DODD: No, no, no. You said—you said yes...

CLINTON: No.

DODD: You thought it made sense to do it.

CLINTON: No, I didn't, Chris. But the point is, what are we going to do with all these illegal immigrants who are driving...

RUSSERT: Senator Clinton, I just want to make sure of what I heard. Do you, the New York senator, Hillary Clinton, support the New York governor's plan to give illegal immigrants a driver's license? You told the New Hampshire paper that it made a lot of sense. Do you support his plan?

CLINTON: You know Tim, this is where everybody plays "gotcha...."

Then Senator Clinton recapitulated why Eliot's plan "makes a lot of sense," but "No," it wasn't "the best thing for any governor to do."

That night, as the Democratic candidates had debated at Drexel University in the City of Brotherly Love, denizens of the Second Floor had critiqued the candidates' performance in cyberspace, focusing on the leading candidates' views about our license plan. My support for Obama and antipathy for Hillary were well known on the Second Floor and had been the catalyst for a rapid-fire back-and-forth involving me and four Clinton loyalists.

[CLINTON LOYALIST 1]: Hillary Clinton just gave the best defense of our license plan on national television that I have heard yet. Brava!!!

[CLINTON LOYALIST 1]: And she's already taking heat for it.

LLOYD: As Cochise said, [Clinton loyalist] listen with forked ear. What I heard was pretty mealy mouthed and equivocating as usual and Edwards and Obama zapped her for it, and Obama supported us without equivocation. Bravissimo! The Mole.

[CLINTON LOYALIST 1]: Fine, you got me there—but she is the only one who has anything to lose by even defending it.

[CLINTON LOYALIST 2]: Agree [with L.C.] she was a disaster. Should have either sold us out (what they'll ultimately [sic] do) or stuck to a tough position. She's giving life to

the emerging, central criticism of her — that she won't take a real position on anything.

The next day, Rudy Giuliani, the then-leading candidate for the Republican nomination for president, launched a broadside attack against Hillary, over her meandering positions on the license plan. He opposed the plan but praised Obama for giving an unequivocal debate answer in support of the plan. Attacks on Hillary continued for the next two weeks and marked the first time she showed real vulnerability, in what many people had predicted would be a Clinton runaway.

Among those betting heavily on Hillary was David Paterson, who had abandoned his almost-certain future as the state's powerful Senate Majority leader, for the largely ceremonial job as Eliot's lieutenant governor. It appeared that David expected Eliot to appoint him to replace Hillary in the United States Senate in the event of Clinton's election as president, which then seemed likely. Whether Eliot would have done so is not known, especially since that would have meant moving either Dean Skelos (Joe Bruno's deputy Majority leader) or Malcolm Smith into the position of succeeding him as governor, because by January 2009, either Skelos or Smith would have succeeded Joe Bruno as president pro-tempore of the Senate.

On the question of whether Eliot would have appointed Paterson to replace Hillary, I don't think Eliot really had an answer, although the question had been on everybody's mind. Regardless of whether he had made any implicit commitment to David, I doubt he would have appointed him to replace Hillary. Even without the benefit of the painful hindsight of a Paterson governorship and assuming that Eliot had an extraordinary ability to repress the high likelihood of his own imminent fall, I do not believe Eliot would have risked placing the State in any two of those four hands. Relative to Skelos or Smith, David Paterson is a veritable Benjamin Disraeli.

As Hillary was being pummeled over the license issue, other assumed allies of Eliot's plan were opposing it or abandoning their early support. The most harmful opposition, with the possible exception of Hillary's, which may have been dispositive, had come from Mayor Mike Bloomberg and Assembly Speaker Shelly Silver. The mayor had worried out loud that giving illegals the same license as lawful residents would render a New York State license ineffective as the photo identification necessary for boarding a domestic flight. That wasn't true, or at least wouldn't be for several years, but it brought into play the contentious issue of "Real ID."

In 2005, the Congress had enacted a law that purported to require states to confirm the lawful resident status of licensed drivers by 2013 otherwise their licenses could not be used to board aircraft. In yet another confusion about a number, which complicated the debate, the actual effective date of the federal mandate was reported to be as early as 2008. Real ID was suspected by civil libertarians to be the centerpiece of the Bush Administration's plot to force everybody in the U.S. to carry a standardized national identity card.

Eliot's response to Bloomberg's stated concerns had been immediate and angry: "He [Bloomberg] is wrong at every level, dead wrong, factually wrong, legally wrong, morally wrong, ethically wrong...." This attack was not typical of the manner in which Eliot otherwise conducted this debate, but had echoed the strident tone of many of his statements earlier in 2007. It also wasn't the first time that Mike Bloomberg had forgotten the boundaries of his authority. He had frequently pronounced or laid his hands on an issue or a thing clearly outside his jurisdiction. Driver's licenses are exclusively a state matter, as Mayor Bloomberg admitted when he said, "It [licenses to illegals] then leads to lots of other problems in terms of voter registration and other things. But it's the governor's call." Bloomberg's meddlesome and inaccurate reaction and Eliot's angry and highly quotable response occurred in the first week of the debate and had made it safer for others to oppose Eliot's plan — since they were challenging an intemperate bully, as Eliot was becoming viewed by many. The most damaging reversals of early support came from Hillary, in the course of five minutes, and from Shelly Silver over a period of several weeks.

Since the license plan did not require legislation, the only way the Legislature could have trumped Eliot was by passing a veto-proof law to nullify the plan. With Shelly's support for the plan, that had been virtually impossible. No bill would emerge from the Assembly, let alone one with the super-majority necessary to override Eliot's veto. However, when Shelly jumped ship, as he had by October 23, 2007, that prospect became likely. The polls on the license initiative were running almost 70 percent against. Daily defections by Democratic legislators made what had seemed unthinkable—passage of a law to block our plan—increasingly likely.

In an effort to save the plan, we advanced a more complicated one. On October 27, 2007, Eliot announced that New York would offer three types of driver's licenses. All state residents, legal or otherwise, could obtain a driver's license marked, "Not valid for federal purposes." A second class of license, pointing toward the standards of the Real ID Act, would also be offered. In order to get this license, the applicant would have had to demonstrate U.S. citizen or lawful resident alien status. This license could be used to board a domestic air flight and would help the Bush Administration make progress on its controversial plan. A third type of license could be obtained by U.S. citizens and nationals frequently travelling to Canada. They could use this license in lieu of a U.S. passport, which otherwise would be required for crossing the border.

With the possible exception of support from frequent travellers to Canada, the three-tiered proposal was widely reviled. It did not mollify those who, out of fear, prejudice or principle, simply did not want illegals to have this "privilege" in any form. The immigrants' rights groups, dominated by Latinos, hated the three-tiered proposal. Eliot had been their hero but seemingly had abandoned them. They viewed the "Not valid for federal purposes" license as a badge of dishonor and pushed back hard. Our observation that any New Yorker, including citizens, could obtain this class of license at a reduced price did not soothe them.

At the late-October breakfast meeting attended by Eliot, Paterson, the Latino legislators and me, the lawmakers expressed their revulsion at the backtracking that the three-tiered proposal signified in their communities. Although it might have come into being over time, as a result of Real ID and the need to simplify crossing the Canadian border, the three-tiered plan was widely reported as a retreat. When he had announced it on October 27, Eliot had been flanked by Homeland Security Secretary Mike Chertoff. Over the years, I had regularly badmouthed Chertoff to Eliot because of a brief, but nasty, experience I had with Mike during the 1980s, while attempting to coordinate some organized crime work the New York AG's office was doing with related work Mike was supervising for U.S. Attorney Rudy Giuliani. Chertoff rudely rebuffed the offer of cooperation and had gotten Rudy to visit Bob Abrams with a request/threat that the AG must back off. For this reason, I had placed Chertoff in my own subjective third and highest tier of weaselhood and warned Eliot that Mike did not work and play well with others.

At their joint appearance, Eliot and Chertoff announced a plan that would give Real ID a chance at success. Chertoff admitted that Eliot had every right to license illegals and that the plan would have made New York and the nation safer. With all that, Mike said, "I do not endorse and I do not think it's a good idea to give undocumented workers licenses or IDs of any kind." Chertoff repeated this position four times in their brief joint public appearance. Whatever benefit Eliot and our proposal might have gotten from Mike's presence was eliminated—and then some. The revised plan was savaged for the previously discussed reasons and its alleged complexity. Senator Chris Dodd described it as an administrative "nightmare."

After the presidential debate, an internal Second Floor drumbeat started, calling on Eliot to pull the plug on the plan before the Democratic-controlled Assembly followed the Republican State Senate in passing a bill to block it. I was the lone dissenter on the senior executive staff. I thought, and told Eliot and my colleagues, that if we believed this plan improved the safety and security of New York, it was worth fighting for, even if we were likely to lose. Most of these internal conversations were held as a group and conducted on a high and principled level. Good documents were circulated, fully airing all points of view about a plan that the vast majority of us supported in principle, but only Eliot and I wanted to defend. The group discussions of whether to fight or fold were held at a senior executive staff retreat on Election Day, November 6, 2007, at Eliot's farmhouse in Gallatin, New York, and during a late-night conference call on November 12.

The Retreat at Eliot's Farm

THE RETREAT HAD been cancelled and rescheduled several times before we finally convened on Election Day. The "official" agenda, and my own, for this meeting kept changing as new events unfolded. One of my items had been to build a Second Floor consensus for removing Malcolm Smith as Senate Minority Leader. However, Smith had recently performed so badly that there seemed to be little utility in beating a dead horse. He had recently dimed us out by saying that the governor had put him up to filing a complaint against Joe Bruno with the

IRS, but that he just couldn't do it, because it just wasn't right. In fact, Malcolm had flubbed the assignment and, when caught, started to point fingers. Our continuing efforts to pursue Bruno in this manner, and to put Malcolm in the middle by using him as as our messenger, had been sheer stupidity—Eliot's, Rich's or both. As Election Day and the retreat approached, TRU was still steaming ahead after more than 100 days, and we were embroiled in the license debate. Eliot's popularity had plummeted, and no high-level managerial changes had been made, save the addition of former lobbyist Bruce Gyory, whose assignment was to create better relations with the Legislature, which, every time we had thought could not get worse, did.

The single issue I would advocate at the retreat was change in the command structure. Eliot, aware of the pervasive dissatisfaction with Rich Baum, had placed an intriguing item on the agenda, about appointing a chief operating officer—the job that Baum and/or Olivia Golden were supposed to already have. The retreat was attended by Eliot, Baum, Golden, Nocenti, Pope, Maloney, Marty Mack, Marlene Turner, Paul Francis, Christine Anderson, Bruce Gyory, Silda, David Paterson, Charles O'Byrne, me and Mike Balboni, our deputy secretary for Homeland Security, who was reluctantly, but vigorously, spearheading the license initiative.

Eliot asked each participant to be candid, but respectful, as we went around the large country dining room table. We were asked to identify what we thought we'd done right, and what had been done wrong, and then to identify what each of us thought must change. Everyone obeyed Eliot's admonition to be respectful. Candor, however, was in short supply. The exceptions involved five people stating in well-understood circumlocutions that Rich Baum had to be reassigned, and Olivia Golden fired. The five were Sean Maloney, Rich's first deputy, Paul Francis, Marty Mack, Peter Pope and me. I was polite, but not subtle, and when Eliot moved to derail the discussion, I unsuccessfully attempted to keep the focus on a staff shakeup. Throughout the discussion, David Paterson whispered to me that he couldn't believe that I was actually saying what I was saying. Paul Francis later apologized to me for failing to support my attempted filibuster when Eliot invoked cloture.

Other than this tense and painful exchange, the retreat had been, for the most part, upbeat, with the hopeful and pervasive sense that things couldn't get any worse. Our spirits had been buoyed by informal exit polls that drifted in, suggesting that our problems were not causing losses for Democrats in local election contests around the state. Although proponents of pulling the plug on the license plan had not gotten a commitment from Eliot at the retreat, it seemed to them that this would eventually happen. I thought differently, since I had Eliot, the only ally who counted.

After departing from Eliot's farm and commiserating with Peter Pope at a coffee shop in nearby Pine Plains, I emailed Eliot with my "postmortem" to the retreat, concluding with this plea:

> **This is so simple that it's pitiful and to think that Rich will ever be able to lead this is just tragically wrongheaded and frankly inexplicable to me from you who is so amaz-**

ingly smart in virtually all other respects. My hope is that you heard and internalized my observations and advice (seconded by so many others today, Sean three times for example). You are my brother and I will fight for you and along with you but we really need these changes to be made. Virtually everything that has gone wrong is rooted there and the problems will continue and proliferate unless you act soon and decisively.

Eliot's only response was to note how well Democrats had done in the local elections.

In the weeks before and after the retreat, Christine Anderson and our new press secretary, Errol Cockfield, fed me to newspaper and magazine reporters doing stories about the administration. These stories focused heavily on the license plan and TRU. I was directed to speak with reporters from the *New York Times*, the *Post*, the *Sun*, the *Times Union*, the *Daily News*, the *New Yorker* and *Vanity Fair*. Christine's perception had been that the stories would come out somewhat better if I were to speak about Eliot, his motives and his mission.

I had established a second career as the singer of Eliot's praises and seer of his manifest destiny. The limited utility of this press office strategy was that the problem with the license plan was not the news coverage. With the major exception of Lou Dobbs' nightly "auto da fé," the press not only played our license initiative pretty straight, but there had been substantial editorial support for the plan, and this had subtly infected the news coverage. In my interviews, I made the case for the plan, including the somewhat disingenuous claim that the three-tiered proposal was something we had said we were going to do all along. Despite the somewhat decent press, public opinion continued to run strongly against the proposal. Democratic officeholders continued to defect, no longer counterbalanced by support from Latino electeds, who felt betrayed.

On November 12, 2007, I accompanied Eliot to an event at the New York Hilton for the State University's liberal arts college in Purchase, New York. Purchase, a school extraordinarily strong in the performing arts, was honoring modern dance legend Merce Cunningham. After Eliot's brief and gracious remarks, focusing on Nelson Rockefeller's legacies in the performing arts and SUNY, we were chatting with a group of friends. Someone raised the license uproar, and Eliot calmly observed that it had caused his popularity rating to decline from near 70 to near 30. Christine Anderson had noticed that one of the assumed friends was a reporter and told Eliot that he would read his observation in the next day's newspaper.

I drew Eliot aside and asked him what he would do if Hillary or Barack called and asked him to pull the plug and deprive the Republicans of what was being perceived as a potential 2008 "wedge issue." Eliot calmly responded that he, not Clinton or Obama, was governor of New York. I took that assurance to the bank and to the conference call late that night, when all but I on the senior staff tried to persuade Eliot to cut bait. I didn't need to argue the plan's merits, as most of those urging Eliot to surrender actually thought that the plan was beneficial. Instead, I argued that we were getting the reputation of backing down from clearly stated principles whenever we were faced with the possibility of defeat. After hearing everyone out about the license plan near midnight November 12, Eliot said that he "had crossed the Rubicon" and would stick with the plan. He asked those trying to change his position to desist.

Early the very next morning, as I was getting ready to leave Manhattan for a trip to SUNY campuses in the North Country, Eliot called me at my home to tell me that Hillary had phoned and asked him to drop the license plan. Eliot's voice was somber and sad, and before I could ask, he said that he had agreed to pull the plug on the plan in Washington, D.C., the next day, November 14, 2007. I appreciated the fact that he called me himself, before I could hear this news any other way. I neither tried to change his mind nor berated him for doing something he clearly didn't want to do. My unexpressed question was how he could have been so resolute the night before, when I had posed the hypothetical that had now come to pass. Instead of asking it, I attempted some soothing small talk about my imminent drive to the Adirondacks, dinner that night with Lake Placid Mayor Jamie Rogers, and lunch the next day with freshman Assemblyman Darrel Aubertine. Who was this guy I was making small talk with? Not Eliot!

That moment was Death Valley for me. It wasn't because the license plan was so damn important. Initially, it had been a good plan, especially given the federal government's consistent failure to comprehensively deal with the multifaceted problems created by the permanent illegal alien population. The revised three-tiered plan, though still a net plus, introduced real problems of administrative complexity and the inevitable stigma and mischief that would have confronted the holders of the "Not valid for federal purposes" driver's licenses. I didn't reckon that this particular moment was the low point because of the spectacular reversal in Eliot's poll numbers, going from 70–30 on Election Day 2006 to roughly 30–70 one year later; it was Eliot's complete reversal in less than ten hours on a position of principle, one stated "publicly" to the senior staff, and privately to me. That caused my spirits to plunge to their nadir and began the process of me emotionally checking out. However, there is a thing about low points: Unless you haven't actually gauged them correctly, there is no place to go but up. That is what the Spitzer Administration started to do on November 14, 2007, as Eliot returned to New York from Washington, D.C.

■ ■ ■

····

Turning the Corner

As we approached the fourth Thursday of November 2007, I had reason to be thankful for things beyond the good health and security of my family. While the manner of Eliot's surrender on the license initiative disillusioned me, I felt that it had created some opportunities. It wasn't going to be a new beginning, nor even an uncluttered landscape, not with three ongoing investigations of TRU still burdening us. However, it had given us the balance of the year to focus on agency initiatives and attempt to produce a better State of the State address and enact a better budget than we had in our first year's efforts. It also had given me some psychic space to attempt the substantial completion of two of my own projects, the reports of the higher education and local government commissions.

I was also thankful that the upstate weather had remained unseasonably mild. The lack of snow in the Finger Lakes, the Southern Tier and the Adirondacks had allowed me and my little team to finish off our visits to all 64 SUNY campuses in a sprint. We had been collecting the views of college presidents, administrators, faculty and students for the higher ed.

commission report and to inform the governor's budget-making process, already well underway.

On November 13, we drove to the top of the Adirondack Park, our fourth 2007 trip to the North Country. The next morning, as Eliot was announcing the abandonment of the license initiative in Washington, D.C., we drove to Saranac Lake to visit the main campus of North Country Community College. This was our 64th and last SUNY stop and had been planned as a triumphant celebration. We took a victory photo at the entrance to the campus. The joy of accomplishing our feat in such a short time span, begun with our visit to SUNY Binghamton on June 25, 2007, had been tempered by our meetings in North Country CC's main classroom building, which was a converted tuberculosis ward built in the early part of the 20th century. The relocation of this shamefully ill-housed community college to a modern facility in Lake Placid, nine miles away, was one of the many small projects subsumed within our major higher education initiative. To me, the North Country campus also symbolized the obsolete and decaying New York that the Spitzer Administration would confront and drag into the 21st century.

Upon my return from the North Country, on the night of November 14, I rejoined the internal budget-making sessions, which had begun in October. The Division of the Budget had prepared large binders for each area of the budget, setting forth on a line-item basis every proposed expenditure, every anticipated source and amount of revenue and cost savings from reduced or eliminated programs.

I had promised myself that I would attain a journeyman's understanding of the budgets for every major program and master those in my areas, especially higher education. The internal budget-making sessions were heady and inspiring, reminding us of why we had come to work for Eliot in the first place. Less than a year into the endeavor, I for one needed this reminder. At "squaretable" sessions attended by 20 or more participants, and almost always by Eliot, a DOB staffer would lead us through an item-by-item review of the proposed expenditures or revenue generators, focusing on those where the proposal involved something new, controversial or quantitatively very large.

Right then and there, we made our cases about the merits of each proposal or offered our own alternatives, with Eliot making the final call or deferring his decision until a later date. He had done this quickly, almost always with a sense of humor, and always demonstrating his detailed understanding of the most arcane and esoteric programs, fees and taxes. There never was a new tax nor one increased, because when we proposed to do that, we called it something else, such as "loophole closing," a "clarification" or a "user fee." Eliot's command at these 2007 meetings reminded me of his master performances during the 2006 transition Policy Advisory Committee sessions. The fall 2007 sessions had been even more impressive, given the sheer number of budget items, the mind-numbing mundaneness of most of these, and all that had happened in the Spitzer Administration up to that point in time.

When the governor's inner circle joined the budget-making process in the fall of 2007, it was already clear that we would have to dash, or at least dampen, the expectations of most major constituent groups when our Executive Budget was released on January 22, 2008. We also knew that the economy was bad and would get worse, forcing us to constantly cut our opening total budget figure and reduce our estimate of revenue. In a perverse but well understood way, we also knew that it would make Eliot's job easier. Though every sector, including health, the environment, education, human services, criminal justice, housing and others, would argue the same things — *"Our area is vital, will save lives, has waited too long, and you promised"* — they would all, on some level, understand the dismal reality of the numbers. When the state's coffers were flush, expectations were far less manageable. The worsening economic conditions weren't going to make our discrete decisions easy, but in the aggregate they would make Eliot's sales job simpler and his moral authority greater.

In meeting after meeting, most attended by Eliot, we made our arguments, made the cuts, painfully squeezed out additional revenue and reached consensus on a few increased expenditures in critical areas. This was the Spitzer Administration at its finest, a group of committed and well-informed professionals making tough and intelligent decisions under the leadership of a philosopher-king.

Though I was in attendance and attentive at the meetings concerning all areas of the budget, in most I said little, though probably more than many there had wanted to hear. I saved my firepower for the discussion of certain taxes and fees that I expected would become lightning rods, for programs involving legal representation of the poor, those providing incentives or disincentives for local governments to become more efficient and, of course, the higher education budget.

The DOB's proposals for higher education were the exception from the otherwise skillful and dispassionate recommendations in virtually every other major area. The DOB understood what public higher education in New York wanted, but seemed antagonistic to those aspirations and had responded punitively. I shuddered when I reviewed the budget division's proposals for SUNY and the City University of New York (CUNY). Placing everyone on short rations might make Eliot's job easier, but that would not be true for the executive staff and the agency heads, who would have to explain these cutbacks to stakeholders all around the state, in hundreds of conversations. I began to see that I might not be as welcome the next time I stopped in at any of the SUNY or CUNY campuses.

With one exception, there was very little in the DOB's higher education budget proposal to fund or even pay lip service to any of the major recommendations that soon would be made in the Commission on Higher Education's (CHE) report to the governor. The budget proposal and the CHE report would appear to be two ships passing in the night. That metaphor would be disconcerting at every SUNY and CUNY campus, and especially at SUNY's world-class Maritime College.

As part of my stump introduction to each president, provost or group of faculty or students, I had said that while the governor had made 2007 the year to focus on primary and secondary education, 2008 would be the year when Eliot's higher education vision would see expression in the CHE report and in the 2008–09 budget. That vision was nowhere to be seen in the DOB's proposal. Indeed, it almost seemed as if the DOB, which was fully aware of the biggest problems confronting the state's public colleges, had decided not merely to ignore, but to exacerbate them.

The budget division's proposals would have reduced funding for all the major programs designed to make it easier for disadvantaged and minority students to attend and graduate from college. State aid to community colleges, which are the entry vehicle for most minority and first-in-family college students, was to be cut, leaving New York's community college tuition roughly four times as high as California's. The budget also proposed that tuition at the state's four-year public colleges be raised by almost 12 percent. This increase was certainly justified, as New York's senior college tuition was half or as little as a third of that in peer states, such as California, Massachusetts, New Jersey and Pennsylvania. But the proposed tuition hike would not have been invested in any of the improvements that the CHE called for, but instead to replace reduced state funding. There was this basic and conspicuous flaw and more to usher in Eliot's "year of higher education."

One of the major recommendations of the CHE, and the one I advocated most forcefully, was a substantial increase in full-time faculty at all the publics. SUNY, but even more so CUNY, had lost thousands of full-time faculty lines over the last generation, the gap being largely filled by adjunct faculty. Although many of these adjuncts are talented and devoted to their students, they could not begin to adequately replace full-time faculty. The CHE recommended the hiring of 2,000 additional full-time faculty at SUNY and CUNY over a five-year period, with 250 of these to be eminent scholars. The DOB proposal had no money for new faculty and, in a variety of ways, would have continued the corrosive trend toward substituting adjuncts for full-timers. And in other areas there was still less. Less incentive for the publics to compete for research money, and ten percent less money for SUNY and CUNY to spend on programs the Division of the Budget deemed not to be related to their "core instructional mission." These non-core programs, such as an institute at SUNY Buffalo doing world-class research into addictions, are the very things that lift a campus and a system from "pretty good" to great and that become magnets for star faculty and students.

Finally, a brand new SUNY school was singled out for termination. In order to save $2,260,000, the Neil D. Levin Institute was targeted for closure. Here, I suspected something more was going on than the obvious need to save money, since with Levin, the savings were so small. The institute was named for a man who had served as New York's superintendent of Insurance, superintendent of Banking and executive director of the Port Authority of New York and New Jersey, that had been housed in the World Trade Center. Neil Levin died heroically on 9/11 after seeing that most of his staff had safely vacated the North Tower, before it collapsed.

The Levin Institute was devoted to globalization studies, with the goal of training managers who would work across borders and cultures. It was developing its own degree programs and helping the other SUNY campuses develop curricula that recognized the importance of globalization and embodied the city and state's desire to remain at the center of an increasingly globalized economy. Levin had built a handsome modern facility on East 55th Street between Madison and Park Avenues. Its president was Garrick Utley, a world-famous journalist and expert on America's image abroad. Paul Tagliabue, a member of the Council on Foreign Relations and former NFL commissioner, was Levin's chairman. The Levin Institute promised to give SUNY, largely unknown in the city, a face and stature in the state's point of entry from, and departure to, the rest of the world.

At Eliot's and my request, Levin had begun formulating proposals for one or more SUNY campuses abroad. The recommendation to shutter Levin blindsided me, and the intensity with which it was being defended by the DOB set it apart from the other proposals. I smelled a rat and heard an echo. I had been told that New York University, a private school, and its president, John Sexton, had staked out globalization studies as NYU's turf, as if New York City, the world's cultural and economic capital, could not accommodate more than one such center of instruction. At that moment, Sexton was surfacing as the fly in the CHE's proposed ointment.

The primary focus of the CHE was public higher education. Sexton, also at the time the chairman of the Board of Trustees of New York's Commission of Independent Colleges and Universities (CICU), of which there are roughly 150, was strongly advocating that more attention and money be spent on the state's private colleges. Sexton and Abe Lackman, CICU's salaried president and former chief of staff for Joe Bruno, were both threatening to dissent from what otherwise would have been either unanimous or broad-consensus CHE recommendations. That the CHE should place greater emphasis on the state's private colleges was a very respectable position, although one with which I disagreed. Shuttering the Levin Institute was something else.

The play, to kill Levin in its crib, was blatant and unvarnished and engendered more internal debate than any other higher education proposal, despite its quantitative triviality. I pleaded with the DOB to back down on this without me having to go to Eliot with my conspiracy theory. They would not. So I did, went to Eliot, and Levin was spared, at least while Eliot was governor. In the 2009–10 Executive Budget, enacted on April 1, 2009, under David Paterson, Levin was zeroed out. Stripped of its appropriation, Levin was left exposed to the vagaries of SUNY internal politics, with its future tenuous, at best. Three weeks after Levin's budget line was eliminated, on April 22, 2009, the director of the division of the Budget, Laura Anglin, was appointed president of CICU, to replace the departing Abe Lackman.

Aside from the fight over Levin, the most contentious issue had been SUNY and CUNY tuition. I proposed, consistent with the CHE's recommendation, that tuition be modestly raised annually, with the additional revenue invested in educational improvements. The DOB had proposed that it be raised, to replace reduced state funding. This was the worst of all possible worlds. Public college tuition increases are treated like live grenades by the Legislature, much in the same way that they handle the matter of their own pay increases. Despite New York's extraordinarily low tuition, the Legislature chronically fails to deal with this issue responsibly and explain to the public that revenue for the state's public colleges must come from somewhere. This was one of the "know nothing" New York traditions that Eliot became governor in order to change. The vastly higher tuition paid by public college students in other states had provided Eliot with plenty of room to educate the electorate. As of 2008, there had not been a SUNY/CUNY four-year-college tuition increase since 2003, and that one had occurred eight years after the previous increase.

While the budget-making meetings were going on, Eliot, Paul Francis, John Reed (CHE executive director) and I met with Shelly Silver and his top aide, Dean Fuleihan. In a statement that, more than any other I heard during the Plague Year, epitomized the irresponsibility of New York's Legislature, Shelly simply said, "We can't raise tuition in a year when we will be getting a salary increase." I waited for Eliot to push back, but he didn't. All I had said was that Shelly knew that none of his members would be in any danger come the next election, and certainly not from enacting a modest tuition increase used to improve the quality of SUNY and CUNY educations.

By the fall of 2007, we needed Shelly. To Eliot, that apparently meant acceding to the drivel Shelly had expressed about public college tuition. After the Speaker left Eliot's office, I pushed back hard and in the next month continued explaining to Eliot that his credibility with the higher education community in large part depended upon how he resolved this issue.

The argument raged on, culminating in a conference call in mid-January, the week before the Executive Budget would be announced. With a room full of people next to Eliot, and me conferenced in on the phone, I took my last shot on this issue. Eliot shut me up with the screaming taunt, "You would have had me out there all alone on the license issue, and you want to do that again!" After the meeting, I promptly emailed Eliot my offer to resign, using the unambiguous government-speak, "I serve at your pleasure." The offer was apparently ignored by him, but not by me. Shortly thereafter, I decided that the best way for me to serve interests that I had come to care deeply about, to serve Eliot and, most importantly, to serve myself and justify the upheaval in my life that working for him had entailed, was to ask Eliot to fulfill the offer he had made to me 15 months before and help me become Chancellor of SUNY. I scheduled a dinner meeting with him, but the earliest date I could arrange was for several weeks later, the evening of February 12, 2008.

Higher education involved "only" $8.2 billion of what initially was a $126.4 billion budget proposal. The paring of all that down to the January 22, 2008, budget proposal amounting to roughly $124.3 billion took up much of the senior executive staff's time for the balance of 2007 and the first few weeks of 2008. Many of the same people involved in budget-making were helping to prepare Eliot's State of the State address, to be delivered on January 9, 2008, and a State of Upstate speech to be delivered on January 16, 2008, in Buffalo.

The two State of the State speeches were going to be Eliot's attempt to make a new start in the new year. When their preparation had begun in the fall of 2007 under the supervision of Peter Pope, there still had been hope that, by year's end, the TRU investigations would be over. The State of the State and the upstate version, a first for any New York governor, had heavy loads to carry. With all official New York present, Eliot would extend olive branches to the Legislature and others he had attacked in 2007, such as Tom DiNapoli. He would lay out his vision for New York in 2008 and beyond, and get everyone ready for the big proposals and significant austerity measures that would be fully described in the budget. The State of Upstate message would summarize the full State of the State but primarily focus on the troubled regions north and west of Albany and propose a $1 billion Upstate Revitalization Fund.

Nearly a year after my plea to Eliot that he hire a full-time high-level speech writer, that still hadn't happened. For the 2008 State of the State, however, we had the Pope. He realized the gravity of the situation and the complexity of taking scores of little speeches submitted by people like me, pairing them down and fashioning them into one great speech of roughly an hour's length. Eliot and Peter proved to be up to the task. The State of the State had to be perfect, or nearly so, in substance and tone because it was going to be heard by a skeptical and hostile audience dominated by state legislators. Those cynical listeners would contrast with the awestruck audience that had celebrated every banal and repetitive utterance in Eliot's mediocre January 3, 2007, address.

The State of the State, which Eliot delivered on January 9, 2008, contained all the elements of a great speech, and each in just the right proportion. It began, and was marbled with, feel-good lines. There were tributes to returning veterans; a moment of silence for Bobbie Bruno, the recently deceased wife of the Majority Leader; acknowledgment of star high-school students; and bouquets for Silda, Eliot's daughters and Bernie and Anne Spitzer. The Tri-Borough Bridge linking Manhattan, Queens and the Bronx was renamed in memory of Robert F. Kennedy as his widow and children received applause. During the salute to returning veterans, Eliot made the first substantive proposal in the speech. I was proud that my assistant, Haley Plourde-Cole, had formulated it, a tuition grant to returning veterans that would cover the full tuition of a SUNY or CUNY college education.

Eliot didn't duck the nastiness of 2007. He confronted it head on, accepted blame for the stridency of his public statements and especially for those that had been directed at the Legislature. He praised legislators whom the year before he had attacked. With each mention of a 2007 accomplishment, and there were just the right number and the right selection, Eliot said that these had been the products of partnership with the Legislature. This was a wise and appropriate reversal of his observation, after the 2007–08 budget enactment, that certain things had not been accomplished in the budget "because there's a legislature."

Eliot confronted the storm clouds hovering over the national and state economies. He introduced the notion that progress in most areas would have to be scaled back in the short term, though not abandoned, with specifics to be revealed in the January 22 budget address. In certain areas it would be full steam ahead, such as state funding for the expanded Child Health Plus insurance program, despite the Bush Administration's veto of expanded funding for "S-CHIP" in 2007.

The speech was particularly strong on what the elder President Bush had referred to as "The Vision Thing." Eliot's vision for New York's bright future involved investment and innovation in education, healthcare, infrastructure, affordable housing and high-value jobs. Eliot assured the audience that all of this was achievable, despite his insistence that it would be accomplished while lowering taxes.

The first specific policy area Eliot addressed was the need to prioritize higher education. As I had said to every one of the more than 1,500 students, faculty and administrators we had met at the state's campuses, "2008 would be the year when the governor prioritized higher education, armed with the recommendations of the commission." Now Eliot was saying it to all of New York State and indeed to the whole world — since I was watching his speech at 1:00 A.M. on a computer in Chang Mai, Thailand.

Of the ten marquee recommendations in the CHE report released a month before, Eliot spotlighted three, including two I had rammed through the CHE. These were the hiring of 2,000 additional full-time faculty at SUNY and CUNY, including 250 eminent scholars, and a mandate for so-called full articulation in the SUNY system. Articulation was our response to the most bitter complaint at the community colleges, about the failure of SUNY four-year colleges to give full recognition for all the credits earned by SUNY community college transfers. The third

CHE recommendation spotlighted by Eliot was a proposed $3 billion Empire State Innovation Fund. Modeled along the lines of National Science Foundation grants, this fund would award research grants for cutting-edge research to public and private colleges in New York State.

During the speech, Eliot had also advanced ideas that went beyond the CHE report. He had spotlighted two specific initiatives at SUNY campuses at the two ends of the state. At the University at Buffalo, he had touted the "UB 2020" plan, which would increase student enrollment from 29,000 in 2008 to 41,000 in 2020 and send upward of 8,000 students to downtown Buffalo.

Eliot also designated the University at Buffalo (UB) as a SUNY flagship and a minute later did the same thing for Stony Brook. Until that moment in the 2008 State of State, the largest public university system in the nation had no flagship, despite the demonstrated wisdom of having such marquee institutions, which improve entire systems, as do Berkeley and UCLA, Austin, Madison, Chapel Hill and others. The CHE had not reached consensus on a proposal for flagships. I had raised the issue with Eliot, and, to his credit, he had been bolder than I would have been. After anointing Stony Brook as a flagship, Eliot spotlighted a killer research consortium in formation at the eastern end of Long Island, involving the Brookhaven National Laboratory, Stony Brook and the Cold Spring Harbor Laboratory, famous for basic research in cancer biology, genomics and neurobiology. At the suggestion of Jim Simons, a billionaire genius who had formerly chaired the mathematics department at Stony Brook, we had been facilitating the formation of this unparalleled research consortium.

Finally, because the Executive Budget would provide neither state funds nor a tuition increase to pay for any of this, Eliot had announced the administration's effort to begin creating a substantial endowment for SUNY and CUNY. He had proposed selling off part of the revenue stream of the New York State Lottery for 20 years, with the goal of increasing the paltry public university endowments by $4 billion. This additional principal would annually provide more than $200 million in new funding to begin to pay for some of Eliot's proposals.

Eliot then moved to a discussion of healthcare. It was a triumph both rhetorical and substantive, because he was able to envision and outline progress in a tough and worsening budget year. Among his priorities was the full state funding of Child Health Plus, designed to enroll 400,000 New York children who had no health insurance. Eliot also proposed a Peace Corps–like program, called Doctors Across New York, to provide financial incentives for young doctors to locate in underserved areas of the state. He made clear that the gains made under the 2007 stem cell initiative would be consolidated and supplemented. Eliot also announced a coordinated attack on type II diabetes and heart disease, which included a childhood-obesity initiative and called for the passage of the Healthy Schools Act. That bill was one part of the big legislative package that had been all but snuffed out by TRU in late July 2007. Other parts of that bundle were mentioned throughout the 2008 State of the State.

The unifying theme of Eliot's speech was economic growth, with virtually every substantive proposal linked to this objective. Eliot outlined his plans for lower taxes, major new infrastructure and affordable housing and touted the work of the local government commission, scheduled to deliver its report in April 2008. He noted that the commission was already facilitating 150 efficiency initiatives, including the potential elimination of an entire county, by ceding its territory to adjacent counties.

Eliot also announced a new property tax commission to be headed by Nassau County Executive Tom Suozzi. This was another feel-good moment. The proposal had allowed Eliot to stroke his rival from the 2006 gubernatorial primary and pretend that a commission would be able to devise a cap on property taxes, while assuring the public that there would be no reduction in school quality. As I listened, my first thought had been of the harsh reality that Californians had experienced as their tax-limiting initiatives bore bitter fruit. Californians got wedged between the "rock" of Proposition 13, making it almost impossible to raise property taxes, and the "hard place" of Proposition 98, which required the state to maintain educational funding at high levels. Suozzi was being asked to help formulate the same hell for New York. A year after Eliot's speech, the California budget would show a deficit of $26 billion, largely the product of arbitrary caps on its local governments' ability to tax. Soon after the State of the State, I would be overheard, and later outed, by a *Newsday* reporter as I talked with Suozzi and expressed the heresy that the only real way to lower property taxes while paying for good schools was to shift the funding burden to progressive income taxation. Nevertheless, a feel-good moment is designed to make the audience feel good. At this crucial 2008 speech, that was an important thing to try doing, and it worked. Even the Republicans put their hands together when Eliot made this bad proposal about capping property taxes.

Invoking the history of the 1970s bailout of New York City by the rest of the state, Eliot then called for a $1 billion Upstate Revitalization Fund, to be heavily subsidized by downstate. He promised that the details of this plan would be the centerpiece of the State of Upstate speech a week later.

Eliot concluded the State of the State with additional conciliatory comments, a call for unity, and more of the vision thing. In what has always been his greatest strength as a public speaker, he did this all very concisely. I don't know whether anyone keeps tabs, but I believe that in each of the major forms of political address, including the stump campaign speech, acceptance of a nomination, concession in an election, victory speech, major policy announcement, inaugural address, yearly "State of Whatever" and resignation, Eliot is either the champion or a contender for the title of Mr. Brevity.

The State of the State was well received and widely praised except by those who were going to criticize any speech Eliot gave, even had he delivered the Gettysburg Address or the Sermon on the Mount. Nick Confessore's article in the *Times*, titled "Niceness Campaign in Albany Gets Nowhere as G.O.P. Pouts," said:

> **Proposals that seemed deliberately aimed at Republican ears drew little response among the Republican Senators, eyebrows remained cocked in skepticism and lips curled into smirks. Protecting children from sexual predators? Eh. Manpower from the state police to aid local enforcement? Big deal. New flagship schools for biotech research in Republican-dominated Long Island and Western New York? Yawn... Only when Mr. Spitzer proposed a huge $1 billion "revitalization fund" to aid the upstate economy did the Legislature's Republicans show evident appreciation.**

With the Republicans' puerile and self-defeating exception, the response to the speech had been very favorable. Mike Bloomberg held a press conference at which he lauded the tone and substance of the speech. The editorials in the major papers echoed this praise, especially concerning Eliot's obvious attempt at conciliation. *Newsday* opined that "Last year, Spitzer was politically tone deaf. On this day he hit close to perfect pitch." The *Daily News* editorial opined, "Gov. Spitzer offered up two bold and potentially landmark ideas in yesterday's State of the State speech: overhauling the public universities and capping local property taxes.... The speech showed he's trying to be collegial. He also wisely dropped last year's shotgun approach."

In addition to the overwhelmingly positive "survey" articles and editorials about the State of the State, there were also many focusing on particular proposals Eliot had offered. The *Daily News* lauded a banking reform proposal aimed at reducing the number of home foreclosures in New York, saying, "the idea deserves a standing ovation" and was "reminiscent of his days as a hard-hitting, pro-consumer attorney general." Throughout the Plague Year, and still today, the yearning for the return of that amazing warrior attorney general is in evidence everywhere. A year after resignation, I was in a Utah hotel lobby with Eliot when a neurosurgeon from San Diego literally grabbed him, started to cry and sobbed, "We needed you so much."

In addition to its comprehensive coverage of the speech, the *New York Times* devoted separate articles to the property tax cap commission and the SUNY proposals. These two initiatives engendered the most buzz and debate. The *Times* article on the public college proposals zeroed in on the presumed lack of tuition reform at SUNY and CUNY, "conspicuously absent, however, from his [Eliot's] speech on Wednesday, was any embrace of the recommendation of a commission on higher education that the state free its public universities to raise tuition without state approval and to charge different prices at different campuses... 'It is off the table for this year' said a top aide to the governor, speaking on condition of anonymity."

The article had been written by the *New York Times'* distinguished higher education reporter Karen Arenson, whom I had courted for months in an effort to spotlight the CHE. Arenson had apparently wrung the admission about tuition out of the so-called top aide, whose neck I wanted to wring, because a tuition increase and reform were immediately plausible, as contrasted with our proposal to "monetize" the lottery to increase the SUNY endowment. That would be a vastly heavier lift and one that would, and did, evoke very strong, principled and emotional resistance. Moreover, when the aide had said tuition was "off the table," the internal discussions about a tuition increase and tuition reform were still going on within the inner circle, or so I had thought. I continued to think that way for another week, until, as I have described, I was shouted down by Eliot and told that, just like on the license initiative, "You would have [had] me out there all alone!"

A week of predominantly positive news coverage and editorial commentary followed Eliot's January 9, 2008, State of the State. There had even been the germ of a positive national story about Eliot to begin to counterbalance the two huge negative nationwide stories that TRU and the license initiative had become. Eliot's vision for New York public higher education was lauded in articles and editorials around the country and most enthusiastically in the *Boston Globe*, the *Courier-Journal* of Louisville, Kentucky, and the *Sunday Oregonian*. The January 13, 2008, edition of that Portland-based paper wrote:

It was a dramatic week, with a major New York politician emerging from a severe political battering with a bold new theme that actually looks to the future. No, not that New York politician [the "No, not that" referring to Hillary, still reeling from the driver's license waffle aftermath] Gov. Eliot Spitzer, who went from Golden Boy honeymoon to can-this-marriage-be-saved in a New York minute, delivered his second State of the State speech, facing a moment of business and employment uncertainty especially in the part of the state north of the New York City Metropolitan area, and came up with a big-ticket solution: Higher Education.

The only substantial reservations expressed about the State of the State speech were neither to the substance nor its tone, but about whether it would be successful in turning the page on the troubles of 2007. The prevailing feeling among the senior staff that night at a dinner held at El Mariachi, a Mexican restaurant in Albany, was that Eliot's address was at least a first big step toward accomplishing that weighty objective.

On January 16, 2008, Eliot delivered his State of Upstate at Buffalo State, a SUNY college located in downtown Buffalo. Buff State is a model for programs that recognize SUNY's responsibility to the state's second-largest-city and takes full advantage of the educational opportunities that its location provides, including one of the world's finest programs in art conservation and restoration. The State of Upstate, delivered in the college's Rockwell Hall, was even more successful than the State of the State, delivered in Albany a week earlier.

The Republican legislators had largely sat on their hands during the State of the State, even when Eliot had praised them and proposed programs that would aid Republican strongholds. The intervening week had taught them that this churlish attitude was unwise, especially in upstate areas virtually on life support. Eliot's upstate speech, which also lasted an hour, consisted of an executive summary of the State of the State, focusing heavily on the proposals with the greatest impact upstate, and a detailed explanation of the $1 billion Upstate Revitalization Fund.

The speech allowed Eliot to display one of his greatest talents, the ability to clearly explain scores of complicated initiatives. Eliot described every component of the Revitalization Fund with references to the communities and institutions that would benefit and with compliments to legislators and local electeds who had championed each cause. For the full State of the State, such specificity would have come across like reading from a technical manual, but for upstaters hanging on by their fingernails, it was the sweet sound of help on the way.

Eliot frequently invoked a SUNY college as the agent of assistance. In this way, he mentioned Binghamton, Geneseo, the University at Buffalo, Morrisville, Monroe Community College, Jefferson Community College, the Albany Nanotechnology College, Buffalo State and the Cornell College of Agriculture and Life Sciences, one of four SUNY colleges at Cornell. As Eliot touted the benefits of the lottery proposal, which would have added a total of $4 billion to the SUNY and CUNY endowments, I was struck by the $200 million figure, which he used to dramatize the yearly benefit to the state's public colleges. Unspoken had been the simple truth that a tuition increase of just $500 at SUNY and CUNY (only the second increase in 13 years) would have yielded more than that $200 million yearly.

The best things about the State of Upstate were simply that it had happened at all, for the very first time, and that it had been delivered in a place that nobody could dispute as befitting the name of the speech. Manhattanites consider Bear Mountain and

West Point, located 50 miles north, as "upstate." The press coverage unanimously applauded the fact that the speech had been delivered in Buffalo, and the upstate coverage had gone beyond acclimation to heartfelt thanks. The "I told you so" Devil whispered in my left ear that I had understood the folly of failing to hold transition events upstate a year before. In the right ear, the Angel had whispered that Eliot had learned something and that it was better late than never.

Afterward, Joe Bruno praised the speech, while noting that the words had to be followed by actions and claiming that Eliot's proposals mimicked those previously made by Senate Republicans. Joe was getting ready for the special election in the North Country to fill the Senate seat that had been vacated by Republican James Wright. If Democratic Assemblyman Darrel Aubertine were to win the election against Republican Assemblyman William Barclay, Joe's dwindling majority would be reduced to a single seat.

Republican Assembly Minority Leader Jim Tedisco, who had no hope of ever being the lower house Speaker, was far more effusive in his praise for the speech. The chorus of praise was joined by most upstate electeds, regardless of party, and by all of the major upstate editorial columns. Specific constituencies, such as those championing small business interests and the environment, applauded the proposals promoting their priorities. In the praise for the State of the State and Upstate speeches, a cautionary note was sounded. Eliot's January 22, 2008, budget message would show whether the words would be backed by deeds.

■ ■ ■

Heading into the Stretch

ON JANUARY 22, 2008, Eliot presented the Executive Budget to the Legislature. This time it appeared that Eliot would stick to his promise that any additions to spending would have to be balanced by equivalent cuts in other programs or additional revenue, not involving taxes. The quicksand of the very bad and worsening economy was strengthening Eliot's hand. A few weeks later, the results in the North Country special election would strengthen him even further.

The Executive Budget achieved most of the objectives Eliot set out for it and indeed most of the priorities announced in the State of the State and Upstate speeches. It included major additional rounds of school aid tied to educational reform, healthcare cost containment and property tax relief. Progress would be sustained in virtually every major infrastructure, transportation, environmental, housing and criminal justice program from the 2007–08 budget year, although in most, the pace would be somewhat slower. Major new initiatives would also be launched, including the Upstate Revitalization Fund, statewide park restoration and funding of the expanded state Child Health Plus program.

Many of the same Second Floor staff who had gone to El Mariachi for dinner after the State of the State address reassembled there on January 22 to celebrate Eliot's successful budget message. With the success of three recent high-profile speeches fresh in their minds, Peter Pope addressed the crowd and toasted to "Turning the Corner." I was in Manhattan celebrating Jan's birthday and somewhat screened off from the infectious optimism. From my vantage point, the corner had not been turned, but at least I could see the contours of an intersection ahead. The Executive Budget, while generally good, also had some avoidable defects. The trend lines in healthcare cost containment and in the allocation of additional school aid were unsettling. Other areas that should have been prioritized, first and foremost public higher education, were not. My greatest concern was that the total projected expenditures were too high, especially given the dual certainties that the Legislature would demand even more spending and that the economy would worsen.

With the exception of a major capital program for SUNY and CUNY, which would result in the construction of a lot of needed structures, mostly bearing the names of sitting state legislators, the prioritization of public higher education proved to be mostly rhetorical. There was nothing in the Executive Budget to fund any of our or the CHE's big proposals. In fact, the campuses would have to effect modest spending reductions across the board. Crises like the severe recession of 2008 present rare opportunities. One had been to focus upon and fund the higher education initiative. Eliot believed that this investment was the one most likely to restore New York to its historic stature and buffer the effect of future economic downturns. The administration's failure to make even moderate investments in higher education was inexcusable.

While higher education was being stiffed, the overall budget grew by rates that we had measured as varying from 5 to 5.9 percent, depending upon which fiscal metric was chosen. The state would have increased its spending at roughly twice the projected rate of inflation. It would have added 2,000 new employees to the state payroll, increasing the total to more than 200,000, an unfortunate magic number.

Comptroller Tom DiNapoli predictably attacked again, criticizing the Executive Budget and the increase in debt, and measured the budget's growth rate at a whopping 7.3 percent. He chose to use a metric that made Eliot look bad. This was Tom's second annual installment of payback for Eliot's attack on his credentials.

The *New York Times* and *Newsday* published positive survey articles as did the *Daily News*. These were followed by others analyzing specific budgetary issues. The voices of New York's electeds were also generally supportive, with Joe Bruno a notable exception. He was preparing for the great battle in the North Country. Bruno had chosen to make the special election in the Adirondacks into a referendum on Eliot Spitzer. Other electeds praised the budget. Mike Bloomberg praised it effusively, continuing the love fest that had begun on January 9, when the mayor had lauded Eliot's State of the State as "the best speech I've ever heard him give." Bloomberg's unrestrained praise was surprising to me, given the existence of several items expected to provoke his ire. The Executive Budget had reduced the amount of new school aid going to New York City by hundreds of millions. The proposed sale of a prime parcel of land north of the Jacob K. Javits Convention Center of New York, on Manhattan's West Side, had also been expected to provoke the mayor's anger, but initially hadn't. Bloomberg's late hits on these issues suggested that his legendary staff had missed these glaring items in their first review of the budget documents.

The consensus verdict of New York's electeds on the Executive Budget was best expressed by Assembly star Mike Gianaris, who said:

> **Everyone recognizes this is a very difficult year budgetwise. While there will definitely be interest groups kicking and screaming about their particular subject areas, the important thing to recognize is there are difficult choices to be made and the governor has struck a good balance.**

The quickly gathering economic storm clouds would have helped Eliot as the budget negotiations progressed.

One established scene in the annual budget ritual is a disagreement among the governor and the legislative leaders about the state's revenue projections. If more money is going to come in, then, more can be spent, as the Legislature habitually desires. During the 2007–08 budget negotiations, the Majority and Minority conferences in the Senate and Assembly each projected substantially higher revenue figures than Eliot, and had used these projections to back their demands for additional spending. Under the 2007 budget reform, the governor and legislative leaders were required to seek agreement on projected revenue. Failing that, the comptroller's projection would become the official number.

The worsening economy had disrupted this reliable pattern in the negotiation of the 2008–09 budget. The Senate Republicans, led by Bruno, had predictably projected $133 million more revenue than Eliot had. The Assembly Republicans had surprisingly disagreed and projected $315 million less than the governor. Shelly's Democratic Assembly conference had projected $615 million less than Eliot, as a prerequisite to their call for higher income taxes, exclusively targeting the rich.

Malcolm Smith, in a continuation of his nonsensical behavior, criticized the Executive Budget ("[W]e aren't controlling spending as much as I think we should") but failed to offer any alternative revenue projection or give a clue as to what the right amount of spending should have been. Malcolm understood that his title conferred the responsibility to speak at certain established moments, but that was as far as his understanding extended. Before the deadline, the legislative leaders and Eliot reached agreement to reduce the revenue projections in the Executive Budget by $250 million.

As the rules of engagement for the final budget confrontation were being defined, the great battle in the northern Adirondacks approached. Eliot and Rich Baum were wisely exploiting Joe Bruno's crudely telegraphed tactic of making the special election into a referendum on Eliot and his first year as governor. They were unleashing the still vast resources of Team Spitzer, but without injecting Eliot directly into the race. The race to fill the seat vacated by Republican James Wright should have been a walkover for the Senate majority.

Unlike much of the rest of New York State, which was trending toward the Democratic Party in voter registration, the North Country was still rock-ribbed Republican. The district contained 78,454 registered Republicans and only 47,094 Democrats, resulting in a seemingly prohibitive advantage. A Democrat had never been elected to the Senate in this district. Republican William Barclay and Democrat Darrel Aubertine initially thought that this was a contest between them, not one between Spitzer and Bruno. They were both popular incumbent members of the Assembly who had claimed their lower house seats on the same day in 2002. Both had deep roots in the North Country. Aubertine was from an old farming family, and Barclay's father had served in the Senate.

Upward of $3 million was spent on the race, an unprecedented sum for that part of the state. Most of this money came from outside the region. Smelling blood, Senator Jeff Klein, a Bronx Democrat, contributed $40,000 of his campaign's funds to the Aubertine campaign, expecting that a win by Darrel would be a major step in Democrats taking control of the Senate for the first time since 1965. When that happened, Klein hoped to replace Malcolm Smith as Majority Leader. I wondered whether Klein's Bronx contributors understood that their money was going to an anti-choice farmer who lived near the Canadian border. Mike Bloomberg, who in June 2007 had abandoned his short-lived status as a Republican, still donated

$500,000 to the North Country Republican senatorial slush fund. Eliot's comment, "[Bloomberg] has been a supporter of the Senate…and that's politics. I'm all for it," reminded me of the many times he had called Joe Bruno "a good friend," each time insulting the intelligence of his audience.

Aside from the enormous wads of money that Eliot and Joe had lobbed in from other parts of the state, the major factors heading into the special election were the Republicans' monstrous advantage in registered voters and our equally large advantage in tactics and skill. Eric Schneiderman, an extremely talented Manhattan-based state senator, had been sent to the North Country for much of the campaign. Eric was skillfully deploying the troops, working with the Spitzer media machine and a former Spitzer campaign manager and coordinating the logistics on site. Rich Baum worked with equal skill from his desk in the Capitol.

The North Country electorate, initially amused and gratified to be the focus of so much statewide attention, soon grew annoyed at the Republicans, who focused their attention on Eliot instead of the district's problems. This misguided strategy was epitomized by a prominent Barclay TV ad featuring a photo of Aubertine and Eliot together. Darrel's smart response had been to hone in on very local issues, including an attack on a fee charged by Barclay's family to salmon fishermen on a river that ran through their property.

An election that should have resulted in a Republican landslide was won by Aubertine with a comfortable five percent margin. The press was unanimous in treating this result as a very big victory for Eliot and an equally great defeat for Joe. The Republicans' tactic of casting the election as a vote on the governor's performance contributed to this interpretation. The good news was that the election result placed a strong wind at the back of all the administration's efforts, most prominently the budget. A bad effect of the special election was that it continued and deepened the Spitzer Administration's obsession with taking the Senate and the wrong-headed assumption that when that happened, most, if not all, of our problems would end.

With 14 months of Malcolm Smith's ineptitude under our belts, it was obvious that a change in Democratic Senate leadership was the first order of business. Malcolm was not the only problem. Other members, in or aspiring to leadership positions in a Democratic-controlled Senate, were also very troublesome. Even Aubertine, the nice guy who had just been elected, was not my cup of tea. Although I try not to trivialize my own vote by casting it for or against a candidate's stance on any single issue, there are exceptions. My daughters' rights to control their own reproductive destinies is one. Aubertine is anti-choice, and Bill Barclay pro. Given the fact that there was very little other than this to differentiate them, I would have voted for the Republican in that election.

I didn't live in the North Country, didn't get to vote in the late-February special election and was busy making my way back to SUNY campuses, some for the third, fourth or fifth time. We had scheduled a series of events at these campuses to promote the endowment initiative. I had additional skin in the game because, several weeks earlier, I had dined with Eliot and disclosed my intention to leave the administration and seek the unfilled position as permanent Chancellor of SUNY, with his expected help. Eliot had so much as offered me the position in October 2006, when there had been a competent permanent chancellor in place, and I had lacked credentials for the job.

Soon after Eliot assumed office in 2007, the SUNY chancellor, Admiral John Ryan, had departed. John Clark had been appointed as interim chancellor. By February 2008, a search for a new permanent chancellor was underway. I was the most popular man in public higher education in New York State, with no close second. I had applied myself and mastered the global issues and the arcania of higher education policy. Although I had never publicly expressed a desire to become chancellor, a score of campus presidents had urged me to seek the position, as had CUNY officials. Many other figures in higher education had also offered their support. So, as the February 12, 2008, dinner date with Eliot approached, I was sure that he would agree that this move made sense for me, for him and for the good of a cause we both cared about deeply.

Tuesday, February 12, 2008, was an Albany day for both Eliot and me. I held meetings throughout the day with local government officials about budget items relating to our efforts to consolidate and regionalize certain local services. I had other meetings involving our renewed effort to eliminate obsolete and redundant public authorities. The bulk of the day had been spent on the higher education push. Eliot held a midday news conference to kick off the endowment drive, which would debut on the University at Buffalo's future downtown campus the next day.

After the news conference, Eliot headed for New York City. As the day wore on, it started to snow and rain on the path between Albany and Manhattan.

Normally, I would have cancelled dinner, given the bad drive ahead of me and the necessity of arriving the next morning in Buffalo for a 9:15 A.M. downtown event. However, I was not going to risk waiting another few weeks for a long and private face-to-face with Eliot. The subject matter was too delicate for a ten- or fifteen-minute chat in the office. As I drove south on the New York Thruway to "The City," Eliot and I spoke four times about the steadily worsening weather conditions and the need to move, later and later, the time of our dinner date at Quatorze Bis on East 79th Street. When I was south of Kingston, Eliot tried to cancel, but I insisted. I invoked whatever was necessary (including his earlier fair-weather chauffeured journey and my hazardous solo drive) to guilt-trip him into keeping our date.

When I arrived at the bistro at about 9:00 P.M., Eliot was already seated and having a Scotch. I immediately explained why I had been so insistent about keeping the date, putting my plan to leave the administration and become SUNY Chancellor directly on the table with our drinks. Eliot appeared distracted and was leaving himself open to become even more so, by having extended chats with the many restaurant patrons who walked over to our table to salute him. Eliot treated my news as he would have the waiter's regrets that, at this late hour, they had run out of the restaurant's signature dish, choucroute garnie. He responded to my declared plan with information that he knew I already knew.

The selection of the chancellor was legally the decision of the SUNY Board of Trustees. That had also been true in 2006, when Eliot had effectively offered me the position. The same had been true in 2007, when I had derailed a weak candidate from being appointed interim chancellor and identified John Clark. Eliot had then informed the trustees that he recommended Clark and, of course, they had obliged. When Eliot had appointed Elmira lawyer Carl Hayden to become chair of the SUNY Board of Trustees, Carl had made his acceptance contingent on Eliot's recognition that choosing the chancellor was the trustees' prerogative. Carl, Eliot and I had all wanted it that way. That would never change the fact that Eliot's wishes would weigh heavily in the board's deliberations, especially given the governor's crucial role in the SUNY budget.

Eliot's preference would count for even more than those of previous governors. He had launched the CHE, had put public higher education front and center in his State of the State, was throwing the full weight of his office behind the endowment plan and had appeared to fully understand the key role that higher education would play in the state's future. So, Eliot's distracted "I'll see what I can do" was disingenuous and annoying. With great help from my staff (and despite resistance and mischief from him and the budget division), I had played the crucial role in creating the one and only prominent and totally positive issue that this governor then possessed.

As the conversation continued and the food came, so did the distractions. Having been with Eliot on scores of such occasions, I knew that he had the power to preempt each well-wisher's desire to have a long chat. He could do that with a polite gesture or a terminating comment. Instead, each intruder was invited to name-drop for as long as he or she wanted. Then, for no apparent reason, Eliot went outside in the middle of dinner in his shirtsleeves and reappeared five minutes later without explanation. To the limited extent that I could get Eliot's attention, I had conveyed my commitment not to leave him until the TRU investigations were wrapped up and the local government and higher education reports and accompanying legislative efforts concluded for the year.

I left the dinner pissed off, but not unduly concerned. Despite his disingenuous recitation about his limited powers, I believed he would push me, and do so strongly and genuinely when the time came. I had a lot going for me at that moment, especially my own skills and the reputation I had built with the higher education community. I was certain that Eliot would push with that tide, and that would be enough.

The kickoff for the endowment campaign on February 13, 2008, in Buffalo, was the best and most beautiful event that I took part in during the Plague Year. Some 400 people had crowded into the old M. Wile industrial building, which was being transformed into the "UB Gateway" for the University at Buffalo's proposed 8,000-student downtown campus. The mood was hopeful and festive because Eliot had named UB as a SUNY flagship in his January 9 State of the State. Lots of happy pictures were taken, and all of the speakers were concise, supportive and laudatory of this embattled governor's struggles and his heroic efforts on their behalf. Among the speakers were

Mayor Byron Brown, UB President John Simpson and local entrepreneur Mike Blumenson. Eliot was happy, glowing and commanding in his characteristically concise speech. He would have been awarded best in show, but for a speech by a female African-American UB law student who previously had earned a B.A. at the university.

Jenna Chrisphonte, a single mother from Queens, New York, had spoken about UB in the way that explains why the term "Alma Mater" had initially been coined. UB had taken her in, remedied the gaps in her high-school education, financially supported her and provided childcare for her daughter. Jenna had earned her undergraduate degree with high honors, and though she hadn't said this, she could have been the subject of a bidding war for her law school matriculation, as most highly credentialed and orally gifted African-American students are likely to be. Her speech moved me, and many others, to tears.

Eliot's endowment drive was off to a fabulous start in the very best place in the state to launch it. In the afterglow, more photos were taken, including the happiest I posed for with Eliot during the year. My little team stayed around Buffalo for the balance of the day for more higher education meetings and a visit to Roswell Park, one of the world-class hospitals in Buffalo that collaborate with UB in medical research and education.

Although we had beaten the odds with our on-time early-morning arrival at Buffalo's notoriously delay-plaqued airport, our luck ran out on the trip home. The return flight was serially delayed by a total of more than seven hours. We killed some time with an orgy at the Anchor Bar, the place where Buffalo chicken wings were invented. After that, we spent five hours at the airport, attempting to sleep on benches, while covering ourselves with maps "the City of Lights".

Near midnight, our flight was granted a waiver so that it could land at LaGuardia later than the 1:00 A.M. cut-off time. Eliot had beaten it out of Buffalo much earlier, right after the endowment event. After several stops in other upstate cities, he flew to D.C. and checked into the Mayflower Hotel. The next day, he would testify before the House of Representatives about the bond insurance crisis then threatening the stability of the financial markets.

The power of the UB event had been such that, had the plane never taken off, we could have floated back to Manhattan on Cloud Nine. I stayed in that frame of mind for the next 25 days, the best of the Spitzer Administration in my opinion. Eliot was hanging tough on the budget. His strength grew significantly after the special election. Many important initiatives that had foundered in 2007, because of TRU and driver's licenses, were resurrected with new force behind them. Among these were components of the legislative package that Rich had assembled in early July 2007. We also renewed our efforts to control the runaway cost of medical malpractice insurance and end the tax-free status of giant Internet merchants who were competing unfairly with brick-and-mortar stores in New York. Though TRU dragged on, and the ineptitude of Feerick, Teitelbaum and Soares took a chunk of our time and occasionally distracted Eliot, the overall trend had been decidedly up, and the mood upbeat.

The final reports of the local government and higher education commissions were near completion. The lottery-monetization proposal, which I had initially dismissed as unrealistic in the near term, was gaining strength, because Eliot was. Had New York become the first state to monetize its lottery, it would have reaped a tremendous first-mover advantage. Investors are always eager for new places to safely park capital. As proposed, this first large monetization might have yielded as much as a $1 billion premium over a similar deal done after others had occurred. The proposal had seemed quixotic for the stumbling Spitzer Administration of just a few months earlier. Eliot's newfound strength had given it a decent chance and the monetization might provide me some real money to work with when I became SUNY Chancellor.

Our public events in support of the lottery/endowment project, starting with the one at UB, had been going extremely well. The many private conversations with editorial boards, potential investors, foundations and opinion leaders had been going even better. One held on February 22, 2008, however, still haunts me. That evening, I met Ed Cox at the Harvard Club on West 44th Street, where he had invited me for drinks. Cox is a prominent New York lawyer who had frequently considered becoming the Republican candidate for United States senator, governor or attorney general, and later was believed to be on the short list for AG had John McCain been elected president.

Cox was a SUNY trustee who took particular interest in the community colleges. He had taken note of the special attention I had given to these schools in my visits and the community college white paper I had submitted to the CHE. When our business conversation ended, Ed asked me to describe my family. After telling him about my kids and Jan, I told Ed that Jan had been a Smith College classmate of his sister-in-law, Julie Nixon. I said that I had met Julie and his brother-in-law, David Eisenhower, at an event at Amherst in the late 1960s and remarked that it must have been "brutal" for his wife, Tricia Nixon, and for Julie, David and himself during the Vietnam era and Watergate.

I apologized to Cox for my part in the brutality, confessing my small contribution to the nasty atmosphere that had confronted Richard Nixon's relatives as they had tried to get their educations at Smith, Amherst, Finch College and Harvard Law. Ed thanked me and said that the pounding they had taken back then had left its mark. I then recalled having heard that Tricia Nixon had for many years lived a reclusive life, rarely leaving the Cox residence in Manhattan. I left the otherwise pleasant meeting feeling slightly depressed, but the down was only momentary.

While Peter Pope's January 22 toast "Turning the Corner" might have been a bit premature, by late February 2008 the feeling of having survived the worst and of moving forward was palpable and widespread on the Second Floor. In late February, I met with Garrick Utley and Paul Tagliabue at Levin Institute about our goal of establishing one or two SUNY campuses in China, India, Turkey, the Persian Gulf or South America. The Stony Brook–Brookhaven–Cold Spring Harbor research consortium had gone from dream to its first concrete steps in late winter. I had been named to the Brookhaven board and was working with the three institutions on the legal structure of the consortium. There was seed money in the Executive Budget for these first steps.

On February 27, 2007, Eliot and I attended an event in Manhattan marking Jim and Marilyn Simons' donation of $60 million to establish a center for geometry and physics at Stony Brook. Eliot spoke and again touted the research consortium and the lottery/endowment proposal. He had done the same the day before, while addressing newly energized students, faculty and administrators who had travelled to the Capitol for "SUNY Day." During the festivities, I addressed hundreds of giddy Stony Brook students, still reveling in that school's designation as a "flagship" by Eliot on January 9. More happy photos were snapped with Eliot, me and these kids.

Recently skeptical people were now starting to listen to Eliot, and it seemed that the stars were finally beginning to align. The brightest star, Jim Simons, told us that his previous contributions of some $150 million to Stony Brook and SUNY would only be the beginning of his and Marilyn's philanthropy, if and when the administration's higher education plans became a reality. The Cornell land grant people and representatives of the Bill and Melinda Gates Foundation met with me to express their support for other components of the CHE blueprint. The UB delegation returned to Albany for the fifth time, bringing a UB 2020 plan revised to show even greater commitment to downtown Buffalo's revival. During that week, of March 3, 2008, I had meetings with many key legislators and held another lottery/endowment event, this time at SUNY's New Paltz liberal arts college, which *Newsweek* named "America's Hottest Small State School" in a 2007 survey.

On Thursday, March 6, the *Times Union's* lead story spotlighted the higher education campaign in an article titled, "Spitzer Adviser Used to Playing Hardball." The article focused on my role in the public college initiative and linked the plan to Eliot's vision for restoring New York to its position as a global economic engine and leader in ideas.

Eliot had been racing around the state in support of the budget and the endowment and was pumping already appropriated funds into affordable housing starts, renewable energy projects and a variety of programs attempting to buffer the cascading waves of home foreclosures. A revenue consensus had been struck among Eliot, Shelly, Bruno, Tedisco and Smith. They had also had agreed on a plan to spur economic development in the state's blighted areas. Bruno and Eliot had joined forces to kill Shelly's plan to surcharge and super-surcharge the income taxes of New York's rich and very rich.

Eliot was sprinting, perhaps toward what he must have known was the premature finish line. I suspect that at some level he must have been aware of that. The first sign, visible to him, that the jig was up appeared in the *New York Times* on Friday, March 7. The *Times* reported that four people had been indicted by a federal grand jury for their roles as organizers and managers of a prostitution ring called the Emperors Club VIP. However, well before this article, Eliot had to have known that the day of reckoning was nigh. A guy as smart and perceptive as he must have picked up some signals with his antennae, perhaps a suspicious stare or near miss during his February 13 stay at the Mayflower Hotel. Regardless, he was sprinting, and a good athlete like Eliot doesn't sprint unless the finish line is in sight.

On Saturday, March 8, 2008, Governor Eliot Spitzer, First Lady Silda Wall Spitzer and Lieutenant Governor David A. Paterson made their last joint proclamation, ironically recognizing "International Women's Day and Women's History Month." I read the proclamation on the seventh day of that very rare, very good week and began the joyful weekend with my wife, my sister-in-law Patty, and two young friends at our home in Chatham. The feeling of ease and goodwill lasted until late Sunday night, with Eliot saying to me, "As of now, you are my counsel... I must resign."

■ ■ ■

61 Hours

W HEN ELIOT AND I finally spoke on the telephone at
10:37 P.M., he told me about his patronage of prostitutes.
The Friday, March 6, indictment of The Emperors Club VIP
escort service and four of its managers had referred to one of the
"Johns" as "Client 9." The *New York Times* had figured out that
this was Eliot and was going to make the information public.
Eliot said that this necessitated his resignation, most likely the
next day. The call lasted no longer than five minutes, ending
with my promise not to abandon him, my rejoinder that he need
not resign and my commitment to be at his apartment by 7:00
A.M. the next morning, as he had requested.

Sixty-one hours elapsed between that Sunday night phone
call and Eliot's short public appearance at 11:40 A.M. Wednesday
March 12, 2008, when he announced his resignation. I experienced that interval like a character in the television drama *24*.
A lot of activity was packed into a short period of time.

Because Eliot had told me that he *"must"* resign, and hadn't
said that he *"wanted"* to, and because I had told him and
believed that he didn't have to, I decided that one of my jobs

was to demonstrate that resignation was not his only option. I decided to make a plan for him to remain governor, despite having recognized that the plan might not work and that even if it did, the period ahead would have made the preceding 15 very rough months seem like a walk in the park. It would also have meant staying by Eliot's side, despite having informed him on the night of February 12 that I wanted out, either to become Chancellor of SUNY or resume the practice of law.

I slept only four of those 61 hours. In the remaining time, I drove from my home in the Berkshires to Eliot's apartment in Manhattan, back to Albany, and then back again to Eliot. I made a public appearance and a speech upstate. I sought out the advice of a handful of people and also gratefully accepted unsolicited recommendations from a few others close enough to me to have my cell phone number and warrant listening to. I met personally or telephonically with several shrinks and spiritual advisers.

During those 61 hours, I responded to three among more than 100 press inquiries and formulated and discussed with Eliot, Silda and Emily (Eliot's sister) my plan for Eliot to remain governor. After Eliot finally rejected this proposal on the morning of March 12, I finalized my own letter of resignation. I stood ten feet from him as he resigned, as I had during his brief public appearance two days earlier.

Eliot's greeting at 6:57 A.M., as I entered the apartment, Silda within earshot, was *"Welcome to a Greek tragedy."* Within minutes, the three of us were seated at a table, where Silda asked me the two toughest questions I have been asked during this affair.

The first, as I previously reported, was the one asked by every-body: *"Did you know about this?"* Then, with Eliot still sitting next to her, Silda asked me, *"Has Jan ever done this to you?"* How odd and oddly phrased, unless you know Silda, too much the lady to directly ask the real question, *"Have you ever you done this to Jan?"* So I answered the intended question, saying, "I have not done this to Jan, nor has she done this to me, but we have done very bad things to each other and gotten through them, and I consider our marriage, though not perfect, to be a great one. You won't have the advantage we had of working through your prob-lems in privacy. You will attempt to do it with the whole world watching and judging you." I thought of this exchange many times in the following months when people, mostly women, asked me whether Silda would leave Eliot, quickly offering their opinion on what she should and/or must do. These women would tell me how outraged they had been when Silda had stood beside Eliot for three minutes and 46 seconds as he spoke at his two public appearances on March 10 and 12.

When I arrived at Eliot and Silda's apartment at Fifth Ave-nue and 79th Street slightly before 7:00 A.M. on March 10, a press contingent had already assembled. It was not heavy, and from their demeanor it seemed that it wasn't clear to them what they were waiting for. During the next eight hours, a massive swarm of reporters and photographers assembled outside the building entrance, equipped with booms, sound trucks and sat-ellite uplinks. When we exited the building for Eliot to travel 50 blocks downtown and east to Third Avenue and 40th Street for the first of his two public appearances, we got to experience the leading edge of the media storm, more intense than any ever before focused on a scandal.

On March 11 and again on March 13, the front page of the *New York Times*, with hundreds of other media outlets merely repeating what it had said, reported what was, on certain key points, a reconstructed and incomplete account of what had transpired in the Spitzer apartment during those three days. Nobody who was actually in the apartment talked to the press about what had happened. The *Times'* account came from Spitzer staffers interpreting what Eliot, Rich Baum and I had told them. The most important topic of discussion in the apartment, reassembled with partial accuracy, was the heated debate about whether Eliot should resign and his vacillating intentions with respect to that issue.

The senior executive staff was nearly unanimous that Eliot should resign immediately, with only Silda and me dissenting. That nearly unanimous opinion was motivated by principle, outrage and a feeling of betrayal, which I did not fault, then or afterward. At first, I understood, but only intellectually, the anger directed at Eliot's apparently massive hypocrisy. Later I would actually "feel" that anger myself, though not as strongly as many others. From the outset, I envisioned the ugliness of the path forward if Eliot battled to maintain his office. However, these strong and valid arguments for prompt resignation were overcome in my mind by opposing factors. I projected a Paterson governorship as even uglier than one under a disgraced but psychologically emancipated Eliot. I was confident that, with the Impostor gone, Eliot would have the strength and ability to govern effectively. However great Eliot's handicaps, I viewed David's as greater, including all the damage already done to various institutions of state government during the preceding 15 months. Moreover, regardless of whether the majority or the minority of Silda and I were right, about whether Eliot should have fought to stay in office, it was my job to give him a plan for survival and the opportunity to keep the promises he had made to the people of New York.

I believed that Eliot should resign only if he was thinking straight and was absolutely sure that he no longer could function as governor. I realized from the second we had spoken the night before, that in one profound way, Eliot had already demonstrated that he did not want to be governor and might never have wanted the job. Furthermore, I hadn't believed that Eliot's desire, to be or not to be, should necessarily have been determinative on the issue of resignation. Elected office holders have a responsibility to the electorate, which should trump their own desires. But not being a shrink, nor wanting to engage in psychobabble, I had simply taken Eliot at his word—when he told me that he wanted to remain governor, but that it wasn't possible.

Eliot said that Speaker Shelly Silver could not control the Assembly, and therefore that body would speedily provide the vote margin for impeachment. I did not doubt Shelly's message to Eliot, that he could not control his members or keep them at bay for a few days in order that these weighty decisions be made in a less hysterical atmosphere. However, I strongly doubted that Shelly could not have at least bought Eliot and New York State a week or more for deliberation and contemplation of the dire consequences of Eliot's resignation. Moreover, I had agreed with Rich Baum's assessment, delivered during a meeting held early Monday morning, that if Eliot managed to hang on he would have become a feeble figurehead.

The question in my mind had been how long Eliot's impotence would have lasted. I thought it would have been for a relatively short time, perhaps until the fall of 2008. There were many legal and constitutional prerogatives possessed by the governor, regardless of the scandal. While waiting for his own likely impeachment in early 2009, Illinois Governor Rod Blagojevich had been able to shove his tainted choice for Barack Obama's replacement in the Senate down the throats of Illinois officialdom, the entire United States Senate and even that of the president-elect. They had all said, "Rod, you can't do that," and he had replied, *"Watch me."*

Soon after I arrived at the Spitzer apartment on March 10, others joined, first Rich Baum, then Emily, then Pam Fox, a close friend of Silda's, and then George Fox, Pam's husband and Eliot's close friend. Eliot had used George's name as an alias during his date with a prostitute at the Mayflower Hotel in Washington, D.C., on February 13. At some point, Michelle Hirschman, Eliot's lawyer from the Paul Weiss law firm, also arrived. Other people whom I did not interact with also came and went.

We huddled in various permutations and combinations for most of the day, with my attention focused on three things—whether Eliot was at risk of suicide, how to comfort Silda, and the formulation of a plan that might allow Eliot to remain governor. Almost immediately after her arrival, Michelle

Hirshman began to tell me things that, had the conversation continued, would have given me information that only Eliot's criminal defense lawyers and Silda needed to have. I stopped the conversation before slipping over the edge. Michelle and her Paul Weiss colleagues, Ted Wells and Mark Pomerantz, didn't need my help, being far more skilled in criminal defense than I. More important, becoming defense counsel would have destroyed my ability to be the Sage Old Guy as Eliot had implicitly requested the evening before when he said, "As of now, you are my counsel." Given Eliot's strong predisposition toward resigning, and the rapid accumulation of opinion in favor of doing it immediately, being phoned in by senior executive staff, it was an uphill battle to prevent Eliot from resigning that Monday.

In the midst of this debate, at a little after 1:00 P.M., the *New York Times* online edition reported that Eliot had been "Client 9" of the Emperors Club VIP prostitution ring, indicted by a Southern District of New York grand jury the week before. I didn't have a plan formulated yet but argued with Eliot, backed by Silda, Emily and his three daughters, that he must not resign that day. I told Eliot that he was acting under *"duress"* and with *"diminished capacity"* and that he could not make a rational decision. At about 2:15 P.M., a statement of resignation was scrapped for the terse statement Eliot made in his appearance at 3:46 P.M.:

Over the past nine years, eight as attorney general and one as governor, I have tried to uphold a vision of progressive politics that would rebuild New York and create opportunity for all. We sought to bring real change to New York,

and that will continue. Today, I want to briefly address a private matter.

I have acted in a way that violates my obligations to my family, that violates my—or any—sense of right and wrong. I apologize first, and most importantly, to my family. I apologize to the public, whom I promised better.

I do not believe that politics in the long run is about individuals. It is about ideas, the public good, and doing what it best for the State of New York.

But I have disappointed and failed to live up to the standard I expected of myself. I must now dedicate some time to regain the trust of my family.

I will not be taking questions. Thank you very much. I will report back to you in short order.

Thank you very much.

Eliot had been so close to resigning, and the hysteria that had broken out so visible and intense, that I realized that I had to give him something tangible, specific and credible to consider, or he would pull the plug as early as the next day, Tuesday, March 11. The plan I put together and presented to Eliot Tuesday and Wednesday morning required him to quickly make another brief public appearance. At this second appearance, Eliot would have said in his own words the essence of what I had drafted and paraphrased for him, Silda and Emily. This was the statement:

On Monday I appeared before you and apologized for conduct which I said was a private matter. I was wrong.

Because of who I am, what I have tried to stand for, and the promises I made to the people of New York State, I realize that my behavior was not private and I must account to you as well as to my family for what I have done. Immediately after making this statement I am leaving the state for roughly a month to get help and treatment for the serious problem I have. I will be in a facility where I will get the help I need. At this moment I am not asking for anything from you or the elected officials of this state other than fair and humane treatment for my wife and daughters during my absence. If upon my return to New York, my fellow citizens and my partners in state government have removed me from office, I will quietly and humbly accept that judgment and return to private life. If I am permitted to return to the state as its governor, I will work tirelessly to regain the trust and faith I have squandered through my personal failings and to fulfill the promises I made to the people who elected me. That is all I have to say at this time other than to say again how sorry I am for letting you down and that I will work hard upon my return either as governor or as a private citizen to make amends. Thank you.

I convinced myself, Silda and Emily that Eliot should make his own version of this statement and undertake the course of conduct and the treatment described. Eliot asked me to estimate the plan's chance of success. I told him that I recommended that he leave the state and get treatment regardless of whether it was likely or not that he would be impeached while he was doing it. I estimated the likelihood of success at some figure above 25 percent, but not much above that. I think my quantitative assessment had been far too conservative. However, I don't believe it would have mattered had I argued convincingly to Eliot, as I now believe, that his chances of remaining governor were better than 50 percent. Eliot had simply been humoring us by going through the exercise of the debate. At that moment, he was in a rush to resign. Eliot no longer wanted to be governor and had not been open to my point of view that his preference should not be dispositive on the weighty issue of resignation.

One measure of Eliot's mind-set that Monday morning had been his declaration to me that he intended to write a book about his term as governor, implicitly indicating that the term was over. He even had a title, one that I thought was lousy and immediately forgot. I responded that I would write one as well, and gave him the title of the book you are reading. In the midst of the escalating inferno, he and I were actually swapping book titles. The incident revealed our similarities and was a sign of our instantly restored kinship. It also said something about both of us, probably bad, or at least neurotic, but I am not sure. After extended final argument on Wednesday morning, Eliot's resolve became clear to Silda, Emily and me. We stopped arguing with him and accepted his decision that he would resign later that day.

The plan for Eliot to try to avoid impeachment and continue as governor, embodied in the statement I had drafted, was simple and built upon a foundation of several truths and admirable American traits. Eliot needed help. Although I don't know, and haven't asked, exactly when his patronage of prostitutes had begun, he must have been engaging in this conduct throughout 2006. I "know" that if for no other reason than because of a distinct personality change that I and others close to him noticed throughout that year, his last as attorney general. Theories and speculation abound, concerning why Eliot would have engaged in conduct that was not just likely, but virtually certain, to destroy his career and grievously hurt his family, friends and the State of New York. However, none that I have heard or hypothesized myself suggests that professional help was not in order. Quite the contrary.

Eliot needed help, and this might have come in many forms from people and institutions with various skills. But, in the same way that a person with cancer might seek spiritual help, he would also be well served in seeking treatment at Memorial Sloan-Kettering. A person in Eliot's apparent condition would have been well served by seeking treatment at the Meadows in Wickenburg, Arizona, and possibly at the Dakota, a facility related to the Meadows, which specializes in sexual compulsion. On March 10 and 11, I contacted these facilities. I told Eliot that I would check into the motel nearest the chosen facility to be his lifeline during the period of his residential treatment.

Jan was mad at me when she learned that I had made this offer to Eliot without first discussing it with her—because I would be absent for at least a month. But, I also suspect there was some vague and unarticulated anger directed at me, some guilt by association, not because I was rumored to be Client 10, but guilt for being so obtuse while my closest friend was off destroying his career and damaging our lives. This attitude was exhibited not only by Jan, but also by others who knew me, as well as by some who didn't. For example, I was frequently described in the press as "still Eliot's close friend," which in context questioned my judgment, past and present.

Americans don't like to kick a guy when he's down or when he's genuinely contrite and seeking help. They also resist doing it when he's not there to defend himself. The plan, requiring Eliot to leave the state and get help, had recognized all these wonderful American traits. Just as important, adopting my plan would have gotten Eliot help that I believed he needed, in an accelerated fashion and in a residential setting far away from New York.

Eliot's month away would also have given New York State a good chance to visit with the "Ghost of Christmas Future." They would have gotten a preview of Governor David Paterson, when he might well have done something incredibly jerky, as he did the day after he was sworn in. Then they might have pondered what a Paterson Administration might be like, especially one with then Senate President Pro Tempore Joe Bruno next in the line of succession.

The justifiable anger and outrage that people felt toward Eliot in the first few days created an unjustified lynch mob atmosphere, whose chemistry is described and analyzed in scholarly works such as J.P. Chaplin's 1959 *Rumor, Fear and the Madness of Crowds*. The classics of mob mentality like *Rumor* mostly predate the Internet age. They cannot describe how the viral spread of information on the Internet and multichannel video and satellite radio platforms exponentially increase the mob effect, in the way an accelerant spreads an arsonist's work. In my upstate/

downstate dashes during the 61 hours, I discovered that my Sirius Satellite Radio service featured a new channel, "Client Nine Radio"—devoted to round-the-clock coverage of the scandal.

Still, I had known that the mood would cool in a relatively short period of time and begin to change as people started the process of searching their own lives and consciences. They would have assessed Eliot's conduct in light of contemporary views about paid sex involving "consenting" adults. I had received calls and email from acquaintances in Australia and France saying that, in their more mature societies, paid sex was no big deal. I also received one from a Russian émigré telling me that, back home, politics occurred "above the waist." People would have compared Eliot's sins to their own and to those of other officeholders, past and present. As I thought about this, both sitting in judgment of Eliot myself and trying to predict how others would judge him, I held certain truths to be self-evident.

We recently had been through many sex scandals involving recent or then-current officeholders. Regularly, it seemed, there were new revelations concerning the extramarital affairs of many others, including semi-deities like Presidents Franklin Roosevelt, John Kennedy and even good old Ike. We all knew that Arkansas Governor Bill Clinton had engaged in "affairs" with state employees, facilitated by other state employees. While president, Clinton had hit on a woman the day after her husband had committed suicide. In the White House, Clinton had inserted a Cuban cigar into the vagina of a young intern entrusted to his care. Yet he had retained his office and quickly returned to such popularity, especially among women, that in

2000 he would have been re-elected in a landslide but for the 22nd Amendment to the United States Constitution.

Contrary to the classic joke that the very popular candidate of the moment would win an imminent election "unless he were caught in bed with a live boy or a dead girl," we all knew highly esteemed members of Congress (highly esteemed by me) who had survived those very situations. Indeed, in my Upper West Side New York City neighborhood, people had wondered out loud why New Jersey Governor Jim McGreevy had resigned "merely" because he had cheated on his wife with a man. They had suspected that there must have been much more, and much worse, to have fueled his hasty retreat—possibly the financial aspects of the relationship with his unqualified homeland security adviser, Golan Cipel.

On the other hand, the conduct Eliot tersely adverted to at his brief public appearances might have been prosecuted as a crime. This particular offense, a violation of the federal Mann Act, had not been prosecuted in analogous circumstances in more than 30 years and was infamously associated with the racially motivated prosecutions of two black celebrities, Chuck Berry and Jack Johnson. The weight of opinion hurled at me at the height of the scandal, and later, was that the aforementioned sexual indiscretions of other politicians were much worse than Eliot's, especially those committed by President William Jefferson Clinton.

As I thought about all of this on an expedited basis, I might have estimated the likelihood of success for my plan much higher than I had, when Eliot had asked me, except for two things. Most important had been the hypocrisy factor. Americans are willing to forgive just about anything, but are much less willing to forgive mere hypocrisy than many actual crimes. Eliot's popularity had been built as the "Sheriff of Wall Street," the crusading attorney general who had righteously, and some said self-righteously, meted out historically severe punishment to those who had breached their fiduciary duties and betrayed the public's trust. While the truth was, and is, that Eliot is not a hypocrite — the facts screamed an instant verdict that he had been guilty of massive hypocrisy. Moreover, Eliot's stridency and fits of temper with his partners in government during the previous 15 months had left few, if any, friends to defend him if he had adopted my plan and gotten treatment out West.

These two factors, hypocrisy and burnt bridges, were the basis for my overly conservative estimate of success for the plan. They also may have been the reason Eliot estimated his chances much lower than I had. His estimate approached zero percent. I don't think Eliot really believed the chances of success were that low. I simply think he hadn't wanted to be governor anymore, for among other reasons, remaining governor would have made him a hypocrite in his own estimation.

After Eliot's public appearance on Monday, March 10, we had caucused briefly and decided to communicate with senior staff that the best way for them to help was simply to do their jobs, to the extent possible, in the midst of the hysteria that was rapidly gaining momentum. We also truthfully told them that no decision about resignation had been made.

Rumors spread that Eliot had decided to resign but was delaying resignation while his lawyers attempted to negotiate a plea bargain with the United States attorney, involving his resignation for lenient treatment. That never happened. Eliot's lawyers knew that federal authorities would not have negotiated such a deal. The United States Attorney properly operates under rules which respect the principle that an elected official's maintenance or departure from office is something for determination in the political realm or by constitutional mechanisms, such as impeachment, designed specifically for this purpose. Nevertheless, this rumor was reported as fact—and repeated thousands of times.

The plea-bargaining, which never occurred, is still being reported, as I write this book more than a year later. I heard Jeff Toobin, a generally reliable and well-informed reporter, repeat it in the coverage of the Rod Blagojevich scandal in early 2009. One correspondent wondered out loud whether the Illinois governor was delaying his resignation in order to arrange the type of deal Eliot Spitzer had tried and failed to get. Toobin, a former federal prosecutor, and an acquaintance of both Eliot and Silda's, erroneously agreed that Eliot had tried. This kind of deal could not happen, because of the same rules that existed when Toobin was a federal prosecutor, a fact frequently mentioned by CNN.

On Monday, March 10, the Second Floor staff was instructed to attempt to do their jobs as best they could. My part of going about the business of running government meant that I would drive back upstate on Tuesday, March 11, for a public appearance and speech in support of the lottery/endowment proposal at Hudson Valley Community College. I had time to continue refining my plan and make many calls during the trips to and from the Capitol. I was constantly on my cell phone during those drives, removing the device from my ear only when I had seen or sensed a state trooper nearby on the New York Thruway. I could not spare the time to be stopped, even if my laminated State Police windshield sign might have warded off the tickets, as it had earlier in the Plague Year. Given the black eye the State Police had taken in TRU, and the madness that had enveloped us during those 61 hours, the summonses for cell phone use might actually have been issued, along with citations for speeding.

My identification of, and contacts with, the Meadows and the Dakota rehabilitation facilities in Arizona proved to be impressively simple. Places that are supposed to help people in need should be easy to contact, but unlike these were, they rarely are. Who was I to have proposed this type of drastic residential treatment without consulting professionals? I had felt empowered to act as I deemed fit and would have proposed a month for Eliot on the Planet Jupiter if I could have arranged it and it might have worked. Nevertheless, I contacted the people I knew in the mental health world and others I knew who had relationships with psychiatrists, psychologists and the schools that trained them. I also contacted certain clergy. Everyone took my call immediately, one benefit of the media storm. I spoke with a Rabbi who had been recommended because of his experience counseling powerful people in times of crisis. I also spoke with eminent shrinks in New York and as far away as Texas.

I even visited my own shrink, a woman I had not seen professionally in almost four years. I called her and said I needed advice and asked for the names and phone numbers of other shrinks noted for dealing with high-profile people in trouble, in order to "help a friend." She just responded, "Lloyd, I have followed your career. I know who and what you're talking about, but you have to come into my office for me to help." And before I could defend on the grounds of insufficient time, she said, "And I will make time whenever you can come in, including right now."

I replied, "This really is not about me or my veiled cry for help."

She said, "Probably not, but you have to come in anyway." So I did right then and received advice, names, contact information, and her parting suggestion that after the smoke settled, I myself should come in for some therapy. Given all that she remembered from sessions past about me and these relationships (Eliot, Silda, Jan, me and the two families), she believed that I would probably need help and it certainly wouldn't do any harm.

During those 61 hours, I received endless requests to comment or appear on television and radio. The *New York Times*, front page and above the fold on March 11, reported with partial accuracy the drama that had taken place in the Spitzer apartment on March 10, including my plea to Eliot that he not resign. On March 10, the *Times* was constantly reporting and updating the story in its online edition. Because of that coverage, I got a lot of calls from all over the world and responded to three. In two of these brief interviews, I tried to dampen the "Eliot will resign any second" rumor being reported as fact, in the same manner that the inaccurate "Eliot's lawyers are plea-bargaining his resignation for leniency" speculation was being reported as the God's honest truth.

I was adamant that the false story that Eliot had decided to resign not take root. A concession has real consequences. I believe that Al Gore would have become president in 2001 had he not clutched and prematurely rushed his concession before rescinding it. A false signal that Eliot would resign might have tipped the balance of sentiment toward impeachment, had he listened to Silda and me and decided to fight on.

During those 61 hours, I did what had come naturally, as I think all the participants did, including Eliot and Silda. When she stood next to him during his two public appearances, it had been natural for her to do that. She had not been asked or told to stand next to him. It was not the product of a choreographic strategy session. If anything, Silda needed to be restrained from performing a far more powerful, and self-destructive, act of support for her man. While it was all happening, it was so clear that everyone understood their roles and played them out to the best of their abilities, without prompting or rehearsal. I knew that Eliot was playing out his leading role with vastly diminished capacity. That is why had we (Silda, Emily and I) not convinced him on Monday to reconsider his intention to resign, I would have attempted to physically restrain him from doing it. I would have done this (and probably gotten myself hurt and arrested in the process) if only to dramatize the point about how rash his decision was and how strongly I felt that he must not do it.

When Eliot finally rejected my plan on Wednesday, March 12, he was not in much better shape than he had been on Monday, when Silda, Emily and I had prevailed upon him not to pull the plug. Had he followed our advice, he likely would be governor today, after a bruising period of very public abuse and punishment. Eliot richly deserved that punishment, and the state deserved to mete it out. The state and its people also were entitled to Eliot, a governor of monumental energy, intellect and vision and one who was vastly better than the Impostor who had governed New York for the previous 15 months. They were entitled to the real Eliot, after he had gotten the shit and hubris knocked out of him. The people of New York State deserved the governor they had elected, unencumbered by the demons that had haunted him every day of his term. New York was entitled to that.

The strong and valid presumption that an elected official serves until death, incapacity, impeachment or the next election intervenes, seems to have been totally lost in contemporary America. In recent years, governors in Connecticut, New Jersey and New York have resigned. The governor of Massachusetts quit his job because he got bored and then toyed with the idea of running for governor of New York. Alaska Governor Sarah Palin treated the abandonment of her office as a badge of honor. One thing that must be said for Bill Clinton, for Mark Sanford and yes, even for the otherwise pitiful Rod Blagojevich, is that each understood that his election required him to serve unless or until he was removed.

Instead of the man New Yorkers had elected, they got David Paterson, a nice and smart guy whom Eliot had selected as his running mate. Eliot had made that choice without satisfying himself that David possessed the only indispensable qualification for being lieutenant governor, and that is the ability to step in immediately and be a good governor. Eliot had failed to check the box in that required field at a time in 2006, when he must have known that David Paterson would become governor. It was just a matter of time.

I am an experienced appellate lawyer, having argued more than a score of important appeals in federal and state appellate courts and one in the High Court itself. Until March 12, 2008, I had been spared the indignity and instant rejection of finishing an oral argument and then having the panel dismiss my appeal, on the spot, from the bench. However, after extended oral argument that Wednesday morning, the one-man panel of Eliot Spitzer rejected my argument, dismissed the appeal, and moved directly to writing the decision on his own fate as governor of New York State.

After Eliot drafted his statement of resignation, the entourage had our chances to throw in edits. The defense lawyers, Michelle, Ted and Mark, made sure that the statement did not suggest an admission to criminal conduct. Those with the more intimate connections, Silda, Emily and me (although Michelle certainly fell into that category as well) were more concerned with tone and history. My only contribution was to clarify the reason that the resignation, which would be announced at 11:40 A.M., March 12, 2008, would become effective much later, at noon on March 17. I wanted Eliot to make clear that he was not trying to hang on for a few more days, although I had pleaded with him to take that additional time and reconsider.

So I inserted language that disclosed that the delay had been at David Paterson's request. David apparently needed that time to prepare, although I doubted then, and know now, that neither five days nor five years would have prepared that man for the job.

As Eliot was finalizing his resignation statement, I was editing mine. I had drafted one, just in case, the day before. I BlackBerry'd the edits to Kathy, sworn to secrecy in Albany, and asked that she shoot a copy back to me in a form ready for me to pull the trigger in an instant.

A few minutes after 11:00 A.M., we loaded into the big black SUVs for the trip downtown. Nothing I had ever experienced firsthand or in fiction prepared me for that two-and-one-half-mile trip. The one cinematic image that came to mind was the last leg of Captain Willard's trip up the Nung River for his rendezvous with evil in the movie *Apocalypse Now*. In the 44-hour interval between the two trips from 79th Street to 40th Street, New York had reorganized itself into a city hosting a spectacle like the Olympics or a World's Fair.

As we exited Eliot's apartment building and travelled along the Fifth Avenue parade route, the streets were lined with press, cameras and tens of thousands of people. Many carried signs or wore t-shirts invoking "Client 9," with the majority of these expressing support or "love" for him. The faces generally wore smiles, but many of those were the nervous or guilty smiles of people witnessing a motorcade headed to a public execution. As we entered the SUVs in front of Eliot's apartment and later exited on 40th Street into a building that fronts on Third Avenue, Eliot apologized to his State Police escorts. They were a group from central casting—tall, lean, strong and handsome men with crew cuts. They were nice, polite, smart guys who had been handpicked for the honor of transporting and protecting the governor.

When we arrived upstairs on the 39th floor, via elevators reserved for the governor's use, Eliot stopped again to apologize—this time to a group of 20-somethings, who worked in the Executive Chamber, including his wonderful "bodyguy," Danny Kanner. Eliot said something about them not losing their faith in government service. I nearly broke down as he did this. The group that had travelled downtown from the apartment surrounded Eliot as he descended the staircase to the 38th floor and the press room where he had spoken Monday and would publicly speak for the last time as governor. Several of us, including me, walked into the room before Eliot and were bombarded by intense rolling volleys of flashes, which continued without abatement from the moment we arrived until we departed three minutes later. Then Eliot stepped to the microphone.

In the past few days, I've begun to atone for my private failings with my wife Silda, my children, and my entire family. The remorse I feel will always be with me. Words cannot describe how grateful I am for the love and compassion they have shown me.

From those to whom much is given, much is expected. I have been given much: the love of my family, the faith and trust of the people of New York, and the chance to lead the state. I am deeply sorry that I did not live up to

what was expected of me. To every New Yorker and to all those who believed in what I tried to stand for, I sincerely apologize. I look at my time as governor with a sense of what might have been, but I also know that as a public servant I, and the remarkable people with whom I worked, have accomplished a great deal. There is much more to be done, and I cannot allow my private failings to disrupt the people's work.

Over the course of my public life I have insisted — I believe correctly — that people, regardless of their position or power, take responsibility for their conduct. I can and will ask no less of myself. For this reason, I am resigning from the office of governor. At Lieutenant Governor Paterson's request, the resignation will be effective Monday, March 17, a date that he believes will permit an orderly transition. I go forward with the belief, as others have said, that as human beings, our greatest glory consists not in never falling but in rising every time we fall.

As I leave public life, I will first do what I need to do to help and heal myself and my family. Then I will try once again, outside of politics, to serve the common good and to move toward the ideals and solutions which I believe can build a future of hope and opportunity for us and for our children. I hope all of New York will join my prayers for my friend David Paterson as he embarks on his new mission. And I thank the public once again for the privilege of service. Thank you very much.

As soon as we arrived back at the top of the stairs on 39, I walked into my office with a view overlooking the U.N., pulled up the email containing my resignation, and pushed "Send" to a group that included Eliot, everyone I could think of on the Second Floor, and the addressee, "Lieutenant Governor David Paterson." I addressed my resignation to David (and not Eliot) because by the effective date of my resignation, April 4, 2008, he would be governor. I sent it as soon as I possibly could to make two points. I had come to work for Eliot, left the law firm I had built in a profession that paid me millions of dollars each year for that and only that reason. Second, I wanted to make it unambiguous that I was resigning before being asked to. In a moment of clairvoyance, I had foreseen the pleasure that David's chief of staff and soon-to-be secretary, Charles O'Byrne, would take in firing most people close to Eliot, while delighting even more as he spared a few whom he liked or had use for during the transition. I wasn't going to give Charles the chance to indulge either of these perverse pleasures with me.

After transmitting my resignation letter, I walked next door to inform Chief of Staff Marlene Turner, who was crying and told me she had or was about to resign as well. We embraced. Then I walked into Eliot's office, but he and Silda were already gone, less than ten minutes after Eliot's public statement. I wanted to do something normal and routine and recalled having had the same instinct on 9/11. That day, after making sure that my family was safe and watching the Twin Towers fall, I returned to my desk and pretended to work for a while before walking home. The family I made contact with that day had included Eliot, whom I told to "get the hell out" of the attorney general's office only a few hundred yards from Ground Zero. Eliot had then walked with his staff up to 40th Street and to the very governor's office where I now stood.

Six and one-half years later, lunch seemed as normal and routine as anything could be. I gathered a bunch of people and instructed them (not asked) that we were going to lunch. One or two were young staffers whom Eliot had just told not to lose their faith in government service. Our group included Haley, Jennica, Peter Pope, Julietta Lozano and, for some reason, Inspector General Kris Hamman, who just happened to be there. We went to Docks Oyster Bar, a nice place in the building, where Sean Maloney and I had recently hosted a Christmas party for the New York City–based governor's staff. This was also a "party" of sorts, and so I ordered a few bottles of wine. Like the attendees of an Irish wake or those sitting Shiva, we tried to keep our conversation on the positive side, focusing on the bright spots and happy anecdotes from the 15 difficult months. I opened and closed the proceedings with a toast to "Governor Eliot Spitzer."

■ ■ ■

What Now?

I CAME CLOSE TO breaking down when Eliot apologized to the young staffers, telling them not to lose their faith in government service, as he was about to descend the staircase and announce his resignation. In the 61 hours, that moment and one with Silda and one with Jan were the only truly emotional moments for me. The rest of that time, I acted and reflexively reacted without feeling much, as litigators learn to, while sacrificing some of their humanity. The emotions began to flow, during the postmortem at Docks, enough at least for a cleansing shower.

When I arrived at Eliot and Silda's apartment on the morning of March 10, my three objectives had been to stop Eliot from resigning, comfort Silda and ascertain whether Eliot was at risk of killing himself. I failed to prevent the resignation. Perhaps my presence had helped Silda a little, but a female entourage had quickly encircled her. This support group, which eventually included Jan, ministered to Silda's needs, helped her with the girls and spoke to the press on her behalf. Silda talked with at least one reporter, who came away from the interview disarmed, like most men who encounter her.

That left the suicide concern. Initially, we hadn't been willing to take any chances and had organized a group of Eliot's male friends, committed to keeping him company when no one else was around and when he would tolerate it. For a while, but not for very long, Eliot indulged this and other heavy-handed attempts to "help" him. It had quickly become clear that he didn't want most of this help, but treated it as part of his punishment. As such, he accepted it gracefully. That demeanor continues to this day when confronted by strangers, as he constantly is, who tell him how much they love, hate, admire, miss or, worst of all, forgive him.

Forgiveness is hard to accept, especially if you haven't forgiven yourself, and if you don't really understand what it is or how to bestow it. At one point, Eliot incredulously asked me how I could have forgiven him. I mumbled some answer, while thinking that I hadn't forgiven him completely, and doubted that I fully understood what that meant anyway. Silda, a Christian woman, understands forgiveness and has bestowed it but cannot fully comprehend how much easier it is to forgive than to be forgiven.

Then there had been the matter of security and transportation for Eliot, Silda and the girls. Former governors are entitled to protection long after they leave office. At the moment Eliot would become a former governor, his predecessor, George Pataki, was still receiving protection. There had been criticism of the $20,000 weekly expense entailed by the continuing State Police detail assigned to the Pataki family. Few families needed security as much as the Spitzers had at that moment in time.

Charles O'Byrne, David's chief of staff, who would assume the position of secretary, began to reveal the tendencies I had foreseen in him. Before David had been sworn in, and before Charles had any authority, he called me to offer Eliot and his family whatever level of State Police protection that we deemed necessary. Two days later, but still before the baton had been passed, Charles called me to warn that if Eliot accepted the protection that he had offered, the new administration might have to publicly criticize him for accepting it "under the circumstances." Happily, I had been able to tell Charles that Eliot had already decided not to accept his legal entitlement. Arrangements were being made for private security and transportation. This was the second time in three days that I had deprived Charles of a nasty pleasure, the first having come with my preemptive resignation letter, which had been reproduced in the *New York Times* before Charles could fire or offer to spare me.

Eliot's refusal of police protection had been wise, especially in the midst of the ongoing investigation of State Police complicity in TRU and the questions being asked by the press about whether Eliot's police bodyguards had been aware of his encounters with prostitutes. Moreover, Eliot hadn't believed he deserved protection, at the public's expense, any more than he deserved forgiveness or to remain governor.

The arrangements for protecting and transporting the family were finalized during a meeting with a private security firm at Eliot's farm on March 17, 2008, an hour or so before David was sworn in as governor. Early that morning, I had driven to the farm from Chatham after dropping off Jan at the Hudson train station. I thought that the moment Eliot ceased being governor would be a dangerous time for him to be alone. After the meeting with the private security company, Eliot and I walked down the hill of his farm to an old barn that was being renovated. We made small talk with the workers, who were awestruck by Eliot's presence at this particular historical moment. We then began the walk back up to the big house, one of three on the property. On the way, we passed one of the smaller houses, called "The Winery," which Eliot and Silda had rented for many years before buying the whole property after the 2006 election. He and I recollected some of the happy moments spent in that little house, including his midnight swearing in as attorney general on January 1, 1999 and the summer outing in 1996 for our new law firm. It was a few minutes before noon, which would mark the formal end of Eliot's governorship.

Along the way, Eliot and I exchanged some gallows humor, including my only half-insincere suggestion that he quickly issue a pardon to Joe Bruno for any state crimes he might have committed up and until 12:00 P.M. March 17, 2008. It would have been a great thing to do for reasons too many and too obvious to count or explain here. After we arrived at the house, the clock struck 12, Eliot ceased being governor, and we were joined by Dr. Daniel Spitzer, Eliot's older brother. The three of us chatted for an hour and I departed, leaving Daniel in charge of the companion detail. That very day, I had become convinced that the cautionary procedure was no longer necessary.

Later, on the drive to the Capitol, I began to focus on myself and my family, and to ponder what I would do. The emotions that had started flowing at Docks five days earlier had broken through in a torrent the night before. On March 16, 2007, Jan and I ventured out to dinner for the first time since the Sunday evening call with Eliot a week before. It was oddly reminiscent of our first trip out for dinner after 9/11. Though the latter "tragedy" had been trivial in comparison, the feeling of "before and after" had been the same on both occasions. Each time, I had been surprised that the restaurant still stood where it had before and that when we ordered, food actually was served. We had gone to one of our favorites, the Blue Plate in Chatham, New York. At the time, I was almost as well known in Chatham as Eliot, a town that follows state government closely and is home to many current, former and would-be senior governmental officials.

Jan and I sat down. In other circumstances, patrons would have come over to say "Hi," but at the end of that particular week they seemed to understand our desire for privacy and to respect it. At some point, the owner came over to say how sorry she was and to "comp" our meal. I thanked but reminded her that I was still Eliot's employee and bound by the "no gifts" Executive Order he had issued on Inauguration Day. Judy's graciousness unfortunately provided an opportunity for a particularly insensitive patron to come over to our table, to prattle on about the Democratic primaries and Obama's success, of which she disapproved almost as much as Eliot's "despicable" behavior. I snapped, and using my considerable powers to punish with words, sent the woman out of the restaurant in tears. Jan became angry with me, and I mad at myself for losing control, but relieved that I was beginning to feel something.

I was also gaining insight into what had given life to the Eliot Impostor of the previous 17 months. Several weeks later, while giving a speech, I gained even more insight into this question, which had plagued me throughout the preceding year. Prior to the revelations, I had been booked to give five speeches from early March to early April 2008. After March 12, I called each institution that had invited me and said, "You don't want me as the speaker at your [upcoming event] as I would be speaking without any authority or power to help your cause." Each institution asked me to keep my commitment. They might have done this out of courtesy or gratitude for past favors or the belief that I still had something important to say or merely out of reluctance to look for a last-minute substitute. They probably were also engaging in what Joan Didion called "Magical Thinking." I certainly was. I had been constantly waking up or turning a corner expecting to find that those terrible things hadn't really happened and that life would proceed as it had.

One of my speeches had been given at Weil Gotshal in Manhattan, on behalf of the New York Legal Assistance Group, a beneficiary of the Spitzer Administration's efforts in support of legal services. My stump speech for such events included a review of the many ways Eliot had already helped this cause and his plans for even greater assistance in the future. I always accredited myself by giving my legal services background and telling several anecdotes from the old days. In one of my "war stories" I described the battle to prevent Presidents Nixon, Ford, Reagan and Bush 41 from drastically restricting the type of work legal services lawyers could do for their clients. I always pointed out that all these attempts to cripple the federally funded Legal Services Corporation had been defeated by a progressive and bipartisan coalition but had finally succeeded during the Clinton Administration.

The Clintons had sacrificed legal services for something else they wanted more. This story had always gotten a rise out of my liberal audiences, as they had often heard Hillary tout her work as chair of the Legal Services Corporation's board, which she had also done during the presidential primary debates. During my speech at Weil Gotshal, I unintentionally went a step further. As I came to the conclusion of the Clinton story, I said, "So every time Hillary Clinton brags about her work as chair of the Legal Services Corporation's board, I want to puke." I certainly felt that way, but hadn't wanted to be so caustic and insulting to my audience, which included many ardent Hillary supporters, including Jan. As I had at the Blue Plate, I lost control. I believe it was because of the mental anguish that enveloped me during this period. I am certain that a similar mechanism had been at work with Eliot during the Plague Year. At key moments, he had clutched or been overwhelmed by the trouble in his mind.

As part of the process of redirecting my attention to my own life and career, I paid another visit to Weil Gotshal, this time to see Ira Millstein, the man who built that massive legal powerhouse. Ira had frequently rendered advice to me in times of crisis. The founding of the small legal powerhouse I had built, and then abandoned to work for Eliot, had occurred after two acts of kindness and advice from Ira.

I confided to Millstein that I felt lost and confused and I ticked off some thoughts about what I might do next. Ira said, "The first thing that you have to get through your head is that you're tarnished." I told him that I knew that, but he said, "No you don't, you're just saying that, you think you aren't, you think that everyone will remember all the good work you were doing, and it was very good, and that they will separate you from Eliot. Forget it, you're wrong, you're tarnished, and the sooner you accept that, the better off you will be."

Ira, as usual, had been spot on. I was tarnished but had thought I wasn't and continued to think that even after I left his beautiful office hanging over the southeast corner of Central Park. Several editorials had already appeared, spotlighting the Spitzer local government and higher education programs as two that should be carried forward by the new administration. Hadn't everyone asked me to fulfill my speaking commitments? I wasn't tarnished and would become Chancellor of SUNY, a prospect Ira dismissed as "silly" when I had mentioned it.

I proceeded to give my higher education speeches, met again with the Levin Institute to further the discussion of SUNY's proposed foreign campus, continued working on the Long Island research consortium, and even did an op-ed piece for the *Times Union* on various proposals for new law schools in SUNY. I convinced myself that the SUNY search committee and board would remember all I had done, lo those few weeks ago.

When I was finally interviewed by the chancellor search committee, stacked with SUNY board members like Ed Cox and campus presidents who had urged me to become chancellor, I gave a great affirmative presentation. It was replete with detailed references to the wants, needs and aspirations of the 64 SUNY campuses I had visited. That tour had become the subject of an editorial in *Newsday*, praising its symbolic significance. I had known that after my opening presentation to the search committee, I would be asked whether my connection to Eliot might hurt SUNY. Being a good appellate advocate, I had posed the question to myself in my opening remarks and answered it preemptively before it had come out of their mouths. Forget about it. Without the slightest acknowledgment that I had just asked and answered the question, the first question posed was, "How can we appoint Eliot Spitzer's best friend as chancellor?" Ira Millstein deserved to witness this.

During the 18 days that I technically worked for David Paterson, I did what I could to neatly tie up my portfolios so they could be turned over to new stewards, if there would be any to receive them. Frequent visits and multiple daily phone calls with Eliot continued, but after one slip-up the email had to be suspended until I got my own BlackBerry. The slip had occurred on March 18, 2008, the day after David's swearing-in, when he and his wife, Michelle, were holding their bizarre first news conference to talk about their extramarital affairs during the previous few years. While this news conference was occurring, Eliot and I exchanged a series of email, later reported in the *New York Times* as follows:

> In the days after he [Eliot] left, he kept in touch with his former aides. He even got a play-by-play of Mr. Paterson's first press conference, during which he and the new governor's wife, Michelle, discussed their extramarital affairs in the Red Room of the State Capitol building.
>
> "Where are u?" Mr. Spitzer wrote that morning to his friend and former aide, Lloyd Constantine.

"I am at farm," Mr. Spitzer continued, referring to his estate in Pine Plains, N.Y. [Actually in Gallatin]

Mr. Constantine, who was then working for the administration of Mr. Paterson as part of the transition, wrote back: "I am in Red Room press conf was scheduled for noon. Promptness is not our friend's strong suit. Has not started yet will call when it concludes."

Mr. Spitzer replied: "Send me bbery when he done. It will be easier if I call u given phones here etc."

At 1:02 P.M., shortly after the press conference, Mr. Constantine offered his analysis:

It's over. David said that in the 99 to 02 period he had a series of affairs at a time when he was jealous. The unspoken part is that he was paying Michelle back for one she had. One of the women was a state employee who did not work for him then, but he has now "inherited." They both went to counseling and their marriage is stronger now than ever. He went public so as not to be burdened by this as he attempts to govern. He came over as honest and sincere as to the facts and the motive for disclosure. I think he more or less put it to rest with one big exception, i.e. the identity of the state employee that he has now inherited and what will happen to her. What a terrible climate in this State.

Although this email exchange with Eliot did not appear in the *New York Times* until much later, I had been tipped off by the press office that it was coming. Danny Hakim and Nick

Confessore, who later would share a Pulitzer Prize for their coverage of our woes, had figured out that Eliot and his distressed confidantes probably had their guards down right after the big bang. The FOIL exemption did not apply to email exchanges between former Governor Spitzer and his inner circle, who were still state employees, cleaning up and clearing out on the Second Floor.

The breach and disclosure of our private correspondence had been gratifying in two respects. Haley and Dan had reminded me of one of my earlier sermons: "Don't ever send an email from work that you wouldn't feel comfortable reading in the *New York Times*." Their verdict was that I had passed this test. Second, the exchange, in portions not quoted, involved me tamping down Eliot's urge to question and criticize David. When he later did that more directly, I admonished him that he was the only person in New York State who had no right to criticize David. Paterson was governor for one, and only one, reason: Eliot had chosen him as his running mate. Eliot had made that choice when he must have known that David was almost certain to become governor. The "almost" qualifier assumed, not that Eliot's conduct would go undetected, an impossibility over the course of 12, eight or even four years, but Eliot's willingness to make a Clintonian fight, which he had been unwilling to do. Eliot had been the starting pitcher who left the bases loaded with an inept reliever coming in. Any runs scored were Eliot's responsibility.

The first week of April 2008 was my last in the governor's office, and I had not tied up all the loose ends on my stuff. That was my fault. I had spent more time on Eliot and my manifest destiny as chancellor than I should have. It had also begun to dawn on me that, no matter how neatly I packaged my portfolios, the higher education, local government efficiency and public authority reform initiatives would go nowhere in the Paterson Administration. In fairness, David just needed to survive in the early going. A nearly on-time, plain-vanilla budget would satisfy that criterion.

On April 2, I met for the last time with the local government staff and commission. They gave me a copy of *Tuesdays with Lloyd,* their tribute to my pontification at our regular weekly meetings and a takeoff on the bestseller *Tuesdays with Morrie* by Mitch Albom. At the commission meeting I apologized because I would not be there when the commission's final report was issued, and for the skepticism that would attach to it and any reform espoused by Eliot Spitzer. The commission primarily comprised current and former mayors, town supervisors, legislators, county executives and two lieutenant governors, Stan Lundine and Al DelBello. They were gracious and put on brave and smiling faces.

That night, there were two farewell parties, one that I hosted and one arranged by my friends in the Division of Criminal Justice. Denise O'Donnell and Letizia Tagliafierro, from that agency, lived in Buffalo and had commuted weekly to Albany. They knew of my affection for their city, whose noble past, current struggles and hoped-for future had consumed so many of my hours and miles. They had gone shopping and assembled a collection of every food or object they could find inscribed with "Buffalo," a buffalo or a Bills or Sabres logo. Later at McGuire's, my favorite restaurant in Albany, we drank and got weepy and talked about the things that might have been.

Sean Maloney, who was empathetic and supportive throughout this rough period, had quickly been elevated to number three in the new administration. He set up an exit interview for me with Paterson, during the second week of April, although my official departure had occurred on April 4. Sean allowed me to keep my credentials until the interview, so I would be spared the emotional jolt of signing in as an outsider. My meeting with David was one of the few that Charles O'Byrne allowed to occur without him being present. While waiting for the appointment outside my former office, already occupied by a new staffer, Basil Paterson walked in. Mr. Paterson, David's dad, greeted me, and I congratulated him on his son's ascension, as I had 15 months earlier at David's inauguration as lieutenant. That had been a beautiful moment, as Mr. Paterson, who in 1970 had become the state's first African-American major party candidate for lieutenant governor, had watched his son enter the Promised Land. Little more than a year later, Basil was bursting at the seams with pride.

David came out to greet and usher me in to his office but had neither "seen" nor detected his father's presence, despite the amazing perceptual powers he has developed to compensate for his blindness. I, like all of Eliot's senior staff, knew that it was my responsibility to help David at such moments and said, "David, your dad has just arrived, so I will wait until you guys are done, however long that is — I'm out of work and have plenty of time."

Basil, then 81 years old but with the energy of a man 30 years younger, laughed and said, "No, Lloyd, you go right in, I am going to be here for a long time."

David's office had been properly denuded of any trace of his predecessor's occupancy and, most obvious to me, the former dominating decoration had been taken off the wall. Eliot had installed a huge and handsome topographical map of New York State on the wall behind the governor's desk. It had been presented to him by his law partners in 1998 as he departed for the Democratic attorney general primary. Superimposed along the border was an ad Constantine & Partners had taken in the *New York Law Journal,* wishing him God's Speed and expressing our confidence in his noble future serving "All of the People of New York State."

My exit discussion with David was pleasant. We liked each other. David had gone out of his way the year before to cultivate a friendship. At the time, he had brought me up to his Third Floor office, far more beautiful than the governor's slightly larger digs on the Second, to meet his new executive staff. David made each member of his staff give me a presentation about their background and responsibilities and pointedly instructed them, in my presence, that they would be at my disposal. He took me to his favorite Albany Italian restaurant for dinner, and we laughed when I presented him with a big bouquet of flowers intended for Michelle, whom I had expected to join us.

Paterson had come out to "Constantinium" in Chatham for several dinners I arranged in his honor. I always called him "Governor," the correct way to address the lieutenant when using one word, as in "Thank you, Governor." When David needed something, I had delivered. He would have reciprocated but for the fact that there was little the lieutenant governor could do for anyone on Eliot's senior staff. But now he could.

I spent most of the hour dispensing advice on what I thought David's priorities should be, and consoling him about the slightly late budget just enacted, with Shelly and Joe exercising free reign at the end. Finally, I raised the chancellor issue. I told David that Eliot and I had guaranteed SUNY Chair Carl Hayden that the choice of a new chancellor would be the board's. It had always been, as a matter of law, but had never actually worked that way, with the governor always telling the trustees whom to appoint. I told David that Eliot's commitment to Hayden embodied a wise policy and hoped he would respect it. However, I also acknowledged that the board would be heavily influenced by the governor's support for, or disapproval of, a candidate, unless they were nuts.

David immediately went beyond my advice to the heart of the matter and promised to meet with me again in May. He said that at the next meeting he would tell me whether he would push for my appointment as Chancellor of SUNY. I departed with complete confidence—not that I had the job—but that the promised meeting would occur. David's memory is damn near perfect. That early April 2008 meeting was the last time I saw David Paterson, though through Sean I had reminded the man, who needed no reminding, of his promise to meet with me again.

A month after the conflagration, Eliot and I were still speaking daily by phone, hacking away on our private BlackBerrys and ready to resume our tennis rivalry. Our face-to-face meetings had dwindled to maybe twice a week. My worst fears for him had been dispelled, and my concerns redirected inward. I decided to travel and engage in as much mindless physical exertion as I could stand for six months, with an option to extend.

With brief stops at home between each trip, I travelled by myself to Utah, then to the Pacific Northwest and later to the Northern California Coast for the longest and most difficult cycling and skiing I have ever done. Later, Jan and I travelled to the south of India, where we scooped up our older daughter, Sarah, and toured Maharashtra, Kerala and Pondicherry. On the 17-hour flight home from Mumbai to Newark, I wrote the prologue to this book and decided there and then that I would try to emulate my son, Isaac, and become a writer.

Before departing on the first of these cathartic journeys, I had lunch with Silda and another, separately, with Eliot. I had been calling Silda regularly, but she hadn't been ready for a public lunch, or at least not one with me. I persisted, and she finally said "Yes" and told me to pick a place that would require us to take a long walk. She made it clear that she wanted to be seen. I called my friend Donatella Arpaia, who had recently opened her sixth restaurant, Mia Dona, on the East Side of Manhattan. It was far enough from Silda and Eliot's apartment on 79th Street to fulfill her command. I requested a corner table and warned Donatella that she might have to move us if things got out of control.

The long walks before and after lunch were great, as were the food and the conversation. Everyone on the path and in the restaurant recognized Silda and probably wondered about the identity of the lucky older guy. They were all smiling and respectful, and our privacy was not disturbed. Whether or not Silda wanted or needed it, I tried to express to her how wonderful it was to be a man in her presence.

A few days earlier, I had "dined" with Eliot in an office he had established in the Crown Building on Fifth Avenue, the headquarters of Spitzer Enterprises, his father's real estate company. The timing of Eliot's resignation had, in one respect, been fortuitous. Bernie had been gravely ill before the dam broke and soon after had been hospitalized in critical condition. Though extraordinarily wealthy, Bernie and Anne Spitzer don't take good care of themselves. Though they are octogenarians beset by numerous chronic ailments, they reject most assistance and fend for themselves in a Spartan manner. After his resignation, Eliot had been able to turn his attention to his parents and primarily to his father's medical condition. I believe that it saved Bernie's life. Eliot had also gone into run the family business while Bernie was recuperating.

We dined that day in Eliot's office on the 22nd floor of the family-owned building, sporting a magnificent view of Central Park to the north. After lunch and a discussion of some ideas Eliot had for the Spitzer real estate empire and my imminent solo trips, we headed off to appointments downtown. I asked Eliot if his car and driver would drop me off on 43rd Street as he headed farther south. He responded, "What driver?"

I replied, "The one we put in place at the meeting with the security company at the farm the day David was sworn in." Eliot told me he had cancelled those arrangements and was walking to and from work and that when he needed to, he took a cab. At the time, the atmosphere in New York was still supercharged—with Eliot and Silda's faces daily on, or near, the front pages of the tabloids. I was dumbstruck and said, "It's gonna be tough to catch a cab at two, and we might get stuck standing there exposed for a long time."

Eliot responded, "This is my city, and I have to take anything they want to give me out there."

I replied, "OK, the taxi can drop me off on the way downtown."

When we got to the street, the traffic was heavy. There were lots of taxis, but they were all occupied. Eliot and I stood on the southwest corner of Fifth and 57th for roughly 12 minutes, until we were finally able to hail an empty cab. There were a few near misses, but each time we had deferred to a woman who had jumped in first, noticed Eliot, and smiled. In those 12 minutes, probably a hundred vehicles stopped to look and wave at Eliot. Virtually every occupied taxi slowed, stopped and saluted. Every bus stopped, and there had been many travelling south in the Fifth Avenue bus lane, right next to the curb where we stood. Every single bus stopped. At first it was a bit intimidating, like the peaks I was headed for on my skis and bike, but after a few minutes it became fun and exhilarating. As we stood next to each other, as we had so many times before, Eliot waved back and gracefully received everything they had and wanted to give him. I was happy to be standing with him, and as proud as I had ever been.

Lloyd Constantine
New York City
Autumn 2009

■ ■ ■

....

ACKNOWLEDGMENTS

I EXPERIENCED THE 18 months chronicled in this book as a plague "year" and was comforted, nursed and ultimately saved by my family. The book begins with me awaking next to Jan in our bedroom in Chatham, and in that same chamber I read to her each successive iteration of the work. She commented, critiqued and made numerous helpful suggestions that improved the book. Jan is my compass, my home and my love.

Once again, as he lovingly did with my first book, *Priceless*, my son, Isaac, provided a fine set of edits, employing his skills as a professional editor as well as his superior talent as an author. He also demanded that I justify to myself and the reader why I wrote the book, why I urged Eliot to make a fight to remain governor and why I maintain to this day that he should have.

Sarah and Elizabeth, our daughters, played a more subtle, but no less important, role. They are my conscience, always buoy my spirits and constantly let me know that they don't care what

I write, whom I sue, how fast my first serve is and whatever else I might achieve or fail at as long as I cook their favorite dishes and am there to be Daddy. The backdrop of this book is much more than a long relationship between two men, but rather the multidimensional interactions of two great families.

Kaplan, my publisher, changed the life of an out-of-work 62-year-old former litigator and civil servant by publishing two books in a six-month span and smoothing my transition to the life of the mind. More than anyone else, the credit or blame for this rests with Don Fehr, Kaplan's editorial director, who shepherded this work and my first book and served along with Isaac as the editor of *Plague Year*. Don also became a friend and mentor in the process.

Copyediting is something that I had barely heard about before *Priceless,* and experienced writers had warned me I would hate. Instead I had the pleasure of working both times with David Johnstone, a wonderful copy editor, skilled intellectual property attorney and prize-winning author in the legal field. David's edits went beyond diction, grammar and capitalization conventions to tone and nuance — all informed by his knowledge of the law and the legal profession.

Constantine Cannon was my professional home before I left to work for Eliot, the place he and I had been law partners and the sanctuary that welcomed me back after the Plague Year and a six-month "walkabout." C|C gave me the time, place and psychic space to write this book. Since many of the people there know and had worked with Eliot, they understood what I had gone through and was going through as I wrote.

Two women at C|C, Melanie Martorell and Evelyn Maldonado, typed every word of the many drafts, as the work slimmed down from a tome to the final version. They corrected my spelling and grammar and made many helpful suggestions because they, like almost everyone at the firm, knew and liked Eliot.

Leah Nelson, a fine young journalist and former C|C paralegal, was my research assistant on this project. Because Leah also is a writer, knows the law and the court system and is my friend, her assistance ranged well beyond finding things and checking facts. She was a second mind in this project, constantly challenging me, like Isaac, to "justify" certain things.

This work was written in two communities, C|C in Manhattan and Constantinium in Chatham, New York. The dirty little secret is that there are two New Yorks, not "one" as Eliot's slogan pretended. There is metropolitan New York City, including "the Island," and there is "upstate." Eliot understood that this dichotomy was destructive and had to be eliminated for the good of both New Yorks. Chatham epitomizes the very best of upstate. The people there are tough, gritty, well-informed and generous of spirit. My friends, especially the proprietor and patrons of Ralph's, Chatham's literary salon, supported this project in countless ways.

Now that I have acknowledged many (but certainly not all) of the people who helped me to write this book, I must also absolve them, i.e., the named and unnamed. Although I checked facts and recollections with many former Second Floor colleagues, none were interviewed. The words, positions and point of view are solely mine as was the decision to write the book.

■ ■ ■

Aught seven and eight was a time
that men of good will
and fine minds
had dreamed, schemed
and strived to create,
Yet quickly it all came
to naught!

INDEX

Index